forming
thinking
writing

THE COMPOSING IMAGINATION

Ann E. Berthoff

University of Massachusetts at Boston

HAYDEN BOOK COMPANY, INC.
Rochelle Park, New Jersey

Library of Congress Cataloging in Publication Data

Berthoff, Ann E
   Forming/thinking/writing.

   (Hayden English language series)
    1. English language--Rhetoric. I. Title.
PE1408.B485   808'.042   78-3485
ISBN 0-8104-6033-5

1 2 3 4 5 6 7 8 9   PRINTING

78 79 80 81 82 83 84 85 86   YEAR

PREFACE

I have stated in the Introduction the philosophical and pedagogical principles underlying this book, but its justification will have to be found in the usefulness and adaptability of the method of composing that it sets forth. I want here to state my intentions and to acknowledge those who have helped me realize them.

A professional, as distinct from an alternately personal and metaphysical, interest in the teaching of composition dates from 1964 when I gave three NDEA lectures to the Greater Philadelphia Council of Teachers of English. Several true believers walked out, as I remember, when I remarked in passing that linguistics had nothing to teach us about the composing process, but there was a generally favorable response to my arguments that an outline, like a blueprint, is appropriate to the final stages of composing, not to the beginnings; that reading and writing should be taught together; that critical and creative writing should not be isolated from one another; that students in both remedial and Advanced Placement sections need all the experience they can get in observing, recording, and observing again, since perception and concept formation are consonant as acts of mind; that what we need to learn to teach are the uses of chaos and the delights of form-finding and form-creating. Father Thomas Loughrey and Robert Boynton of the Council urged me to write a textbook incorporating these ideas. Ten years later I started on that project; it has been my good fortune to have Bob Boynton as my editor, encouraging and guiding my endeavor.

One of my chief concerns has been to write a book which teachers of literature could respect, yet which would not be devoted to "writing about literature." I wanted students to have the opportunity to read selections of good prose on important matters and to write experimentally about a wide range of experiences, including the experience of reading and thinking. I have also hoped to write a book that could develop an awareness that language has social and political dimensions. I was thinking about this book during the days of campus protest against American action in Indochina, when I shared the hope of many that thoughtful, substantial changes in attitudes toward education could be institutionalized. They have not been, and one result is that illiteracy is by now a national crisis. I will be glad if this book can help forestall a return to drill; I am hopeful that it will encourage conceptions of "creativity" as something other than "nonlinear" and "nonverbal" solutions to "the communication problem."

Friends and colleagues have offered warnings and encouragement. Best of all, they have been willing to put theory and suggested practice to the test in their own classrooms. I have learned as much from their experiences as I have from my own. For their very helpful responses to "Assisted Invitations," a pilot project for this book, I want to thank Jonathan Bishop, T. Y. Booth, Joan Bridi, Gillian F. Brown, Florence S. DeVecchi, Brenda S. Engel, Robert Foulke, Elizabeth S. Harris, Jane P. Marx, Ruth M. Mathewson, Anne W. Mattill, Martha Orrick, Sherman Paul, U. T. Summers, R. C. Townsend, and Aileen Ward. I am grateful for the thoughtful criticism I've had from colleagues at the University of Massachusetts at Boston: Harriet Feinberg, Alan Helms, Susan Horton, Richard Lyons, Monica McAlpine, Louise Mendillo, Emily Meyer, Rosamond Rosenmeier, and George Slover. Several of my students from Advanced Composition were willing to read various sections from different perspectives and to put some of the assignments to work in their own tutoring and teaching. Kristin Bomegen, Art Morrill, Bill Morse, Jean Parsons, Rebecca Saunders, and Peter Zimmer have been especially helpful. And for help in emerging from chaos, I want to thank Ronnie Groff, Hélène Guidice, and Vic Schwarz at Hayden.

I am very grateful to Samuel Hynes, who invited me in 1965 to develop a course in experimental writing for upperclassmen at Swarthmore College. When James Broderick suggested several years later that I experiment with approaches to freshman composition at the newly established Boston Campus of the University of Massachusetts, I had the chance to discover how many of the problems in teaching composition were "universal," no matter what the age or background of students. I am grateful to both for their support and encouragement and for their searching questions about some of the premises and conclusions of the book-in-progress.

Leo Marx, whose interest in the pedagogy of composition derives from an understanding that writing and thinking are profoundly related, has raised with patience and persistence the kinds of questions that guide and comfort so that one can find the strength to reexamine fundamental principles. And from Josephine Miles I have learned more than from anyone else about the relationship of a philosophy of language to ideas about teaching writing. The encouragement I have had from these extraordinary teachers has been important to me at all stages of composing.

Insofar as this book reflects my teaching experience, it has been nurtured chiefly by the late Carolyn A. Blackmer, who was mentor and guide in the first years of my classroom career, nearly thirty years ago. She taught me how to read Whitehead and Peirce and to trust the power of the human mind, despite a young teacher's inclination to believe that there was little evidence for its existence. Our daily trip home on the Boston and Maine (bringing back to North Station a carload each of lobsters and tired teachers) was a three-year seminar in forming, thinking, and writing. I like to think that she would have approved this attempt to encourage students to explore how it is that, as she used to say, *form finds form* and "to grow," as I. A. Richards has said, "in capacity, practical and intelligential" as a result. The book is dedicated to her memory.

ANN E. BERTHOFF

Concord, Massachusetts

CONTENTS

INTRODUCTION:
PHILOSOPHY AND PEDAGOGY

This book is intended for those who want to teach composition primarily and centrally and not just as an adjunct to the study of poetry, short fiction, and essays. It will probably not have much appeal for those who consider that the composition course must be primarily concerned with writing as self-expression, because that view generally is accompanied by a deep suspicion of method—and the heart of this book is a method of composing. Certainly I am concerned with both the person and the expressive function of language, but since language also has referential and heuristic functions, personal expression is seen here neither as the chief end nor as the principal means of composition. The book will not appeal to teachers who prefer to work with manuals and guides and a rigid syllabus. There are no special "study questions" because the whole book is a study question. I learned a lot in writing it, and I am hopeful that teachers will learn a lot in using it, adapting it to their needs.

This is a book about the composing process that provides continuing opportunities to put theory into practice; it does not simply line up exercises that demonstrate theoretical points. Most rhetorics, it seems to me, assert a principle that is then illustrated with trivial examples; the student is left wondering how to apply the principle to the problems faced in writing real

1

papers. I have tried to present both logical and rhetorical principles in conjunction with exercises in composing and to show how the choices we make when we write can be made more intelligently and with a greater sense of control if we have a method. The book provides a rational sequence of writing exercises in conjunction with theory and analysis, but it has a flexible structure; the book won't take over the course unless that is what is wanted.

I begin with meaning, not with thought ("Think of what you want to say . . .") or language ("Choose the words which you feel would fit your idea best . . ."); we will never get the two concepts together unless we begin with them together. The making of meaning is the work of the active mind, of what used to be called the *imagination*—that power to create, to discover, to respond to forms of all kinds. My guiding philosophical principle is that this form-finding and form-creating is a natural activity; the book's central pedagogical principle is that we teach our students *how* to form by teaching them *that* they form. Man is the forming animal, the *animal symbolicum,* as the philosopher Ernst Cassirer put it.

This book embodies a philosophy of composition, but it centrally concerns actual acts of composing, not just thoughts about composing. It offers not rules and exhortations but *assisted invitations* to students of composition to discover *what they are trying to do and thereby how to do it.* This language comes from I.A. Richards, who once claimed that what we need in teaching reading and writing is "not so much some improved philosophic and psychological doctrine, though no one should despise that, as sets of sequenced exercises through which . . . people could explore, *for themselves,* their own abilities and grow in capacity, practical and intelligential, as a result. In most cases, perhaps, this amounts to offering them *assisted invitations* to attempt to find out just what they are trying to do and thereby how to do it." *

The assisted invitations in this book are at once forming, thinking, and writing exercises. They offer occasions for students to experience the composing process as a matter of forming concepts, making meaning, finding and creating forms. I have used the word *composing* throughout the book to mean any such

---

* *Design for Escape* (New York: Harcourt, 1968), p. 111. Italics in the original.

act of mind.* The assisted invitations to write experimentally are intended to teach that "pre-writing" is writing; that getting started is as important a phase of composing as getting it together and getting it finished; that in all phases, composing is forming. A composition is a bundle of parts: students are invited to explore for themselves how discovering the parts and developing ways of bundling them are interdependent operations. The ambiguities and complexities of composing are right there from the beginning because I believe that elements of what we want to end with must be present in some form from the first; otherwise, we will never get to them. Furthermore, in these suggestions for composing practice, I have included both critical and creative writing, since both exercise the forming power of the active mind: the imagination is engaged in a process of making meaning, which may take the form of image or argument, story or discursive demonstration. I don't believe that students should have to wait until graduate seminars to learn that storytelling and exposition have a lot in common or that finding forms of feeling exercises the mind. The misconception of affective and cognitive *domains* is responsible for much of the trouble we have currently in teaching reading and writing. A philosophically—and psychologically—sound differentiation can be made between two kinds of abstraction: that which forms by means of successive generalizations and that which forms without conscious, deliberate generalizing. (We don't see a chair by generalizing about it.) For the purposes of developing a method of composing, however, the similarities and continuities are more important than the differences.

The real test of any method for carrying through any process is not how well it works in the proving ground, but the quality of the guidance it offers elsewhere. Students should be encouraged to make this book's method their own by putting it to work in the writing they do for other courses. The central purpose of all English courses is surely to teach reading and writing; the best way to see what's happening is not to try to mea-

---

* I have depended on the terms *forming*, *meaning*, and *composing* and have seldom used the terms *symbol* and *abstraction*, since they are heavily burdened with meanings that are irrelevant to my purposes. But, of course, all these concepts are related. A useful formulation of the relationships is this statement by Susanne K. Langer: "The perception of form arises . . . from the process of symbolization, and the perception of form is abstraction." ["On a New Definition of 'Symbol,'" *Philosophical Sketches* (Baltimore: Johns Hopkins, 1968), p. 62.]

sure "proficiency in the language arts" or "basic skills," but to
note how students go about composing in all areas of their aca-
demic life. Meanwhile, the assistance offered in the composition
class should be substantial and pointed but not exhaustive, and it
should assure that students have the experience of mastery as a
safeguard against frustration and despair. (I'm suspicious of any
approach that requires students to produce a piece of terrible
writing before teaching can begin.) Students can gain that mastery more easily from a dozen starts than from a single finished
job. The principle that students of composition should be encouraged to discover continually is that unless several things
happen simultaneously in composing, composing doesn't happen.

In my view, any exercise—perceptual, grammatical, expressive, rhetorical, logical—can have heuristic value only if students know what they are trying to do. Discovering how to work
is contingent on exploring what is to be done: a method of composing should continually ensure that the *how* and the *what* and
the *why* are seen and experienced in dialectical relationship.
There are two consequences of this methodological principle:
one is that the exercises will be carefully limited in scope; the
other is that, since what is being presented is "everything at
once," there will be lots of repetition.

The first consequence—short writing assignments—means
that teachers can afford to encourage students to compose continually, habitually. The fact that short "papers"—single paragraphs, selected sentences—are easier to read than 500-Word
Themes means that there can be more time for conferences;
more time for considered responses; more energy to give to
an ongoing review of writing careers. Teachers don't have to
read everything that students using this book produce; indeed,
they *shouldn't* read everything. Students reading one another's
work is the best alternative, especially if it's combined with discussion in small groups. Knowing that there is an attentive
reader whose critical questions you can learn to make your own
ahead of time is an experience every writer should have. But
whether papers are read by the instructor or not, they should
not be "graded." * Although the writing exercises are generally

---

* Measurement is appropriate to what can be measured. Apples and eggs
are graded according to their dimensions, freshness and soundness
being presupposed. Compositions can be factored and judged in terms
analogous to those used in judging apples and eggs, but the price is
high: we begin to attend to the factors and not to the process. But to

short, I have tried to counteract the feeling that they don't lead anywhere ("When do we come to paragraphs?") by including all along the way suggestions for composing in units larger than the sentence and the paragraph. I suggest that students keep a journal of observations while working in Part I and include there paragraphs and essays developed from such journals. Many of the exercises in Part II could develop into themes, papers, and essays.

The second consequence of teaching a method of composing in which everything is happening simultaneously is that there will be a great deal of repetition. This can work to everyone's advantage, since repetition is, after all, a fundamental aspect of form. Every principle of composing gets presented and re-presented in this book—explained and demonstrated and explained again. Every teacher I know agrees that the fundamentals of composing have to be presented, analyzed, demonstrated over and again. (In my experience, the first of several explanations of classification, say, might take 2 weeks, but the next time around, when classification shows up again as an aspect of paragraphing, it might be handled in a single class.) The challenge is to make that repetition have a cumulative effect by having students see how principle and practice are related. There is a spiraling effect in each of the several composition courses I teach, and I have tried to write the book so that this can happen for those who use it. The book is consequently full of echoes, but they are there for the reader to apprehend and enjoy. I have seldom allowed myself to say, "As you will remember . . ." or "We have seen how . . .": if it isn't remembered, the mere mention will not help, and if it is remembered, why spoil the fun?

This book is neither handbook, nor rhetoric, nor reader, although it serves some of the functions of each. It offers detailed procedures for revision, which is an integral part of the composing process, as correction is not. I have included a brief analysis of some common errors, showing how paraphrasing and establishing context and other techniques can help to locate faulty structures and to repair them. The book is centrally concerned with rhetoric as the study of the relationship of language

---

say that writing should not be graded is not to say that it should not be evaluated. I would prefer a system in which progress reports prepared in conference with the student, a final review of the folder or notebook made by the instructor, and a review of papers from other courses or an extra-course competency exam read by the instructor and his/her colleagues form the basis for an assessment ideally expressed in terms of *pass* or *incomplete*.

and thought. Rhetoric is only superficially a matter of evaluating audience and adjusting tone; it has deeper foundations that we can discover only insofar as we develop a philosophy of knowledge, a theory of imagination.* A "rhetoric" should, therefore, be concerned not just with sorting out topics and places but with exploring the dialectic of names and purposes, images and concepts, thinking and forming. The Paragraph Sequences in Parts I and III provide a philosophical framework for the method of composing set forth in Part II. The passages offered for study are complex, and the effort they require is considerable, but that is the only kind of reading which has heuristic value for students of composition; I believe that students like to think, if they think they can. One of the chief themes of this book is that the acts of mind involved in critical reading, in making sense of texts, are the same as those in operation when we compose: how we construe is how we construct. The passages appearing throughout the book are meant to illustrate kinds of writing, principles of composing, and the process of forming concepts; they are not intended simply to offer topics. Just as the appreciation of music is not furthered by asking students to describe what the music makes them think of, so the appreciation of literature—or any other kind of discourse—is not encouraged by using it to stimulate response. †

Part I includes a sequence of eight passages—one or two paragraphs each—on how we see relationships; *seeing relationships* is the book's working concept of thinking. Part II includes 30-odd paragraphs that illustrate rhetorical and logical principles. Part III, which reviews the method of composing presented in Part II and demonstrates ways of adapting it to the process of critical reading, includes two sequences of paragraphs: one set is about composing works of art; the other concerns the relationship of interpretation and context in scientific, linguistic, and historical inquiry. Almost all selections in the book have been kitchen-tested; my students have found them challenging and interesting—and frequently amusing. The concepts in Paragraph Sequence III are frequently difficult to grasp, but the entire book provides a context and they support and explain one another.

---

* I have made this case in "From Problem-solving to a Theory of Imagination," *College English*, 33 (1972), 636–649. Reprinted in *Rhetoric and Composition: A Sourcebook for Teachers*, ed. Richard L. Graves (Rochelle Park, N.J.: Hayden Book Co., 1976).

† The case against using literature in this way is argued persuasively by C. S. Lewis in *An Experiment in Criticism* (Oxford, 1961).

The method of composing is not tied to these or any other selections appearing in the book; it is adaptable, for instance, to a composition course that includes reading books on a single theme. Reading and writing, I believe, should always be taught together. The danger is, of course, that in the literature course, composing will be restricted to such formats as The Book Report and The Term Paper and that in the composition course, reading will move to the center, pushing writing to the edges where Drill-for-Skill lurks. But the risk must be taken because composing is best nurtured by interpreting texts as well as experience. A course in composition that includes reading offers the best chance of encouraging students "to explore, for themselves, their own abilities and grow in capacity, practical and intelligential, as a result."

part i

THE MAKING OF MEANING

Introduction: Assisted Invitations to Explore the Composing Process

This book teaches a method of composing that focuses on the ways in which writing is related to everything you do when you make sense of the world. This method is meant to serve both the inexperienced writer and the student who has written many papers but who finds the next one almost impossibly difficult. Here are some things about composing which this book can teach you:

- How to get started writing
- What to do next
- How to get started again when you come to a dead end
- How to repeat yourself on purpose with effects that you are controlling
- How to define, limit, expand, eliminate, amalgamate, subordinate, coordinate, recapitulate
- How to know when to stop

A method of composing isn't a set of rules, but it does provide guidelines and procedures. A method helps you find your way around, but it is not like a map, since a map for one territory is not much use in another—and there's no such thing as a general map. But if you have a method, you can make your own map according to the terrain and the nature of transport, depending on where you want to go and how far you want to travel. A method of composing is a critical method, a way of getting thinking started and keeping it going. The more you can learn about composing, the better able you will be to argue with yourself and others; to take notes and study for exams; to read poems and textbooks; to think through problems and to formulate questions that practically answer themselves. The main justification for learning a method of composing is that it can help you think clearly.

This book offers down-to-earth suggestions as well as general principles; theory and practice need one another because principles are easily forgotten unless they are put to the test, and practical suggestions can't be counted on to help you more than once, unless they are grounded in principle. Invitations to explore what is involved in the composing process, how it is related to the everyday use of your mind, are indicated by this little sign: ℘

They are *assisted invitations;* that is to say, all exercises and suggestions for composing practice are accompanied by explanations and analyses.

Whatever you really learn, you teach yourself. If you only learn what you are told, then you are only keeping in mind, for a longer or shorter interval, what was put there by somebody else. What you really learn is what you discover—and you learn to discover by questioning. This book offers you assisted invitations to learn to question what it is that you do when you compose and thereby how to do it better—more easily, more quickly, more confidently.

Nothing in the book is important only for itself: everything is intended to encourage you to adapt the method of composing to your own needs. This method takes advantage of the fact that when you do anything, the *what* and the *how* depend on one another. The more you can learn about what goes on when you compose, the more you will learn about how to compose. In order for that to happen, the composing process has to be slowed down; in this book, everything gets repeated. My hope is that the repetition will have a cumulative, not a deadening effect, but I can't be sure. Something that you find perfectly obvious will be obscure to someone else, and something that is self-evident to another reader may give you trouble. Developing a method of composing means explaining explanations, writing about writing, thinking about thinking; sometimes that can make you dizzy. But if you find a sentence that makes no sense, don't reread it until you've finished the paragraph. Then, if things are still obscure, go back and reread. The second time around, rereading a sentence can be useful, but you should avoid backtracking until you see what's ahead. Learning to read critically means, for one thing, finding what it is that you don't understand.

Throughout this book, I have taken the stand that learning to write is a way of learning to think and that thinking requires knowing how to discover and put to use the resources of language. Part I concerns the relationship of language and thought, the ways we have of making meaning. Part II develops a method of composing that is seen as a matter of forming concepts, developing ideas as a way of shaping your language. Part III offers advice about how to use this method in both critical reading and critical writing.

1. The Composing Process Is a Continuum

You don't suddenly become another person when you sit down to write, though that may be what it feels like sometimes. Composing means putting things together—and that is something you do all the time. When you take in a scene or an event or a piece of news, you are interpreting, putting things together to make sense. When you see what is happening or understand what has happened or imagine what might happen, you are composing: figuring out relationships, working out implications, drawing conclusions. What is currently called "getting your head together" used to be known as "composing yourself."

When we think, we compose: we put this with that; we line things up; we group and classify and categorize; we emphasize or pass over, start and stop and start up again, repeating ourselves, contradicting, hedging, declaring and questioning, lying and denying. Even in dreaming we are composing, although for different purposes and in a mode different from the ones common to waking hours. When we read, we *re*-compose, juxtaposing this character with that character, the theory with the supporting evidence, the argument with the alleged facts, etc. We compare premises and conclusions, ifs and thens, the beginning of the story with the ending, seeing what goes together to make up the whole, seeing how the composition is put together, enjoying it, learning from it.

Composing—putting things together—is a continuum, a process that continues without any sharp breaks. Making sense of the world is composing. It includes being puzzled, being mistaken, and then suddenly seeing things for what they probably are; making wrong—unproductive, unsatisfactory, incorrect, inaccurate—identifications and assessments and correcting them or giving them up and getting some new ones. And all these things happen when we write: writing is like the composing we do all the time when we respond to the world, make up our minds, try to figure out things again. We aren't born knowing how to write, but we are born knowing how to know how.

Although writing has a lot in common with that composing we could simply call *consciousness*, writing doesn't just happen as a matter of course; the writer has to make it happen. Writing is not a "natural-born" capacity that we normally and necessarily develop, the way a child learns to walk and talk. Nor is learning to write like learning the facts in an anatomy text or making a Shaker footstool out of a kit. When you write, you don't follow somebody else's scheme; you design your own. As a writer, you learn to make words behave the way you want them to.

Up to a point, writing can be explained and taught as a skill. And it can be demonstrated, as dovetailing the joints of a drawer can be demonstrated. Composing means working with words, and, in some ways, that is a skill comparable to working with wood. But woodcraft is not just assembling some pre-cut forms, nor is wordcraft gluing statements together. Composing is more than a skill, though the writer must be skilled with words and syntactic structures, just as a cabinetmaker has to know how to use a gimlet and an auger. Composing is more than craft, and it requires more than skill, because working with words requires working with meanings, and meanings are not like walnut planks or golfballs or bulldozers or typewriters or anything else that simply requires skilled handling. Learning to write is not a matter of learning the rules that govern the use of the semicolon or the names of sentence structures, nor is it a matter of manipulating words; it is a matter of making meanings, and that is the work of the active mind.

Writing, as it is discussed in this book, involves you in thinking about thinking and the making of meanings by means of language. That doesn't mean that you must have a detailed knowledge of neurophysiology and linguistics any more than a swimmer needs a theory of hydrostatics. But having some knowledge of how the mind makes meanings is the way to understand how writing has to do with making sense of the world and thus to take advantage of the fact that the composing process is a continuum, an unbroken and continuing activity. The work of the active mind is seeing relationships, finding forms, making meanings: when we write, we are doing in a particular way what we are already doing when we make sense of the world. We are composers by virtue of being human.

You don't have to philosophize or master psychological theories in order to learn to write, but it's important and, I think, comforting to know that the means of making meaning which you depend on when you make sense of the world and when you write are in part made for you by your brain and by language itself. You don't have to learn to focus your eyes or to control the responses of your eardrums. You don't have to re-invent English grammar when you compose a sentence (though you may have to learn to adjust your ways of using it to those of your reader) any more than you have to take grammar lessons to learn to talk. What you do within the limits provided by language and perception, how you use them to make meanings, is up to you, but you don't begin from scratch.

2. Observing; Observing Your Observations; Observations on Observing

What you do when you make sense of the world involves the same acts of mind as those involved when you write: that's what it means to say that the composing process is a continuum. Keeping a journal of observations is one way to see how your mind works; since the active mind is a composer, there's something to be learned by observing it in operation. (*Journal* comes from the French word *jour*, day; a journal is a daily record.) Poets are often addicted to journals, because they know that the composing process is going on all the time and that they need a record of the dialogue between them and the world. Of course, a journal has the practical value of teaching concentration and account-taking. A poet I once knew was hired as a research assistant to an anesthesiologist. The job was to observe the appearance, reactions, speech, behavior, etc., of children before and after surgery and she got it not because of A's in biochemistry (she had had no pre-med) but because the doctor guessed correctly that her powers of observation were highly developed.

Writing every day about what you're looking at is the best way I know to discover the interdependence of language and thought. The journalist of observations is in a good position to appreciate this wise formulation of Kant about human understanding: Percepts without concepts are empty; concepts without percepts are blind.

Deliberately observing your observations and interpreting your interpretations sounds like being self-conscious and, in a sense, it is: you are the one who is aware of what is going on and you are also the one responsible for the going on; you are the do-er, the agent. To be deliberately aware of what you're doing is a consciousness of self. But thinking about thinking is not the same kind of operation as thinking about how to serve in a game of tennis or what to do with your lips when you're learning to play an instrument or what to do with your feet when you're learning to dance. In such cases, self-consciousness is what you have to get over. Learning a skill involves immersing yourself in the rhythm of the activity so that you "think" with your whole body; concentrating on what-the-agent-is-doing is therefore a distraction. For the student of composition, however, concentration on what you're doing in making meanings is the best way of learning to write.

Here is the procedure I'm suggesting for keeping a journal of observations. Get yourself a notebook small enough to be easily carried around, but not tiny; a 9¼ × 6 spiral is ideal, one bound at the side rather than the top. For about a week, write in it for 10 minutes each day in response to some natural object. This object shouldn't be something you're familiar with (instead of an apple, take a pomegranate or a Seckel pear) and it shouldn't be a rock or a pebble, since they are not *organic,* and one of the points of this looking/seeing is to learn something about *organization.* Address yourself to the object; ask it questions; let it answer back; write down the dialogue. Record your observations and observe your observations. Follow your mind in its course: the composing process rather than a composition is your concern, but if what you're composing seems to have a will of its own, follow its lead; you may be surprised to see where it takes you. At the end of a week or so, see if you can compose a couple of paragraphs setting forth the meanings you have made.

If the observing becomes tedious (and it will) stay with it, regardless; if it becomes intolerable, get yourself another object. I offer my students a choice from several cigar boxes full of bird feathers, crab legs, shells, dried seaweed, seed pods, various weeds, pine cones, two or three puff balls and oak galls, bits of bark with fungus, etc., but they sometimes prefer their own twigs and bones and parsnips.

               ∾ To get started, here is an assisted invitation to learn to observe carefully by drawing. This lesson on contour drawing comes from Kimon Nikolaïdes's *The Natural Way to Draw*, which has been called the best "how-to" book ever written about anything.

Materials: Use a 3B (medium soft) drawing pencil with a very fine point (sharpened on sandpaper) and a piece of cream-colored manila wrapping paper about 15 by 20 inches in size. Fasten the paper with large paper clips to a piece of stiff cardboard. Do not use an eraser.

Sit close to the model or object you intend to draw and lean forward in your chair. Focus your eyes on some point, any point will do, along the contour of the model. (The contour approximates what is usually spoken of as the outline or edge.) Place the point of your pencil on the paper. Imagine that your pencil point is touching the model instead of the paper. Without taking your eyes off the model, *wait* until you are *convinced* that the pencil is touching that point on the model upon which your eyes are fastened.

Then move your eye *slowly* along the contour of the model and move the pencil *slowly* along the paper. As you do this, keep the conviction that the pencil point is actually touching the contour. Be guided more by the sense of touch than by sight. *This means that you must draw without looking at the paper,* continuously looking at the model.

Exactly coordinate the pencil with the eye. Your eye may be tempted at first to move faster than your pencil, but do not let it get ahead. Consider only the point that you are working on at the moment with no regard for any other part of the figure.

Often you will find that the contour you are drawing will leave the edge of the figure and turn inside, coming eventually to an apparent end. When this happens, glance down at the paper several times during the course of one study, but do not draw while you are looking at the paper. As in the beginning, place the pencil point on the paper, fix your eyes on the model, and wait until you are convinced that the pencil is touching the model before you draw.

Not all the contours lie along the outer edge of the figure. For example, if you have a front view of the face, you will see the definite contours along the nose and the mouth, which have no apparent connection with the contours at the edge. As far as the time for your study permits, draw these "inside contours" exactly as you draw the outside ones. Draw anything that your pencil can rest on and be guided along. *Develop the absolute conviction that you are touching the model.*

This exercise should be done slowly, searchingly, sensitively. Take your time. Do not be too impatient or too quick. There is no point in finishing any one contour study. In fact, a contour study is not a thing that can be "finished." It is having a particular type of experience, which can continue as long as you have the patience to look. If in the time allowed you get only half way around the figure, it doesn't matter. So much the better! But if you finish long before the time is up, the chances are that you are not approaching the study in the right way. A contour drawing is like climbing a mountain as contrasted with flying over it in an airplane. It is not a quick glance at the mountain from far away, but a slow, painstaking climb over it, step by step.

You might be interested in this comment by another art teacher (Frederic Gore, *Painting: Some Basic Principles*) about the relationship of naming and identifying, drawing and defining.

To put a line round something is to name it and to attempt to enumerate its characteristics. It is a form of definition. Children arrive at the same time at a stage when they draw objects and when they name them. It is difficult for any of us to draw in line something which we cannot name—that is to put a line round something which we cannot separate intellectually from its surroundings. If we draw a nameless thing, we automatically ask what it is while we draw it, and attempt to see a likeness in it to something which we can name. Both to draw things and to name things are attempts to identify and understand objects, situations, conditions and relationships. A particular function of line in drawing is (like naming) to define objects. With a line we first draw nouns. Later we describe relationships: physical situations, the geometry of space, psychological situations, movement. In the traditional European school of drawing (the heritage from Massacio, through Raphael to Ingres), contour defines objects and gives them their precise structure and character, while tone (shading) is largely used to state generalities of form—the physical characteristics which all objects share alike—planes and structural relationships, space, lighting conditions. A cube or a cylinder may be given solidity by tone, but it is defined as a cube or a cylinder by line. Whenever we wish to give individuality, precise definition and character to a figure in life drawing or to a head or anything else which we put in a drawing, we find that we must pursue the contour ruthlessly and search out the form by means of outline. The more particular we wish to be the more ruthless we must be. The characteristic shape is in the contour. If in a painting we see a line which is enclosed, we presuppose an object and try to recognize what it is.

Now read some passages from student journals, a couple of meditative essays based on journals, and a feature article for a newspaper written after such journal practice. They are offered not as models but as authentic responses to encourage you in your own observations:

Emily's Walnut Husk

Sept 3 Soft moss-like thread worn crust fruit pit white fluff gulleys ridges touchable cracking mold cheeky tip twig anteater insect animal

Sept 4 pointed pursed lips pouting prune spots shadow. Shadow looks like a battery, or blimp, or bottle, or fire extinguisher. Shadow looks like something man-made, technological; difference between shadow and object . . . inorganic/organic . . . dead/alive. Shadow so smooth, not ridged. Feels like velvet. Looks fragile, feels solid although crusty. Temptation to peel it. Sand embedded, almost glued. Nothing comes off on my fingers. What's inside? Skull of an animal. Angry profile.

Sept 5 Sturdy. About to kiss. Makes wooden, knocking sound. Little hairs. Musty smell. A mask, a puppet—seems alive but feels and sounds inanimate.

Sept 6 Tongue sticking out. Eight spokes, ridges, radiating from tip . . . they go haywire White spots like a disease . . . it rolled in talcum powder . . . transforming into whiteness? . . . aging. Twig trying to grow out at fat end . . . stopped in the middle of giving birth.

Sept 7 Ridges are like a map. Science fiction, another planet, a world. Falling off the edge, thin end is an enormous cliff. Trails, ocean, hills, inhabitants so tiny. Each speck, each fleck of fuzz lives there—or is a city—a country Wherever it is placed, it dominates, everything else is background like an aerial photo. Is there a world inside it? It's a capsule, it's going to take off, it's so still, the way a loaded object is charged but immobile. It's alive, vibrating. Still. Solitary. Stuck. Lonely.

Sept 8 It eats through the thin end. Ridges are rolls of fat or bulges showing ingestion. It's old and wrinkled and overfed and sitting there stuffed. Cracks at fat end—bursting and brittle. Soft, velvety/hard, crusty: an aged creature. So old, so delicate, sturdy but soft. Aged, wizened, grandparent, elder. Wise. Senior fruit.

Sept 9 Smooth side. Still has a snout. Piece of thread going across like a mantle, a sash. Draped regally, or like a snake on Medusa. Something refined about it, casually elegant. Mole or Mouse King. Fruit King. About to be propelled forward at a stately regal pace, a slow-motion scurry. White padding on behind so he can sit upright. Little feet underneath? Hold it and it's furry, squeeze it and it's hard like wood. Drop it and it crumbles a bit and makes knocking sound . . . not a furry little creature after all, only when you don't touch it.

Sept 10 The shell has crumbed off in places. Vulnerable. Suddenly capable of disintegrating. Greyer color inside. Insides are peeking out. Fur rubbed, chipped away . . . mange. A wound. Three heights, dimensions now: Tallest ridge, smooth surface, beneath the surface. Valleys. An old planet, devastated. An old creature deteriorating. The snout is still impish. It will keep on moving no matter what. Pursed lips smiling. Indestructible. What's been attacking it? Poor thing.

Sept 11 From head-on, the thread covers his nose—as if he's pushing through some wilderness, on the move and plowing past obstacles, one of which catches on his nose. He's in motion, the snout is angry, determined, the body is getting cut up, wounded, assaulted along the way, and time goes by and he gets older but he keeps on going, leading with his nose, peering out sharply with the eyes that are dents, that are ridges. White spots on his body like dust, cracking shell from the dry air, wrinkles around the face from fatigue and age and grimacing.

Sept 12 The fat end is tearing off. The creature is being ravaged. I've been careless with the object. It is slowly being destroyed. There is a patch of whiteness inside the end that's breaking. Does the white spotting come from inside? The outside is a sham, the real life is inside, hiding, deceiving me. But to explore it more I'd have to take it totally apart, dissect it, and that would mean ruining it, interfering, destroying it. It is coveting a secret. The shell is just a mask. But the inside that's now exposed is hard to the touch. Indestructible. It won't let me in. Its attitude is still the same, the face determined, aggressive. If the back fell completely off, would it change expression?

Sept 13 I feel so guilty, I put it carelessly in the pouch of my bag day after day, and now it's coming apart. But the thing is looking at me spitefully, nothing will really stop it. The angry profile is really smirking. It's now the end of our time together, and it's acting like it's got one up on me. I'm sick of it. It still looks valiant, like a charger, a little Mouse, Fruit Soldier. Slightly wounded but triumphant.

Bill's Blue Jay Feather

Friday 8 a.m. As I sit down to contemplate my feather—before I ever begin to really look at it, I have several *ideas* about it in my mind. So to dispose of them (somewhat) before I really begin—this is (I believe) a blue jay feather. That is a bird feather, with a thousand immediate connotations for me. For now I will *try* to leave the blue jay behind, however, and begin to simply look at it as an object.

The feather is about 5 inches long, and lies comfortably in my flattened palm. It is not wide; the sense of its size is along the length of the central spine, not across it. The spine itself is fine, lustrous, and very tough. At its white tip it is bare, and translucent, but about half an inch from the tip a gray black stain appears, and gradually replaces the white.

As the darker color begins strands of the feather itself start to appear—very soft, fine, and random in their formlessness. As the eye moves up the quill, however, the strands quickly become longer and more regular in their flow—and upward sweep turning slightly in upon the quill, and down, near the tip, so that each strand fits lightly under the tip of the next. Looking at the outside of the feather (as it would have been on the bird) the right side sweeps much more emphatically upward than the left, showing barely half the width of the latter. While the color of the right side of the feather changes from its original light grey to a rich blue almost before the strands have organized themselves into a uniform sweep, the left side remains obstinately grey for nearly an inch before the same bright blue begins to appear at the roots of the strands. From here, as the width of the feather expands, the dark grey remains an edging on the feather of a static width, while the blue arrowhead continues to expand as the eye follows the feather toward the tip. Thus, the feather is, basically, a rich blue, with the dark quill a line through this field, and the grey strand tips an edge along the left of the field.

This pattern dominates the feather, with only two exceptions. By far the most obvious is the tip of the feather, where blue and black both end abruptly on a sure white field broken only by the dark quill. The line of change is perpendicular to the quill, so that the strands, as they curve upward, each pass from their original color into white.

Sunday a.m. The second exception is along the narrower blue part of the feather, to the right of the quill. Appearing at the midpoint vertically of the blue field is a short, thick grey hash mark across the blue field perpendicular to the quill— the length of it from quill to the feather's edge, while the width is about half that. This mark is repeated four more times between the first one and the white band—now lighter, now darker, but always similar in shape. The marks appear to be superimposed over the blue field, yet they show the same lustre as the background.

The reverse side of the feather is hardly so interesting as the outside, for, although the pattern and texture of the reverse are repeated, the color is dominantly grey, with only a hint of the brilliant blue. In fact, this hint of blue, apparent only along the edge of the narrow side of the feather, is only a result of the curl of the strands—the back of each blue strand is actually completely grey.

Monday a.m. The perfect and balanced form so far set down by this description must be qualified by noting the slightly irregular edges of the feather. The edge itself is defined by the successive curling upward of one strand after another, and, as these curlings vary in degree from one strand to the next, slight irregularities in the edge are produced. A smooth, fine edge will suddenly be disrupted and dive inward as several exceptional strands are overcurled and turn back too sharply to blend in the edge pattern. Here, if closely observed, the strands assume their own individual identities, and the larger pattern is broken. But never for long; soon a more standardized strand will reset the dominant pattern, and the edge will be reasserted once again. Thus, the edge continues right up to the white tip. Here, as the strand lengths decline at the very end of the quill, each one's individual existence again becomes manifest—they become too short and bristly to maintain the pattern, becoming distinct branches out of the whole of the feather.

Tuesday p.m. Reading over this last paragraph and looking at the feather, I have just realized that the white tip is transparent —I can see through it as it lies on the page. I am not seeing between the strands, but through them. Looking down the feather again, it is not transparent in the blue/grey zone, until the grey pales considerably near the point of the quill. It must be the pigmentation of the strands which blocks the passage of the light, as it only penetrates where the darker colors are either absent or faint.

This feather is a marvelous thing, but what does it accomplish? Why don't birds have hair, or fur? It is water-resistant, I believe, because of its sheen, its fine texture, its regularity. But couldn't the water penetrate *between* such feathers? It does not strike me as a particularly efficient heat retainer, and although I am sure that it would give increased lift for flight, what is the point of covering the body with such feathers?

Wednesday a.m. Today is the last time I plan to write on my feather. As I look at it, it strikes me as completely familiar, with nothing (?) left to discover. But just say that, and I find something more. The feather is not two-dimensional as I thought, but actually shows a curve, both along the length and across its width looking down on the feather (i.e., on the outside), the edges curl upward just slightly, creating a gentle trough along the quill. And the quill itself is not straight; if laid on a flat surface it shows a steady arch above the table. In fact, it is this arch which, combined with the color and sweep of the strands, gives the feather its grace.

David's Milkweed Pod

Thursday, Sept. 2 I have set the milkweed pod on top of my digital clock and my minutes of observation are very neatly numbered for me. The first thing I notice is the damage incurred to the pod while it got carried around in the pocket of my coat. It has split slightly at the end of its seams, and its fur is slightly matted and worn. Its shape is similar to the shape of a large, fat goldfish. Its color is a nice light brown, the color of a mouse. In rereading that sentence I notice that "nice" is a totally unnecessary word that doesn't tell anybody what color brown the milkweed pod is.

This exercise is going to make me babble, I can see. I can observe my observations, observe myself trying to structure my observations ahead of time so that they will come out in ordered, "literary" paragraphs.

Friday The first thing I observe is that in plugging in my typewriter, I have unplugged my clock. That seemed like an awfully long minute. I tell myself to look at the pod, to center myself around it, so that at least my babble originates its drifting there. I stare at the pod, making associations; thinking about a book I read called the *Psychology of Meditation* that talked about meditating on objects. Then I think about a poem I read that used a pod as a sexual metaphor.

Saturday "Hello pod," my brain says to itself, feeling already a degree of familiarity. I notice faint lines running the length of the pod, like the grooves on smooth bark. Little bumps and nodules interrupt the grooves at random points. Short, white hairs stick out the seams. I realize I haven't really touched it to see what it feels like, and so I reach out and stroke it and it is very soft.

Sunday I think about the milkweed pod in terms of time. Probably no observable changes will happen in the week or so I observe it, but I know it's changing, drying out and transforming. It seems sterile and devoid of purpose, sitting there on my shelf. I get the urge to open the window and throw it out. For awhile the pod seems to be less an inanimate object and more a part of ongoing process. I think about the hundreds of potential milkweed plants contained inside the pod, and then remember when I was a child my father breaking open the stem of a milkweed plant and squeezing the milk onto a wart on his hand. He claimed that it cured warts, but I don't remember if it did or not.

Monday It occurs to me to smell the pod. Nothing very distinct, but then my sense of smell was never very acute. I can be in the same room with a hundred pieces of toast burning and never quiver a nostril. In this particular instance, however, I do not feel too deprived, since what I do smell has the faint odor of the dust bag in a vacuum cleaner. What I have really observed here is the limitations of my observational powers.

  I realize also that this journal would probably be different if I was writing it just for my private self. I am aware of the audience, mainly you, Mrs. Berthoff, and try to picture you reading this by the fireside of some Concord home.

Tuesday I set the pod out on the kitchen table so I could type there, and when I came back one of my roommates had picked the pod apart. I was already feeling overwhelmed at the possibilities of what there was to write about, and this made it seem like an infinity made more infinite. All there really is time to do in the 5 or 10 minutes that I look at it is to pull a few sentences down out of the brain static that gets generated. This gets me to thinking about what thought is like before it becomes sentences, which would be very hard to express in sentences. I've been thinking and writing for 5 minutes, and I've hardly said a word about the pod.

Wednesday I think I'll start off with more description. Dark, oval seeds cover a thick body of very light silken material, like cornsilk only more fragile. The seeds are overlapped in a pattern exactly like shingles on a roof. My thoughts spread out in associational chains from this fact. First of all I note that

I would probably not make this comparison if I hadn't worked on roofs. Then I wonder if most people notice the pattern of shingles, and wonder if that comparison would reach the mind's eye of most people. I feel that it is important for a writer to worry about that.

Another chain began with noticing the pattern, and was concerned with function. I realized that I knew the function of the pattern on a roof (to prevent leaks) but that I didn't know the function of the pattern on a seed pod.

Thursday All the seeds are falling off from the silk. I can't figure this out, because it seems to me that the seeds should be firmly attached, each to its own tuft of silk, so that they can float on the wind. The only explanation I can think of is that because the skin has been torn off, the inside is drier than it should be. Or maybe as the seed dries out on the wind it drops to the ground like a parachuter jumping out of an airplane. I doubt it, but the idea sounded good.

Martha's Bit of Branch

Here's a bit of branch, long since broken from its tree. All the juices have drained from this husk, but if you look closely at the core you can see the channels where they ran. The pith has splintered vertically, not across the stump; that tells you something about the direction of transport. Up and down food and drink were carried, from root to leaf and back again. (How water can be pushed so high, no one quite knows. The laws of hydraulics are broken by the tree, which follows secret laws of its own.) Nothing runs here now and there is no sign of root or leaf. Dried out like this, you might think such a fragment had been fixed and preserved forever—were it not for the sprinkling of fungus along its length, invisibly reducing organic back to inorganic stuff. Life is chewing away at death, reclaiming immortal matter.

There's a paragraph, a bundle of words split off from experience. Could a reader tell which way the currents that fed it ran? To one who knows the history of its composition, it seems impossible that any clues could be found in those splintered ends. See, the process of criticism is already starting to pull it apart. I wait to discover what new shapes will spring from its decomposing.

Suzanne's Crab Leg *

What am I looking at? What are these particles of shell, lying broken on a sheet of paper? And what are these dried filaments? Are they connective tissue, transparent and fragile, encrusted with sand, no longer able to bear the wrench and pull of the living, moving crab inside? Why is it that the upper part of the crab's leg is shattered, while the claw itself is nearly intact? Does the tubular, curved, tusk-like shape give the claw strength, or is it thicker and more resilient? I wonder—do those evil little teeth on the inner edge of each "jaw" of the claw contribute to its unbreakability? And why, in the drying-out and aging process, does the upper leg lose its resiliency so much more than the claw?

And what is there to see when I focus in close? Is it a process of close focus that reveals the complexities of surface and blurs the perception of forms? Why am I now more conscious of the play of orange toward the tip and cream toward the upper part of the claw? Is the ability to notice a shiny streak along the ridge (how is it I never *noticed* the ridge along the outside of the claw?) a function of concentrating on surface to the exclusion of form?

And now what happens when I move back again? Why am I conscious, now, as I wasn't before, of the arrangement of these forms on the white blue-lined sheet of paper? What roughness of claw teeth, fineness, abrasiveness of speckles of sand, what hungry, cave-like space interior to the claw's joint, bereft of its contiguous parts do I see? What happens to my mind as it moves in and out and over these forms, surfaces, textures, spaces?

What statement can I make that means as much as a query?

What mental process, what level of perception does the question keep pushing me toward, what statement would it close me off from, forcing a false start with each sentence? What happens when I touch these fragments, turn them over, rub my finger over the sand deposited inside, meditate on the salty, watery, sandy, sea-grassy life these forms belonged to when they were whole? What part of the whole is a crab, after all? What does it know of a windy

---

* Note that the sentences in this essay are all in the form of questions.

afternoon in early summer, of the glassy slick of water on
sand that its motions disturb only slightly? Does it feel and
sense its structural wholeness, fresh and pungent flesh
protected by a hard but resilient outside bone? Doesn't it
know it belongs there and not here, dry and fragmented on
my paper, in my electric-heated, sun-filled winter bedroom
on Waltham Street? Why did it get there in such a broken
condition, if not due to the detached curiosity of Ann
Berthoff, if not to the indifference and pocketbook-disorder
of Suzanne Lynch, if not to the testing and naughtiness of
my son's friend Thomas? Did you break it, Ann and Suzanne and Thomas, or was it broken already, when the
water level went down and left it drying and dying in last
summer's sun?

Rebecca's Water Lily

I began this semester with an assignment to describe a purple lily pod, which I found exciting and liberating. I had this
lovely object and the freedom to say anything I liked about
it, since in describing it I could describe how it affected me
and what it suggested to me. I turned it into an image of the
transience of life, the secretiveness of nature, the spring
and fall of the individual creature; I made sexual metaphors
from its intensity of color, and generalized to my personal
sense or experience of fall and the cold. I was amazed at the
sense of freedom, of being able to be myself in this new way.
The full significance of this first, self-consciously used image
was not apparent until much later.

The dried-up lily pod is still with me; sometimes perched
on my dictionary, usually on the floor of my room. I remember the day most of its stem, which I had loved for its
winding length, broke off, and today I notice that part of
the leaf itself has crumbled. It stayed and moved with
me through a significant period of time, along with other
gathered up images and fascinations. We move along, my
images and I, like a tidal wall of water—strong because they
carry meaning. I make them change, and mutate; I rearrange them and I suppose they change me. I wouldn't focus
on them so if they did not rearrange my thinking too.

It broke my heart (or would have, had I let it—I knew the
experience was not over) when the stem of the leaf broke
off since that was precisely what I'd liked. I broke it; it was

no accident, though one likes to think that these things just happen, life goes on, etc. But in addition to the calendars I keep, my journals, and all the photos I take—all pictures of time marked as it moves—I still have the pod, and I'm awfully glad I didn't throw it away when I got so anxious about my own abilities. All those times it mocked me (actually it more resembles a hungry, wretched cat now than anything that could mock), all those times it reminded me of my inability to work; how it tried to remain on the floor with the dust but I in some perverse mood always returned it to my desk—how hard it was to learn to live with chaos. The symbol of what was exciting at first has come full circle and makes me glad I still have it, battered as it is. It holds my meaning—I found my way through a section of time, and understanding.

Robin's Fish Trip

Why didn't somebody tell me? Why didn't you tell me? During the 7 years I've lived in Boston, I've been dragged to concerts, coerced into buying various record albums, and had my sanity questioned for not seeing certain films. But in all that time, no one has ever insisted that I visit the New England Aquarium. If I hadn't been sent there on a writing assignment, I might have missed out forever on the most involving museum in this area.

The Aquarium is such an exciting visual experience that I was talking to myself in wonder before I got off the first floor. You must go and see for yourself. The Aquarium opens at 9 A.M. It's important to arrive early before the endless busloads of schoolchildren disrupt the silent and intimate setting created by the very low lighting. The Aquarium uses the concept of theatre and entertainment in its interior layout. In the semidarkness, as in a theatre, one's sense of both privacy and involvement are heightened and a very personal experience is possible. Tanks of varying sizes are mounted into the walls and lighted from behind. Like small stages they present a particular view of aquatic conditions or explain the complex relationships of sea plants and animals to one another and to us. In each tank there is at least one creature whose brilliant colors or fantastic shape stand out wonderfully, luring us through the half-light to the next tank.

The Aquarium manages to present an enormous amount of information and a great variety of exhibits in a simple direct manner. I learned about underwater sounds (the ocean, it turns out, is a pretty noisy place), and got some static from an electric fish when I pushed the button in front of its tank. I was warned against poisonous stingrays, man-eating sharks, and the dangerous shellfish-out-of-season! Printed information is mounted in colored letters, along with photographs, on plexiglass and then illuminated from behind. Some exhibits have recorded information which plays when you press a button. All the tanks are placed on opposite ends of each floor. The side walls are either left in shadow or have pictures of whales and sharks painted in large, outline form.

The real first floor is actually a wide, shallow pool in which penguins and sharks live in apparent harmony. Around this pool runs a slightly elevated walkway, and from its center rises the three-story, cylindrical glass tank. Another walkway spirals right around the sides of this enormous tank until it reaches the top floor where you can look down into the water and realize just how broad the tank is. Going up this ascending walkway is just like walking through Harvard Square on any warm Sunday afternoon. I just couldn't believe what I saw. Giant sea-turtles with shells like batiked leather, the world's fattest fish, sharks with quick, subtle movements, and hundreds of fish of every size, including a deflated blowfish and one poor creature with a healed-over bite taken right out of its back. Every hour a diver goes to the bottom and feeds the turtles and smaller fish, while the sharks turn terrifying arcs through his rising air bubbles. This feeding procedure became a strange water ballet, which set off for me a chain of associations on our relation to the sea and our place with these creatures in the evolutionary chain.

All these musings were lost when I got back down to the first floor exit and came upon the sea otters. These little animals have the same effect on order as the Marx Brothers, tearing about their area and bathing pool in a total frenzy. The glass boundary was the only reason I was able to keep from picking one up and taking it home. The otters actually seem to wave as they swim on their backs and perform series of difficult underwater somersaults, squeaking all the while. If their appeal isn't enough to encourage you to visit the

Aquarium, go anyway! I promise that you will find yourself wondering, as I did, why no one ever told you about the
New England Aquarium.

3. Seeing Relationships: Paragraph Sequence I

The subject of these short paragraphs by poets, philosophers, artists, and psychologists is the mind in action. Each is
followed by a brief comment that generally relates the points
made in the paragraphs to the composing process. You are then
offered *assisted invitations* to do some experimental thinking
and writing. These are indicated by the little sign: ࿓

Sometimes a particular composing exercise is suggested;
sometimes I simply say "consider," although, of course, you can
write out your "consideration." If you use the left-hand side of
the open double page of a notebook—use your journal of observations—for notes and queries about the reading, then you could
write on the right-hand side, following the assisted invitations,
to find out what you are doing when you make sense of the world.

The experiments do not increase in difficulty; in fact, they
may become simpler. There are no right answers. The experiments
are ways of exploring the composing process as an ongoing
operation, which includes getting ideas, seeing the point, thinking something out, inventing, arguing, dreaming—writing
things down all along the way. Keeping everything together will
enable you to return to an experiment and rediscover what it is
about and, perhaps, to give it another go. Anything your instructor wants to read can be transcribed, but this is your notebook,
a way for you to listen in on the inner dialogue you carry on
when you are thinking.

Sensory Knowing: Muir's Girnel

Our diet was a curious one by town standards. We went without many necessaries, or what are considered necessaries—
beef, for instance—and had a great number of luxuries which
we did not know to be luxuries, such as plovers' eggs, trout,
crab, and lobster: I ate so much crab and lobster as a boy
that I have never been able to enjoy them since. Our staples
were homemade oat bannocks and barley bannocks, butter,
eggs, and home-made cheese, which we had in abundance;

white bread, bought at the Wyre shop, was looked upon as a luxury. In the kitchen there was a big girnel with a sliding top; inside it was divided in two, one compartment being filled with oatmeal and the other with barley-meal. The meal had to be pressed firmly down, otherwise it would not keep. The girnel, when the top was slid back, gave out a thick, sleepy smell, which seemed to go to my head and make me drowsy. It was connected with a nightmare which I often had, in which my body seemed to swell to a great size and then slowly dwindle again, while the drowsy smell of meal filled my nostrils. It is from smell that we get our most intense realization of the solidity of things. The smell of meal pressed tightly down in the girnel made me realize its *mass*, though I could see only its surface, which was smooth and looked quite shallow. My nightmares probably came from an apprehension of the mere bulk of life, the feeling that the world is so tightly crammed with solid, bulging objects that there is not enough room for all of them: a nightmare feeling powerfully conveyed in the stories of Franz Kafka.

Edwin Muir, *An Autobiography*

Human beings learn in childhood to read the book of nature. You come to understand what to expect when you tease a cat or toss a pebble in a pool or touch a hot stove. You don't have to go to school to learn how to judge distance or to tell whether it's early or late afternoon (assuming that you aren't suddenly transported to a different latitude). We learn in terms of the space things take up, the time things take to happen. We live in a world of space and time because it is of such a world that our senses give report. Learning to make sense of that world, discovering physical dimensions and the psychological limits of experience, is the work of childhood. It can be the happiest work we ever do—or the grimmest; more and more frequently for American children, it is simply missing. Watching a television program about burrs and frogs can't give you the same experience as exploring a vacant lot; seeing a documentary about life in an inner city slum is not the same thing as the remembered experience of being cold and hungry.

                  ❧ 1. Muir observes that it is smell which gives us "our most intense realization of the solidity of things." What sense, would you say, gives

us our most intense realization of the fluidity of things?
Tell about how you know from your own experience.

2. Can you remember an early occasion when you were
conscious of *space* as well as of something little or big
in space? Describe it.

3. Look up the "seven wonders of the world." How
many were (are) famous because of size? What does
your discovery tell you?

4. Maria Montessori, one of the great women of our
century, realized that what children learn they teach
themselves, and that they can be totally involved—
body, mind, soul—in that endeavor. In her schools, she
developed a "prepared environment" to provide for
Rome slum children occasions that would encourage the
kind of experience from which children learn. I don't remember that she had any girnels on hand, but you
might be interested in reading how she designed the
equipment for her school. She gives a full account in
The Montessori Method, but almost any book by or about
Montessori will describe the prepared environment.

5. Edwin Muir's poems include several in which his
boyhood in the Orkney Islands provides the imagery.
Read, for an example, "The Horses." He was also a
critic and, with his wife, the translator of Franz Kafka,
whom he mentions in this passage. One of Kafka's
stories that can give you an idea of this power of dis-
torting the dimensions of the physical world so that we
seem to be sitting in on a dream is "The Bucket Rider."
In "The Burrow" and "Metamorphosis" the physical
scale of experience becomes a metaphysical theme.

6. The environment of the country and the environment of the city are different; the world of space and
time is the same. How do you think a city child might
first gain a sense of mass?

Physiognomic Knowing: Gombrich's Ping/Pong

. . . What is called "synesthesia," the splashing over of impressions from one sense modality to another, is a fact to
which all languages testify. They work both ways—from
sight to sound and from sound to sight. We speak of loud
colors or of bright sounds, and everyone knows what we

mean. Nor are the ear and the eye the only senses that are thus converging to a common center. There is touch in such terms as "velvety voice" and "a cold light," taste with "sweet harmonies" of colors or sounds, and so on through countless permutations. . . . Synesthesia concerns relationships. I have tried out this suggestion in a party game. It consists of creating the simplest imaginable medium in which relationships can still be expressed, a language of two words only—let us call them "ping" and "pong." If these were all we had and we had to name an elephant and a cat, which would be ping and which pong? I think the answer is clear. Or hot soup and ice cream. To me, at least, ice cream is ping and soup pong. Or Rembrandt and Watteau? Surely in that case Rembrandt would be pong and Watteau ping. I do not maintain that it always works, that two blocks are sufficient to categorize all relationships. We find people differing about day and night and male and female, but perhaps these different answers would be reduced to unanimity if the question were differently framed: pretty girls are ping and matrons pong; it may depend on which aspect of womanhood the person has in mind, just as the motherly, enveloping aspect of night is pong, but its sharp, cold, and menacing physiognomy may be ping to some.

E. H. Gombrich, Art and Illusion

Elephants, Rembrandt, and soup have nothing in common except that when they are placed in opposition with something else of a certain kind to be symbolized by "ping," they are "pong." It's hard to see if an elephant could ever be a *ping*, but if you put a cold soup—*gazpacho*—in opposition with chili, soup might then be *ping*. Rembrandt's shadows help make him *pong*, but shadows in a summer grave could be *ping* if they are in opposition to a stormy sea.

All of this categorizing has to do with how the interior of your mouth is shaped when you say *ping* or *pong* and how the sounds those words make are associated with objects. In making sense of the world, we use all our senses and associate one sense experience with another. But we also judge character and temperament and develop our expectations about feelings and ideas on the basis of those experiences. This game can teach you a lot about the interaction of sensory experience and thinking, which is seeing relationships.

➦ 1. Categorize as *ping* or
pong two things of the same kind: two items of clothing,
two cars, two games, etc. Exchange your *ping/pong* list
with someone and see how much agreement there is on
the *pings* and *pongs*.
2. The eighteenth century philosophers were fascinated
by the notion that one sense corresponds to another.
Locke reasoned that the color yellow could be explained
to a blind man as being analogous to the sound of a
trumpet. Try describing your favorite colors in terms of
sound. Or how about sounds as colors—"the blues"?

Interpretation: Arnheim's Droodles

Visual knowledge and correct expectation will facilitate
perception whereas inappropriate concepts will delay or im-
pede it. . . . A Japanese reads without difficulty ideographs
so small that a Westerner needs a magnifying glass to discern them, not because the Japanese have more acute eyesight
but because they hold the *kanji* characters in visual storage.
For similar reasons, bird watchers, hunters, mariners, phy-
sicians or microbiologists often seem endowed with super-
human powers of vision. And the average layman of today
has no trouble perceiving human figures or animals in Im-
pressionist paintings that looked like assortments of meaningless color patches eighty years ago.

It should be noted that the effect of such "preperceived"
images depends not simply on how often their prototypes
have been met in the past but also quite importantly on
what the nature of the given context seems to call for. What
one expects to see depends considerably on what "belongs"
in that particular place. The perception of familiar kinds
of objects, then, is inseparably related to norm images the
observer harbors in his mind.

Rudolf Arnheim, *Visual Thinking*

We construe—figure out what we're hearing or seeing—on
the basis of what we have seen, but also according to what we
think we might be seeing or hearing. Once, in the days before
jet travel when transatlantic planes had to make fueling stops,
I found myself in Iceland. After three months in Europe hearing very little English, I had expected that customers at the
coffee bar in Reykjavik would be speaking Icelandic. I took in

with fascination the strange and wonderful sounds of a language I associated with stirring epic and wild, primitive song. As I listened, it became clear that what I was hearing was my native tongue spoken by two G.I.s from the Bronx.

                 ∾ 1. Consider the role of expectation in instances of recognition, false and correct, from your own experience.

2. What role does expectation play in cryptography? In jokes?

3. Arnheim suggests that "droodles," which are "playful examples of visual paradoxes ingeniously exploited" can provide "good study material for any explorer of visual perception." One of his students created this droodle, captioned "Olive dropping into martini glass" or "Close-up of girl in bikini." One of my students, who has gone into the contracting business, saw it as "Hip roof with a paint bucket on the porch." How did he get that image? Can you see it as something else? Draw your own droodle. Ask your friends for captions.

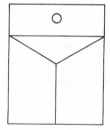

Oppositional Structures: Ogden's Starfish

Opposites . . . may be either the two extremes of a scale or the two sides of a cut, the cut marking the point of neutrality, the absence of either of two opposed characters in the field of opposition. . . . The symbolic forms which have been developed in ordinary language for the expression of these distinctions have been crystalized not only in terms of two-dimensional projection, but also in a very special relation to the human body.

In the first place, the spatial cut has been identified with the body itself, and more specifically with its vertical axis, in the opposition of *sides*, right and left, and the opposed rectilinear directions, right and left, along the arms in a horizontal position. Secondly, the *extremes* of the scale are represented by the head and feet, the two opposite ends of a single continuum, measured primarily upward, from the base to the top, as with the minimum and maximum of the thermometer. Hence the convention whereby *In front of* and *Behind*, which also give us the opposition of Before and After, Future and Past, are diagrammatically on the horizontal line of right and left—in terms of the position of the body (facing either right or left) and of a progress along the line; while Up and Down are primarily movements from one extreme of the vertical scale to the other.

This dependence of our symbolization of opposition on the symmetry of the body is emphasized when we consider the oppositional requirements of such an actinian as the star-fish. We, too, have elaborated secondary oppositions for the upper and lower *surface*, the opposite ends of a *diameter*, *radial* opposition, etc.; but since they are not "our" surface, "our" diameter, and "our" radius, neither our primary projections and diagrams nor our linguistic metaphors are in these terms.

C. K. Ogden, Opposition

Ogden's explanation of two fundamental kinds of opposition —the cut and the scale—can lead to interesting speculations about how we orient ourselves in the world of space and time. Paul Klee's notes on balance and symmetry will remind you of what you already know if you've ever done any layout for a newspaper, designed a poster, arranged furniture, decorated a store window or tried to teach someone to ride a bicycle. Klee was one of the most influential of modern painters. In his classes at the *Bauhaus*, a center for the study of design in all the arts, he taught the principles of motion and form by means of such exercises as these from his *Pedagogical Sketchbook* which explain how we read the environment according to our bodily orientation in time and space.

Re-cognition: Barfield's House

A little reflection shows that all *meaning*—even of the most primitive kind—is dependent on the possession of some measure of this power [the capacity to recognize significant

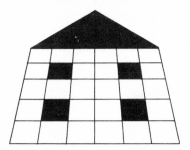

Once more the vertical

Why is this representation of a house wall incorrect? It isn't wrong logically. The lower window openings are closer to the eye than the upper ones, which means they are "larger" perspectively. As representation of a floor pattern, this perspective rendering could be easily accepted. This picture is therefore incorrect not logically but psychologically, because every creature, in order to preserve his balance, insists on seeing actual verticals projected as such.

The tightrope walker with his pole. Horizontality: The Horizon as actuality.

Horizontality: The Horizon as supposition.

The vertical indicates the straight path and the erect posture or the position of the creature. The horizontal indicates his height, his horizon. Both are completely realistic, static facts.

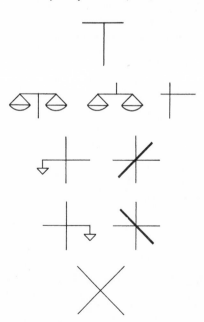

The scale

The tightrope walker is emphatically concerned about his balance. He calculates the gravity on both ends. He is the scale.

The essence of the scale is the crossing of perpendicular and horizontal.

Disturbed balance and its effect.

Correction through counterweight, and the resulting counter-effect.

Combination of both effects, or diagonal cross (symmetrical balance as restoration).

Nonsymmetrical balance

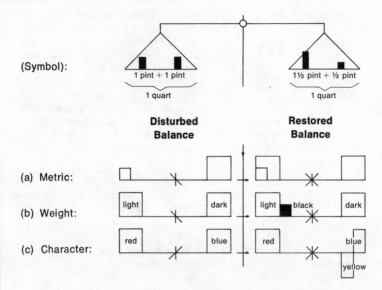

(Symbol):

1 pint + 1 pint   1½ pint + ½ pint

1 quart   1 quart

Disturbed Balance   **Restored Balance**

(a) Metric:

(b) Weight: light   dark   light   black   dark

(c) Character: red   blue   red   blue   yellow

Left: Overloaded through the heavy dark, the axis AB has dropped from a to A, and has risen from b to B. Its original horizontal position was ab. Both axes, ab and AB, have the point C as a common pivot. As the result of a turn around this point, left-dark is now lower than right-light. To restore balance, black is added to the right-light.

Or: I am stumbling toward left and reach out toward right to prevent a fall.

Right: The upper portion of my body is too heavy. The vertical axis shifts toward left and I would fall if correction did not take place in time by broadening the base through a step outward of my left leg.

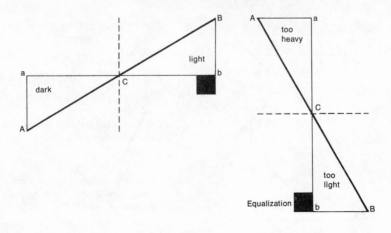

resemblances and analogies]. Where it was wholly absent, the entire phenomenal cosmos must be extinguished. All sounds would fuse into one meaningless roar, all sights into one chaotic panorama, amid which no individual objects —not even color itself—would be distinguishable. Let the reader imagine for a moment that he is standing in the midst of a normal and familiar environment—houses, trees, grass, sky, etc.—when, suddenly, he is deprived by some supernatural stroke of every vestige of memory—and not only of memory, but also of all those assimilated, forgotten experiences which comprise his power of *recognition.* He is asked to assume that, in spite of this, he still retains the full measure of his cognitive faculty as an adult. It will appear, I think, that for the first few moments his consciousness—if it can bear that name—will be deprived not merely of all thought, but even of all perception—unless we choose to suppose a certain unimaginable minimum, a kind of panorama of various light, which he will confront with a vacant and uncomprehending stare. It is not merely that he will be unable to realize that that square, red and white object is a "house," and to form concepts of an inside with walls and ceilings—he will not even be able to see it *as* a square, red and white object. For the most elementary distinctions of form and color are only apprehended by us with the help of the concepts which we have come to unite with the pure sense-datum. And these concepts we acquire and fix, as we grow up, with the help of words—such as *square, red,* etc. On the basis of past perceptions, using language as a kind of storehouse, we gradually build up our ideas, and it is only these which enable us to become "conscious," as human beings, of the world around us.

Owen Barfield, *Poetic Diction*

The osprey dives from a great height above a broad river and takes off again with a fish in its talons; the boy runs after the ball, dodging cars in the busy street, snatching it just in time from in front of a truck. Are the two acts of the same kind? The cat about to give birth to her first kitten looks pained and perplexed, but the minute the first kitten pops out, she licks it, nudges it into place by a nipple, eats the afterbirth and gets ready for kitten No. 2; the pianist looks over the score for a minute or so and then plays it through without pause. Are the two acts comparable?

Re-cognition means *re-knowing*—but what is *knowing?* For a student of composition, it is instructive to keep asking that question: How do I know? What do I know? How do I know I know? Do I know my knowledge?

Barfield's difficult book is about the making of meanings by all those who use language; that's you and I and the poets, but not cats or fish hawks or even cute chimpanzees.

        ❧ 1. What does "coming to your senses" mean in the case of regaining consciousness after fainting? How about suddenly seeing that you've been mistaken about something important? Describe the experiences.

2. Look up accounts of persons who, having been blind or deaf since birth, are by surgical means given those senses. How do their experiences tally with what Barfield imagines would happen if we lost the power to recognize?

3. What role does "recognition," in Barfield's sense, play in the dilemmas of science fiction? Write a recognition scene from a chapter you could call "Galactic Roar." (Barfield notes that without the power of recognition, "all sounds would fuse into a meaningless roar.")

4. There are certain kinds of aphasia (loss of language power because of brain damage) in which a person can recognize objects but not their names; in other forms, the name will be recognized but not the object. Read Kurt Goldstein's *Human Behavior* for a fascinating account of early work in this field of psychology with soldiers wounded in the first World War.

Forming: Langer's "Things"

Our merest sense-experience is a process of formulation. The world that actually meets our senses is not a world of "things," about which we are invited to discover facts as soon as we have codified the necessary logical language to do so; the world of pure sensation is so complex, so fluid and full, that sheer sensitivity to stimuli would only encounter what William James has called (in characteristic phrase) "a blooming, buzzing confusion." Out of this bedlam our sense organs must select certain predominant forms, if they are to make report of *things* and not of mere dissolving sensa. The eye and ear must have their logic—their "categories of understanding," if you like the Kantian idiom, or their "primary imagination," in Coleridge's version of the same concept. An object is not a datum, but a form construed by the sensitive and intelligent organ, a form which is at once an experienced individual thing and a symbol for the concept of it, for this *sort of thing.*

. . . Mental life begins with our mere physiological constitution. A little reflection shows us that, since no experience occurs more than once, so-called "repeated" experiences are really *analogous* occurrences, all fitting a form that was abstracted on the first occasion. *Familiarity* is nothing but the quality of fitting very neatly into the form of a previous experience. I believe our ingrained habit of hypostatizing impressions, of seeing *things* and not sense-data, rests on the fact that we promptly and unconsciously abstract a form from each sensory experience, and use this form to *conceive* the experience as a whole, as a "thing."

Susanne K. Langer, Philosophy in a New Key

In the daily entries in your journal of observations, you can begin to test the truth of Langer's argument. Perception, which is a process of composing, involves differentiation and selection, amalgamation and elimination. As you describe your "thing," you are selecting and differentiating, saying what it reminds you of, setting it apart from others of the same kind. You can listen in on your own thoughts to find out how it is that what you see becomes familiar.

           1. When you are studying a difficult passage like Langer's, it's a good idea to read it straight through first. Then compare the final sentence with the opening sentence and see if you understand how the last one repeats the first. Then reread. Finally, look up the words that you still can't make sense of (*hypostatizing?*) and reread.

2. For the final sentence, is *form finds form* an adequate "translation"? Why or why not?

3. You know the old story of how the blind men described the elephant: can you describe the object of your observations in terms only of touch?

4. Consider seeing each of the things listed below for the first time. Then describe the appearance and your experience. You can do this in narrative form: "When we reached the top of the hill, there we saw below us on the plain. . . ."

> a man on horseback
> snow
> a used-car lot
> a metropolis

Forms of Limitation: Whitehead's Squirrel

That day in the history of mankind when the vague appreciation of multitude was transformed into the exact observation of number, human beings made a long stride in the comprehension of that interweaving of form necessary for the higher life which is the disclosure of Good.

I remember an incident proving that at least some squirrels have not passed this borderline of civilization. We were in a charming camp situated amidst woodland bordering a Vermont lake. A squirrel had made its nest in our main sitting-room, placing it in a hole in brickwork around the fireplace. One day she decided that her family had grown up beyond the nursery stage. So, one by one, she carried them out to the edge of the woodland. As I remember across the years, there were three children. But when the mother had placed them on the rock outside, the family group looked to her very different from its grouping within the nest. She was vaguely disturbed, and ran backwards and forwards two or three times to make quite sure that no squirrel had been left behind. She was unable to count, nor had she identified them by christening them with names. All she knew was that the vague multitude on the rock seemed very unlike the vague multitude in the nest. Her family experiences lacked the perception of the exact limitation imposed by number. As a result she was mildly and vaguely disturbed. If the mother could have counted, she would have experienced the determinate satisfaction of a job well-done in the rearing of three children; or, in the case of loss, she would have suffered vivid pain from the absence of a determinate child. But she lacked adequate experience of any precise form of limitation.

Thus the rise in vivid experience of the Good and of the Bad depends upon the intuition of exact forms of limitation. Among such forms number has a chief place.

Alfred North Whitehead, *Modes of Thought*

Whitehead's contention in the chapter from which this passage is taken is that, although the feelings we have about the Good are often associated with infinitude (absence of limits), it is our capacity to count, to move from a sense of "vague multitude" to a "precise form of limitation" that allows us to suffer and enjoy moral feelings. Enumerating and naming are vital to the development of a specifically human moral sense.

      1. What devices for "counting" have you developed other than numbers? What ways do you have of remembering license numbers and phone numbers, etc.?

2. You probably know some counting games (e.g., "One potato, two potato, three potato, four . . ."). Write one for the squirrel.

3. Argue that the need for counting might have a biological basis, as well as having moral implications.

4. Does a cat suffer the same confusion when she moves her litter?

5. Consider the "Old Woman Who Lived in a Shoe" ("She had so many children she didn't know what to do . . ."). How is her dilemma different from the squirrel's?

Thinking about Thinking: Burke's Trout

All living organisms interpret many of the signs about them. A trout, having snatched at a hook but having had the good luck to escape with a rip in his jaw, may even show by his wiliness thereafter that he can revise his critical appraisals. His experience has led him to form a new judgment, which we should verbalize as a nicer discrimination between food and bait. A different kind of bait may outwit him, if it lacks the appearances by which he happens to distinguish "jaw-ripping food." And perhaps he passes up many a morsel of genuine food simply because it happens to have the characters which he, as the result of his informing experience, has learned to take as the sign of bait. I do not mean to imply that the sullen fish has thought all this out. I mean simply that in his altered response, for a greater or lesser period following the hook episode, he manifests the changed behavior that goes with a new meaning, he has a more educated way of reading the signs. It does not matter how conscious or unconscious one chooses to imagine this critical step; we need only note here the outward manifestation of a revised judgment.

Our great advantage over this sophisticated trout would seem to be that we can greatly extend the scope of the critical process. Man can be methodical in his attempts to decide what the difference between bait and food might be. Unfortunately, as Thorstein Veblen has pointed out, invention is the mother of necessity: the very power of criticism has enabled man to build up cultural structures so complex that still greater powers of criticism are needed before he can distinguish between the food-processes and bait-processes concealed beneath his cultural tangles. His greater critical capacity has increased not only the range of his solutions, but also the range of his problems. Orientation can go wrong. Consider, for instance, what conquest over the environment we have attained through our powers of abstraction, of generalization; and then consider the stupid national or racial wars which have been fought precisely because these abstractions were taken for realities. No slight critical ability is required for one to have as his deepest enemy a people thousands of miles away. When criticism can do so much for us, it may have got us just to the point where we greatly require still better criticism. Though all organisms are critics in the sense that they interpret the signs about them, the experimental speculative technique made available by speech would seem to single out the human species as the only one possessing an equipment for going beyond the criticism of experience to a criticism of criticism. We not only interpret the characters of events (manifesting in our responses all the graduations of fear, apprehension, expectation, assurance, for which there are rough behavioristic counterparts in animals)—we may also interpret our interpretations.

Kenneth Burke, *Permanence and Change*

Kenneth Burke's disquisition on how a trout responds to the world makes the point that it is language that enables non-trouts to go beyond the interpretation of signs to the interpretation of interpretations. The trout lives in a world of stimuli and responses; nontrouts live in a world of meanings. Even if it is called "verbal behavior" in an attempt to bridge the worlds of animal and human life, *language* as a mediation differs profoundly from *language* as a system of signals. The retinal cells act according to certain codes that are stored neurologically, but when we look at something, when we see relationships, there are numberless other intervening acts by which the brain/mind transforms signals into symbols. Throughout this book there are passages from the writings of psychologists and philosophers about the nature and character of those transformations; for now, what we need to note is that interpreting our interpretations is made possible because language gives us a means of making meanings.

         1. "No chimpanzee thinks he thinks": that is the poet W. H. Auden's way of putting the point about the world of meanings in which we live. Thinking about thinking; observing your observations; interpreting our interpretations: How would you explain these formulations?

2. What's the difference between Kenneth Burke's trout and a trout in a Walt Disney animated cartoon? What does *animation* mean?

3. How would you explain the difference between Morse *Code* and a *code* of ethics?

4. Form Finds Form

When you're faced with a blank piece of paper, what you need in order to get started is not philosophy but a method; nevertheless, if a method is not going to degenerate into a set of do's and don't's, it must have a philosophical foundation. A method should be grounded in certain principles that can account for what you do when you compose. Those principles all concern the making of meaning. Here they are in summary form:

The composing process by which we make meanings is a continuum. We don't take in the world like a camera or a set of recording devices. The mind is an agent, not a passive receiver; experience isn't poured into it. The active mind is a composer and everything we respond to, we compose.

Things are "really" there, but what is "really" there we can't see. For instance, you look in front of you and see a solid object—say a table, which is usually the philosopher's favorite example. Modern physics tells us that this table is really an event, but we don't see electrons moving in that frenzy of activity that makes the table an event. We do not have eyes that can take in that scene; if we did, it would be quite a focusing job to move from submicroscopic levels to those required to see objects in space. An electron microscope, which transforms in an exceedingly complex manner, could give us a picture of one infinitely small portion of that excited mass, but it would be in no way relevant to the experience or knowledge we have of the piece of furniture we put the cups and saucers on. We don't have x-ray eyes, because human life does not require such vision and indeed would be impossible if we saw inner structure rather than contour and color. We can judge dimension and mass and depth of field because the space in which we move requires such perception. The brain puts things together, composing the percepts by which we can make sense of the world. We don't just "have" a visual experience and then by thinking "have" a mental experience: the mutual dependence of seeing and knowing is what a modern psychologist has in mind when he speaks of "the intelligent eye." That is very ancient wisdom: our word *idea* derives from a Greek word that originally meant both *I have seen* and *I know*.

Meanings are relationships. Seeing means "seeing relationships," whether we're talking about seeing as *perception* or seeing as *understanding*. "I see what you mean" means "I understand how you put that together so that it makes sense." The way we make sense of the world is to see something *with respect to, in terms of, in relation to* something else. We can't make sense of one thing by itself; it must be seen as being *like* another thing; or *next to, across from, coming after* another thing; or as a *repetition* of another thing. *Something* makes sense—is meaningful—only if it is taken with *something else*.

Now, just as the retinal cells and the rest of the brain compose the relationships we see/perceive, so the active mind composes the relationships we see/understand. Relationships, whether perceptual or conceptual, are compositions. We perceive and understand relationships in terms of space and time and causality. The way we *know* reality, the ways we have of seeing relationships, are encompassed by those three terms, space, time, causality: they are what the philosopher Kant called the "categories of human understanding." We see/know outline, contour, color, texture; we judge size, volume, distance, rate of speed, direction; we apprehend succession, whether it's a chain of happenings—"one damned thing after another"—or a complicated story or play or joke; we can figure out the cause if we see the effect, and we can guess the effect if we know the cause. Of course, we will be frequently mistaken (Is it a man or a bird?); having the capacity to understand means having the capacity to misunderstand. The categories of understanding are not guarantors of the truth; that is why we need to be critical in our thinking, to learn a method that will guide us in interpreting our interpretations.

There must be a means of making meanings. One of the chief meanings of meaning is *mediation,* "the means by which." We can neither apprehend (take in, gather, make sense of) reality nor express an idea without a means of doing so. Everything we know, we know in some form; there is no *im*mediate knowledge. (*In-,* which can be a sign of the negative, changes to *im-* before *m.*) We don't "have" meanings that we then put into words. Language is not a set of pigeon holes into which we put things, ideas, feelings. We discover meanings in the process of working (and playing) with the means language provides.

Language is our readiest means of making meaning. Linguistic forms correspond to perceptual forms. Seeing that the circles move out from where the stone is tossed is comparable to saying/thinking: "If I toss the stone in the pool, it will then mark the center of a series of expanding circles." Or, more simply, "Look what I can make happen!" Making meanings with language is like making sense of the world. Telling left from right is like telling beginnings from ends, both when we watch something happen and when we tell a story about how it did happen. Differentiating dark from light, figure from ground, the shore bird from reeds and grasses may take practice and experience, but it involves the same acts of mind as are involved when we follow an argument or answer a question.

The way meanings are put together by means of language matches our experience of how things are related in time and space and the way causes and effects reflect and control one another. *Form finds form* is a short-hand way of saying all this. It's a way of representing both *feedback*—the guidance we get from the means we are using—and what one philosopher (I. A. Richards) has called *feedforward*—the capacity to formulate the choices we make when we are putting things together, seeing relationships, interpreting our experience, making meanings.

part ii

A METHOD OF COMPOSING

Introduction: The Auditor and the Sheep Dog

To observe carefully, to think cogently, to write coherently: these are all forming activities. If you consider the composing process as a continuum of forming, then you can take advantage of the fact that you are born a composer. The way you make sense of the world is the way you write: how you construe is how you construct. You can set about learning to write, confident that composition is not a matter of hammering together words and phrases, sentences and paragraphs, according to standard patterns that somebody else tells you to superimpose. It's a matter, rather, of learning how to use the forms of language to discover the forms of thought and vice versa. By conceiving of meanings not as things but as relationships, you can avoid the futile question of which comes "first"—the chicken or the egg dilemma—and explore instead the mutual dependence of choosing and limiting, identifying and differentiating, finding and creating forms. You can discard the faulty notion that when you compose, "you figure out what you want to say before you write," and accept, instead, this more helpful slogan: *You can't know what you mean until you hear what you say.* Like *form finds form,* this formula suggests the mutual dependence of ends and means, which is at the heart of composition.

Studying the composing process can teach you that ideas are not floating in the air, waiting to be brought down to earth; thoughts are not nonverbal butterflies that you catch with a verbal butterfly net.* The relationship between thought and language is dialectical: ideas are conceived by language; language is generated by thought. (*Conceive, generate:* sexual metaphors are indispensable in describing the life of the mind unless you want to consider the mind a machine and speak of *products.* Composing, in this book, is considered as an organic process, not a mechanical one.)

A composition is a bundle of parts. When you compose, you "get it together," but the "it" is not a matter of things or "words"; what you get together in composing is relationships, meanings. In composing, you make parts into wholes; you compose the way you think—by seeing relationships, by naming, defining, and articulating relationships. What makes it hard is that you have to do two things at once: you have to bundle the parts as if you knew what the whole was going to be and you have to figure out the whole in order to decide which parts are going to fit and which are not. The only way to do that is to keep everything tentative, recognizing that getting the parts together, figuring out the whole, is a dialectical process.

Dialectic is the term we will use throughout this book to name the mutual dependence of language and thought, all the ways in which a word finds a thought and a thought, a word. The most useful definition for our purposes comes from I. A. Richards who calls dialectic a *continuing audit of meaning.*† Just as a bookkeeper has to account for income and expenditures in order to balance credits and debits, an audit of meanings would have to balance what one sentence seems to say against what others seem to say; how one way of saying something compares with another; what one word seems to refer to in a certain context with what it seems to refer to in another. Of course, *audit* also has to do with listening. In composing, you have to be your own auditor in both senses: you have to listen in on the inner dialogue, which is thinking, and you have to be able to

---

* I. A. Richards puts the matter this way in "The Future of Poetry," reprinted in *So Much Nearer: Essays Towards a World English* (New York: Harcourt, 1968), p. 175.

† See *How to Read a Page* (Boston: Beacon, 1959), p. 240 and *Speculative Instruments* (New York: Harcourt, 1955), p. 109.

balance the account of what you've been hearing against what is set down on paper.

In all its phases, composing is conversation you are having with yourself—or *selves*, since you are speaker, audience, and critic all at once. You do the talking, the answering, and the kibbitzing. When you are making meaning in sentences, gathering sentences to compose paragraphs and paragraphs to construct arguments, you are doing the same kind of thing you do when you carry on a conversation. But then why is it, generally speaking, more difficult to write than it is to talk? (I say "generally speaking" because all of us find occasionally that putting something on paper is a lot easier than saying it, speaking it right out to an actual person.) What is there about conversation that's missing when we write? An actual audience, of course.

From an audience, we get feedback, a response that lets us know the effect of our words, a response that helps determine what we say next. Furthermore, in conversation we depend on slang and informal expressions; we are uninhibited except by our sense of propriety about what our audience should hear or could stand to hear. If we get stalled, we can hem and haw and stutter and gesture until we find the words we need; we can count on lowering our voices or raising them to make a point; we can take back anything we wish we hadn't said. When we talk, we stop, wander, get off the track, get back on again. All of this oral composing is easier for most of us most of the time because our sense of the audience keeps us alert to what needs to be said or re-said or un-said.

Learning to write means learning to listen in on the inner dialogue. When you are really listening to a lecture or a discussion, you feel involved; you are recreating the discourse—what's being said—in your head. When you are really listening, you are silently thinking. You can listen in on your own thoughts when you are the "lecturer" and the discussant. Learning to write is a way of making that inner dialogue make sense to others.

The method of composing that is set down in this book is dialectical. The words *dialogue* and *dialectic* are cognate, which means "born together." Each names a linguistic activity or process in which a "twoness" is made one. The following four sections are intended to help you develop a *dialectical* method for making the inner *dialogue* make sense to others. It allows you to take advantage of the fact that every operation involved in composition—naming, opposing, defining—involves all the others. A dialectical method of composing helps you avoid making hard and fast decisions ahead of time. As Melville remarked, "There are some enterprises in which a careful disorderliness is the true method." Composing by our method is not like plodding down one row and up the next with a mule, and it certainly is not like a tractor tearing along making beautiful, entirely regular patterns. Our method works like a Scottish sheep dog bringing in the sheep: she races back and forth, driving the flock in one direction signaled by the shepherd, but acting in response to the developing occasions, nudging here, circling there; rushing back to round up a stray, dashing ahead to cut off an advance in the wrong direction. When you compose, you are the shepherd and the sheep dog and it's up to you to decide whether you want the sheep in fold, fank, or field and to know how to get them there.

Assisted invitations to try out the method of composing set forth in the following three sections are indicated as before by the sign: ❧

Sometimes you are invited to write on a particular topic in a particular way, to compose within narrow limits; in other instances, you are invited to discuss certain conventions or to consider one point or another, with no particular writing suggested. But that doesn't mean that you therefore do no writing: developing your own topics is part of your job as a writer and you will have opportunities to practice that skill. When the discussions are carried on in class, it's a good idea to save time for everybody, including the instructor, to write. After a 15-minute discussion—or argument—there is generally plenty to write about, to write with and from.

All the assisted invitations are meant to help you bridge from theory—the *what* and *why*—to practice—the *how*. The exercises offer you a chance to practice on a small scale, but the whole point of a method is that it should help you in real writing. My assumption is that you will be working on papers assigned in other courses while you are studying this book; my hope is that you will make this method of composing your own, adapting it to your needs, putting it to use in writing those papers.

You can use your journal of observations when you respond to the assisted invitations. It will help you be your own audience-critic if you save the left-hand side of the open double page for notes, quotations, drawings, and what we will be calling *chaos* and *oppositions*. Use the right-hand side for composing sentences and paragraphs. Or vice versa: it doesn't matter, so long as you use the facing pages as a way of representing the dialogue/dialectic of the composing process.

1. Getting Started

Listing and Classifying: Purposes and Presuppositions

A list of names is a composition: it presents simple information in simple form. A list names the *contents* or it names the *members of a series*. The table of contents in a cookbook; a label on a paint can; a line-up of ballplayers; a program telling us that the pianist will play first the Haydn E♭ Major Sonata (Hoboken 52) and then the Mozart B♭ Major Sonata, K. 570: These are all lists whose function is to tell us what's *in* something or what comes *before* what.

Such lists don't make very good reading; only compulsive readers study the breakfast cereal box. Most lists are not meant to entertain us, but only to inform. However, a list can become an expressive composition if the form it takes is predominant. If we sense rhythm and balance, an opening out and a gathering in, then we have no mere catalog. The difference between a paint can label and Leporello's list of Don Giovanni's conquests; between a stock clerk reading the shelves and a child's counting game; between a chronicle of "begats" and a creed; between a recipe for fish chowder and a litany, is the predominance of form—the balance, order, rhythm that gives us the sense of a lively whole.

The only use most of us have for a formal list is to help us remember certain items by memorizing their names. Medical students pass on to those who come after them dozens of dirty rhymes whose sound patterns lighten the task of learning, say, the vessels and tissues of the wrist cross section in the proper sequence. In *mnemonic* devices (Mnemosyne is the mother of the Muses and goddess of Memory), the role of rhythm and pattern is to fix the names in mind. The form of the list may please us, but that is not its chief purpose. Other kinds of formal lists might help us remember, but their chief function would be to make us feel part of a ceremony, to lift us out of our private selves, and give us a sense of being a member of a community.

To see how a writer goes about creating a form by means of which he can assemble various items is to learn something very important about composing. Lists are composed; they don't just happen.

Isaak Walton's *The Compleat Angler*, written in the seventeenth century, concerns everything you ever wanted to know about fishing and aren't afraid to ask your old friend *Piscator*

(Fisherman). Walton's book is about the sport of angling, but it's also a meditation on Man and the rest of Creation, on the beauties of the Earth, the fact of mortality and the promise of eternal life. Walton can go with no strain from a short discourse on the soul to a recipe for carp (stuffed with oranges and anchovy butter). He writes in dialogue form, one of the oldest forms in which philosophy can be written; it's an inner dialogue being brought out into the open. The novice fisherman, who gets hooks caught in his thumb and can't tell a pike from a pickerel, asks leading questions which Piscator then answers with directions and explanations—and recipes. A great deal of information has to be set down, but in a pleasing form. The modern procedure would be to publish the anecdotes in one volume and the "how-to's" in another, but *The Compleat Angler* was written to provide both instruction and delight and to show how they are related. Here is Piscator's catalog of trout flies:

And now, good Master, proceed to your promised direction for making and ordering my Artificial Fly.

PISC. My honest Scholar, I will do it, for it is a debt due unto you by my promise. And because you shall not think yourself more engaged to me than indeed you really are, I will freely give you such directions as were lately given to me by an ingenious Brother of the Angle, an honest man, and a most excellent fly-fisher.

You are to note, that there are twelve kinds of artificial-made Flies to angle with upon the top of the water. Note by the way, that the fittest season of using these is a blustering, windy day, when the waters are so troubled that the natural fly cannot be seen, or rest upon them. The first is the Dun-fly, in March: the body is made of dun wool, the wings of the partridge's feathers. The second is another Dun-fly: the body of black wool, and the wings made of the black drake's feathers, and of the feathers under his tail. The third is the Stone-fly, in April: the body is made of black wool, made yellow under the wings, and under the tail, and so made with wings of the drake. The fourth is the Ruddy-fly, in the beginning of May: the body made of red wool wrapt about with black silk, and the feathers are the wings of the drake; with the feathers of a red capon also, which hang dangling on his sides next to the tail. The fifth is the yellow or greenish fly, in May likewise: the body made of yellow wool, and the wings made of the red cock's hackle or tail.

The sixth is the Black-fly, in May also: the body made of black wool, and lapped about with the herle of a peacock's tail; the wings are made of the wings of a brown capon with his blue feathers in his head. The seventh is the Sad-yellow-fly in June: the body is made of black wool, with a yellow list on either side, and the wings taken off the wings of a buzzard, bound with black braked hemp. The eighth is the Moorish-fly: made with the body of duskish wool, and the wings made with the blackish mail of the drake. The ninth is the Tawny-fly, good until the middle of June: the body of tawny wool, the wings made contrary one against the other, made of the whitish mail of the wild-drake. The tenth is the Wasp-fly, in July: the body made of black wool, lapped about with yellow silk; the wings made of the feathers of the drake, or of the buzzard. The eleventh is the Shell-fly, good in mid-July: the body made of greenish wool, lapped about with the herle of a peacock's tail, and the wings made of the wings of the buzzard. The twelfth is the dark Drake-fly, good in August: the body made with black wool, lapped about with black silk; his wings are made with the mail of the black-drake, with a black head. Thus have you a jury of flies likely to betray and condemn all the Trouts in the river.

This list-maker knows what he is talking about and he knows what he wants to say—a happy state of affairs for any composer. Piscator gets across the general idea of a trout fly by describing in minute detail the materials that it is to be made from and where they are to be obtained, how the parts are to be assembled, and when each fly is to be used. One fly after another is described according to a pattern which makes it easy for the reader to refer to the list to find out *which* fly to use *when* and *how* to make it out of *what*. The list is designed for easy reference and the metaphor that closes it neatly reminds us of the purpose of these 12 flies.

Composing a list involves organizing names according to some purpose. The act of drawing up the list is also a way of discovering purposes. If your shopping list is arranged by stores in the order in which you pass them on the street, then that order will itself suggest items for your list. Remembering that the bookshop is next to Eastern Mountain Sports where you intend—an *intention* is a purpose—to pick up the backpack you've ordered might lead to adding a book to your list; the listing process helped you discover a further purpose: *Pick up backpack* led to *Get spy novel for Shep.*

Purposes generate lists and listing helps discover purposes. Here are some assisted invitations to see how that works.

        ❧ If you know a lot about cars, make a list of what you would want to remember to check or ask about when you shop for a second-hand car. Then make a version of your list for someone who doesn't know anything about cars except how to drive. Compare the two lists: Which is longer? Which was harder to compose? Why?

        ❧ Draw up a Christmas list. Is there any order to it? What purpose has determined that order?

You can think of a list as answers to a set of questions: *purposes* answer *needs.* Here are some lists in the form of a record. They are taken from the pocket diary of a farmer and surveyor living in Dubuque County, Iowa, over a century ago. (He was my great-grandfather and the family legend is that he was not a lovable man, a notion that is perhaps suggested by this record.) From these lists, what can you tell about the needs and purposes of William I. Anderson? Of any prairie farmer in the mid-nineteenth century?

January   *Saturday 10*   *1857*
Killd old Dice

Sunday 11
out hunting a dutch gal
got none

Tuesday 13
cheese & crackers   20
staid all night at A. D. A.
Bot corn of Boss Straton   25
Took ADA the 3rd load of wood
made 9 dolars

January   SATURDAY 10   1857

Killed old Dra

SUNDAY 11

out hunting at dutch gal
got none

MONDAY 12

January   TUESDAY 13   1857

cheese & cruckers 2º 20
Staid all night at A D A
Bot cow of Asa Straton 25
took at D A the 3 rd load
of wood   make 9 dolas

WEDNESDAY 14

Bot lamp & fluid & can 370
Pair of shirts silk 400 Baskett 50
figs 10 cent Patent tether 25 cents
Ink of Ratory 50 cents Hood & flonell
for Baby 2 45 corn of Straton 25
at home Jerry is off at some
foolb affair at Mc Kees
went to see hibird woman monkey 25

THURSDAY 15

off to Moores to swap
Otter for corn

January   FRIDAY 16   1857

Bot Davis Pain Killer 25
got the surryge mended 25
corn at Dubeque took a small
load of curly sugartree wood it Bot
got Dubeque stain at Neely
Aniversary of the Mask
degree for N W I A

SATURDAY 17

got mares shod 135 cents
Bot shoes for sudan 140
Paid Stout & co for lumber 1080
Coffee Paid 200 Bot of Bass 0
10 gal Molasses 950 & 50 lbs
of sugar 600 dollars did not pay
got home from Nass a little

SUNDAY 18

January   MONDAY 19   1857

TUESDAY 20

WEDNESDAY 21

helped to bury G Duglass
Bot nails to fix roost
for hens & fiend them

Wednesday 14
Bot lamp & fluid & can   370
Pair of shirts silk   400   Baskett   50
figs   10 cents   Patent leather   25 cents
Ink of Ratory   50 cents   Hood & flannel
for Baby   245   corn of Straton   25
at home   Gerry is off at some
fooll affair at Mikes
went to see Hibrid Woman monkey   25

Thursday 15
off to Moores to swap
otter for corn

Friday 16
Bot Davis Pain Killer   25
got the suryinge mended   25
corn at Dubuque   took a small
load of curly sugar maple wood   ADA
got Dubuque staid at Neebys
Aniversary of the Mark   degree for Wm I A

Saturday 17
got mares shod   135 cents
Bot shose for Susan   140
Paid Stants & co for lumber   1080
Coffee Paid   200   Bot of Brecht
10 gal Molasses   950 & 50 lbs
of sugar   600 dollars did not pay
got home froze Nose a little

Wednesday 21
helpd to bury G Duglass
Bot nails to fix roost
for hens & pend them

(*Note:* Some of the terms are obscure, others are illegible.
ADA stands for Andrew D. Anderson, William I.'s brother.
The "dutch gal" refers to a German servant; he found one
eventually to whom he paid $24.20 for working from April
6 to September 25. The "degree" mentioned is a Masonic
honor.)

Studying how lists are drawn up and considering the principles by which they are organized can teach a writer some very
important things about the composing process.

∾ Make up a grocery list and
keep it on hand for use during the discussion to follow.

Grocery lists are highly personal compositions. They are
often written in a kind of shorthand, a code that saves time
but that could cause confusion. A 25-year study of grocery lists
abandoned in shopping carts convinces me that few people make
out a list which anybody else could safely use.

- Why did you get this flour?
- You said to get flour. That's what the list said.
- I didn't say Pillsbury's.
- I got flour; you said flour.
- Don't you know I always get Gluten Beauty?
- The list said flour.
- Well, I didn't mean just any flour.
- You didn't say that.
  Etc.

I've found that the composition students who draw up the
most efficient grocery lists are householders. An experienced
shopper knows how to save time not only in making the list but
also in using it. Efficient lists are often schematized according to
the area in the store where certain items are to be found; indeed,
some lists could serve as floor plans. (*Scheme* or *schema* derives
from the Greek word for *shape* or *plan*. Note that these words
are both nouns and verbs.)

lemon	p. chips	Thuringer
P.E.I.	gerkhins	
B. lettuce	kidney beans	hamburger
leeks	coffee	o j
tom	sugar	milk
red onions	spaghetti	Monterey J
	marinara	
pie crusts		bread
Ital gr b		

You can read the schematized list as you would a map,
orienting yourself at the entrance. If you read up from the bottom right-hand corner and from right to left across the top, with
side trips into the center and then down the left-hand column,
you will have done a tour of the store, ending at the checkout
counter. Here is the list again as a floor plan:

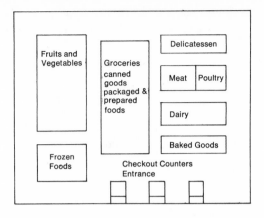

The schematized list/map represents the order in which the merchandise is displayed. And, of course, that order is determined by various requirements and needs, physical and psychological: food that must be refrigerated will generally be along the walls since this is where the pipes and electrical lines are; advertising specials will be placed at various eye-catching points, etc. The merchant/architect/planner organizes the store with various purposes in mind, just as you organize a list with purposes in mind. We find something more easily if we know what we're looking for; both the list and the layout of the store are meant to facilitate that. You can see how this works if you consider how the order of various names on the list offers clues for decoding certain items that are not intelligible by themselves: *lemon, leeks, red onions* help us make sense out of *tom* (*tomatoes*); *P.E.I.* is harder, but if you find yourself among the leeks and tomatoes you might catch sight of a bag of potatoes from *Prince Edward Island.*

                       ❧ Using the floor plan as a guide, decode the other mysteries in our list.

Each of the groups of items is a *class:* when you compose a list, you are *classifying.* A parsnip is a parsnip is a parsnip, but it is also a vegetable. Classifying is *renaming* so that one item can be grouped with others of the same kind. *Vegetable* is a class name given to certain edible plants. A parsnip has characteristics in common with carrots and potatoes and all "such like" that grow not on vines but underground (I've heard a parsnip called a "honky carrot"); they form a subclass called *root vegetables.* When carrots and potatoes are grouped not only with lettuce but with pears and raspberries and apples, they are seen as members of a larger class, *fruits and vegetables.* The more kinds that can be included, the more general the class.

Degree of generality	Class-name
general	merchandise, groceries produce
specific	fruits and vegetables vegetables root vegetables
particular	parsnips "this parsnip"

In any kind of list, one word suggests another; one name joins another and another until you have a class that you then name: you rename the names. A class is a form that finds forms —not only members that belong to that class but other classes as well. One thing leads to another, we say; one thing makes you think of another; one class finds another class, not just other members. "Produce" finds not only pears and raspberries, eggplant and acorn squash, but "meat" and "dairy."

The names you choose for your classes will depend on the *context of situation.* When you look for parsnips in the produce department, that name is appropriate to the situation: you are buying an item that the grocer finds convenient to keep with other fresh *products* that need to be kept cool and ventilated and sometimes watered. The names listed on a menu, on the other hand, would be entirely different. You would write *salad,* not *produce; creamed parsnips,* not *root vegetables; radishes,* not *fruits and vegetables.*

The reason why a menu does not make a very good shopping list is that it belongs to a different context of situation. Suppose that you shop with a menu as your guide: if the menu reads "Hamburger," you first have to translate that shorthand to "dill pickles, catsup, sliced tomatoes, sliced onions, mustard, hamburger rolls—and hamburger." Then you have to disregard terms that are relevant to cooking and preparation only, eliminating any items you already have or adding quantities needed.

∾ Translate the names of these menu items into names appropriate for a shopping list:

Green Salad
Lasagna
Ice Cream
Coffee

You can see that the menu determines the shopping list, but shopping can in turn determine the menu. If the menu calls for hamburgers and you discover when you get to the meat counter that the ground beef is sold out and that steak is $2.99 a pound, that situation could force revision of the menu and, hence, of the shopping list.

∾ How can you use the situation (the hamburgerless meat department), the schematized list, and the need for a revised menu to help you save the picnic?

∾ For what context of situation would such class names as *protein, minerals, carbohydrates*, etc., be appropriate?

A list is a composition even though it is composed with just words, not sentences and paragraphs. The listmaker knows the relationships that those words stand for, the groups and classes and sequences that the list indicates in a succinct and economical way. Each item of a list could be expanded to a sentence. "Rice, carrots, green peppers, tea" could be developed in this way: "If there are going to be 20 people for supper and I have only $10.00 for groceries and if the cupboard is bare, which it seems to be, I'd better get out the regimental rice cooker and make vegetable curry; tea would be the thing to go with the curry and since I have only a little leftover Lapsang Souchong, I'd better get a quarter pound of spiced Indian: that'll fill them up."

You can also think of the items of a list as a set of answers to certain questions. When you draw up a list, you are addressing yourself to certain needs that can be stated as questions. Thus, *baking soda* on a grocery list is an answer to these questions: "Do I need baking soda? Does that cake recipe call for baking powder or vinegar and baking soda? Is there any baking soda left from last summer when I used a lot on bee stings?" But *baking soda* on the grocery list does not answer questions that are not raised in the context of situation, which is shopping for kitchen and household supplies. It is not, for instance, an answer to the question, "What is the common household product whose chemical formula is HCO_3?" A shopper would have to be able to differentiate baking soda from washing soda, but he wouldn't have to know the chemical formulae to do so.

Any one list answers only certain questions, not all possible questions about all possible purposes it may serve. If we had to take into account every need, we would be fated to draw up an endless list and we might never get anything done because we would never get the list ready. (For some compulsive list-composers, this is precisely the point: lists substitute for actions.) You need to eat, but that need is not part of the context of situation in which grocery lists are composed; it is a presupposition, an assumption that does not have to be proved or argued or deliberately considered.

∾ "What do I need to stay alive?" is not normally a useful beginning for composing a shopping list, but what are some extraordinary circumstances in which that question would indeed determine the menu? Describe them.

Just how much we usually take for granted in making a list can be discovered if you try to determine the presuppositions of the list-maker. Here is Leon's grocery list and his analysis of the presuppositions:

milk—2½ gals	juice—1 can fr grape
bread—2 loaves	cookies—1 pkg.
eggs—1 doz	apples—1 bag
steak—1½ lb N.Y. sirloin	cake—1 frozen
bacon—1 lb	chips—1 large bag
peanut butter—1 sm jar	canned ravioli—1 can
jelly—1 jar	potato salad—1 lb tub
salami—½ lb Genoa	cole slaw—¾ lb tub
butter—1 lb	tuna—1 small can
2 diff TV dinners—frozen	mayonnaise—1 sm jar
cereal—1 box	celery—1 pkg

In composing the grocery list, certain presumptions or presuppositions were made. That is, several things were taken for granted. Among these are:

that I will be living
that I will go shopping to purchase these items
that I will want or need these items
that I will not be shopping for another week after this trip
that I am the only one who will be eating the foods listed
that I can pay for these purchases
that I will eat three meals per day, plus snacks
that the amounts purchased are sufficient for my intentions
that the items listed are available

The presuppositions of a list can be obscure or fairly self-evident. Here, of course, the analyst is the list-maker, so he has more to go on than the list itself in reconstructing the context of situation, but you can sometimes tell just from the list what sort of person the list-maker is. You don't have to be a Sherlock Holmes to read the items of a list as clues to the character of the list-maker and the circumstances in which he or she lives.

∾ Using your powers of detection, write a characterization of this list-maker.

Shop for supper (scrapple, syrup)
Ask for scraps for Wicked Willie
Renew subsc to *The Friendly Agitator*
Write letters about the bombing
3:30 silent vigil, P.O.
5:00 Chiropractor (phone Marilyn about ride)
Start green afghan for Dan

∾ Make out a list of planned activities for the day so that a reader could fairly deduce three things about the list-maker.

∾ What are William I. Anderson's presuppositions? (See pages 53–55.)

∾ Louise has argued that lists are "WASP" doings, and that the chief thing one can learn about a list-maker is that he or she does not feel powerless and is probably not powerless. Could you

make a list disproving this assertion? Does list-making
play a role in consciousness-raising groups? Why?
What is the difference between making lists and being
able to make lists?

       ∾ What are the presupposi-
tions of this mnemonic list?

> *Market Arch Race and Vine*
> *Chestnut Walnut Spruce and Pine.*

       ∾ Write out the directions for
getting someplace by car or public transportation. Assume that the list will be used by someone who is familiar with the area.
Then write out the directions for the same trip assuming that the list will be used by someone from out of
state.
Compare the lists: what presuppositions can you identify in list No. 1?

One meaning of meaning is *mediation;* another is *purpose.*
To ask what a list *means* is to ask what it says and what it is for,
what purposes it serves. A list can be used to remind you of
what's to be done or to record what has been done. When you
check off a list, it's like making another list. The composing
process involves this kind of comparison between intention and
achievement, between purposes that have been fulfilled and those
that are still unrealized.

       ∾ Suppose that you are the
chief organizer of a public meeting. You have four com-
mittees reporting to you. What are they? Compose the
lists they submit to you. Then compose the master list
that will guide your organizing efforts.

       ∾ Analyze your list. Here is a
checklist for the purpose:

> order
> schematization
> classes
> purposes and needs
> presuppositions

Would anyone else be able to use your master list? Why
or why not?

Naming and Defining: Chaos and Dialectic

Listing is the composing process in a nutshell. Composing a list may be a simple act, something we do rather thoughtlessly; nevertheless, virtually every aspect of composing is represented in listing: naming, grouping, classifying, sequencing, ordering, revising. Each of these operations can involve the other, which is why it's so difficult to talk about composition: everything leads to everything else. A good course in composition could be entitled "Related Everything." The term we are using for the interdependence of all the operations involved in composing is *dialectic*. Your job as a composer is to guide the dialectic. If you can remember that composing begins with naming, which is a kind of defining, and ends with definition, which is a kind of naming, you'll have a slogan that can help you keep the dialectic lively.

        ❧ Step 1. Write down at least 20 words at random in response to this figure. In your inner dialogue, you can ask, "What do I see?" and "What does this figure make me think of?" Take 5 minutes.

Step 2. Across from each noun, set down a verb appropriate to the figure; e.g., *tree . . . grows.*

Step 3. Choose one of your words and see if any of the other words cluster around it. What context of situation is being developed that allows this clustering to happen?

Step 4. What is the most general name (other than "thing"), the one which could include other names, the way "produce" includes parsnips, pears, lettuce, apples, etc.? If there is no such word in your chaos, can you

Fig. 1.

develop one by combining two or three words from your chaos? Can you add a new one?

Step 5. Choose two words from the chaos of names that seem farthest apart and write one sentence in which they both appear. Does this sentence create a context of situation or is it nonsense?

Step 6. Can you form two—and *only* two—classes that include *all* your names? (The names needn't be equally distributed.) How would you rename these sets?

Step 7. Using any of your original chaos and any new names generated as you grouped and sorted, write a few sentences in which you consider the figure.

Getting started when you're composing means getting names. They don't come out of the air: you generate them in responding to pictures, images, objects, questions, answers, statements—to what you see and read and hear and feel. These names provide the essential source for a writer: they provide chaos.

Here is a good description of chaos from Mary Shelley, the author of *Frankenstein,* who explains in an introduction to a later edition of that famous tale just where it came from.

Everything must have a beginning . . . and that beginning must be linked to something that went before. The Hindus give the world an elephant to support it, but they make the elephant stand upon a tortoise. Invention, it must be humbly admitted, does not consist in creating out of void, but out of chaos; the materials must, in the first place, be afforded*: it can give form to dark, shapeless substances but cannot bring into being the substance itself. In all matters of discovery and invention, even of those that appertain to the imagination, we are continually reminded of the story of Columbus and his egg.† Invention consists in the capacity of

---

* "Afforded" means "on hand"; the materials must be "there."

† "When Columbus' friends taunted him, saying that discovering America was really easy since one only had to point west and keep going, he asked them to stand an egg on end. They tried but failed. Then Columbus took the egg, flattened one end and stood it up. Naturally his friends protested that they had thought the egg could not be damaged. His friends had assumed for the egg problem limits which did not in fact exist. But they had also assumed that it would not be possible to point west and keep on sailing. This feat of navigation seemed easy only after Columbus had shown that their assumptions were imaginary." [Edward de Bono, *The Use of Lateral Thinking* (London, 1967), pp. 88–89.]

seizing on the capabilities of a subject and in the power of moulding and fashioning ideas suggested to it.

The chaos that invention—both critical and creative—needs is generated by naming. Naming is the primary act of composition: a writer needs to develop the habit of generating chaos as a way of getting the composing process started. In the Biblical account of Creation, the Lord God gives Adam the duty (honor? pleasure? right?) to name the beasts; it's a way of saying that language and creation enter the world at the same time.

Having a chaos on hand can save you from neatly ordering a few names into a strict "outline" and starting to "write it up" before you have done any real exploring. If you commit yourself to one scheme, one definite plan, then anything unexpected can only cause trouble. "Staying on the track" becomes a virtue in itself, despite the fact that that track might be leading into a swamp of the self-evident. But, of course, the aim of composing is not to tolerate chaos for its own sake but to learn to put up with it while you discover ways of emerging. That can be less difficult than generating chaos in the first place because, for one thing, the mind doesn't like chaos; ordering is its natural activity. A method of composing should help you take advantage of that fact.

You can think of ordering as a dialectic of chaos and form. Explanations of how compositions get made—whether they are of clay or marble, words or gestures, tones or lines—try to account for the origins and beginnings by finding some way of representing that dialectic. Here is one artist's comment:

> I begin logically with chaos; it is the most natural start. In so doing, I feel at rest because I may, at first, be chaos myself. This is the maternal hand. . . . [Later] I give myself a conscious jolt and squeeze my way into the narrow confines of linear representation. Then everything goes quite well, for I have trained hard and thoroughly in that field. It's convenient to have the right to be chaos to start with.

Paul Klee is explaining that once he has a chaos, he can then deliberately choose to "squeeze [his] way into the narrow confines of linear representation." Translated into more general terms, Klee's description lets us see that a chaos both affords the materials and encourages the ordering process. Klee knew that he needed those "confines," but he also knew that by themselves, without chaos, they were powerless. No composer can choose until he has a sense of the alternatives, and they are defined by limits. Those "confines" Klee speaks of provided for him the limits that are essential to creation. The best formulation I know of this principle of composition is Allen Tate's definition of a poet as "one who is willing to come under the bondage of limitations— if he can find them."

The ways we order a chaos of names are the same as those by which we make sense of the world: we see and know in terms of space, time, and causality. The philosopher Kant called these the "categories of understanding." If you check through the words in your chaos, you'll find that every one of them names Fig. 1 as a *spatial* form or a *temporal* form or as something that *causes* something or is itself an *effect*. The spatial form of Fig. 1 is obvious: it has a shape; it occupies space. What kind of spatial form depends on who's looking and what kind of setting the figure is given. The words you set down in your chaos probably include names for that shape like *tree* or *river mouth;* if you have a word like *lightning,* you can see that the spatial form takes on a temporal dimension. A picture or a drawing of lightning records its shape, but it also captures a moment in the passage of time. You can represent a streak of lightning by means of an arrangement of lines, but that pattern also stands for the moment in which the lightning flashed across the sky, the happening itself. Whether the spatial or temporal aspect of a figure is emphasized depends on how you look at it, how you construe it.

Here is Irene's comment on Fig. 1:

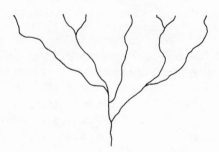

Assuming, for the moment, the tree-like qualities of this grouping of lines, the point of convergence (the trunk) is not grounded; it is in a suspended state of imbalance. If incomplete then, this "down" design might be more apropos as:

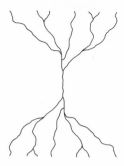

(Grandma Moses was asked how she painted. She answered, "Down. I paint the sky, then the trees, then the land.")

The way you look at something creates a context, and once a context is supposed, further particulars are suggested; that's the dialectic in operation. Matching verbs with nouns is a first step towards tentatively setting up a context. *Tree/grows* suggests, perhaps, other trees. You can set one tree next to another—and another and another; the line of trees is being inspected by a man (or is it a bear?) in a Scout hat with a chin strap; there's a little camp fire smoking in the foreground: pretty soon, you'll have a poster warning of forest fires.

Here are some assisted invitations to construe and construct.

〰 Add lines (all straight) that convert these two lines to a sketch that represents something you could name and that would be recognizable.

〰 What happens to the way you see the figure above when you name a location? How many events can you think of that this figure could represent?

∾ Whenever you watch something happening, you are seeing/knowing in spatial, temporal, and/or causal terms. Consider how you interpret the trajectory of a baseball; the flight of a broad-winged hawk; the track of a spaceship.

∾ I once asked a poet if she could name something that would not fit into the categories of space, time, and/or causality and she said almost immediately, "My eyes." Another poet might say that eyes represent the interaction of all three. Write a short paragraph (or poem) that gives form to one or the other conviction.

Fig. 2.

∾ The more things a figure could represent, the more generalized it is, just as *"produce"* is a more general term than *"fruits and vegetables,"* which is more general than *"apples and carrots."* See if you can develop a term—a word or a phrase— that is general enough to include Figs. 2, 3, and 4 and specific enough to exclude Figs. 5 and 6. Is the term you decide on the same as the one you identified in Step 4, p. 63–64?

Fig. 3.

Fig. 4.

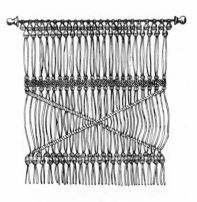

Fig. 5.

Fig. 6.

If you look at a tree in winter, you see both the bare branches and the pattern they make. That pattern is what the tree has in common with anything else that has that shape and structure. The pattern is the figure the tree makes, and you see it precisely because you see resemblances in shape and outline and structure between the bare tree and similar forms. Sometimes the pattern will be more emphatic than the object. If you look down from a high cliff or an airplane and see the mouth of a river, it may look like a triangle; from that perspective, the design the river makes is more apparent than the particular details of mudcracks, marinas, and waves. Indeed, the characteristic shape of a river mouth is called a *delta*, after the Greek letter of that name: Δ.

A bare tree might not look like a triangle because the linear pattern of its branches is more apparent than the outline, but a bare tree does look like a river mouth in which tributaries, however faint, are discernible. The bare tree and the river mouth both have a central element with subsidiary elements going off from it—*branching* off. The class name that gathers these examples and everything else that is organized in this way is *branching system*.

HDWDWW? and Opposing: Specification and Substantiation

The composing process is a continuum: seeing and thinking and writing are all ways of forming. We begin to make sense of the world in the very act of perception. The process of selection and differentiation is implicit in seeing; forming is dependent on seeing how one thing is like another, how it is different from others. This same process of re-cognition continues when we name in response to spatial and temporal forms. Selection and differentiation—forming—is implicit in naming just as it is in perceiving.

Most writing you will do in course work will not be in response to things—objects, landscapes, figures, etc.—but to ideas. Nevertheless, since you don't become somebody else when you sit down to write, it makes sense to claim that what you do when you interpret an idea or a passage of writing is not fundamentally different from what you do when you interpret an object. Writing involves the same acts of mind as does making sense of the world: you construct the same way you construe.

When you figure out what you're looking at, you name and compare, classify and rename: you do the same things when you write. Thinking is a matter of seeing relationships—relationships of parts to wholes, of items in a sequence, of causes and effects; composition is a matter of seeing and naming relationships, of putting the relationships together, ordering them.

A composition is a bundle of parts: you get the parts by generating a chaos of names and you bundle them as you identify and rename the relationships among them. Listing is the simplest way to bundle the parts, but when your purposes are more complex than a list can serve, then you need to know other ways of bundling, other ways of organizing chaos. If you're going to explain, describe, define, narrate, argue, or promulge— which is Walt Whitman's word for *promulgate*—then you will need to know just what and how much to say about what. A method of composing should offer means of establishing context so that you can develop criteria for judging what specification is needed. Specifying is the way of classifying, of characterizing what goes in which group; as you specify, you give substance to the general. You can't decide how to go about that by asking, "What do I mean?" That question must itself be converted to more specific questions.

The two most serviceable means of generating critical questions that can help you order chaos are very simple and infinitely adaptable: one is asking, *How does who do what and why?* which we will abbreviate from now on as HDWDWW? The other is drawing a line down the middle of the page in order to generate oppositions. Both are means of starting the process of naming and defining and of keeping it going.

"How does who do what and why?" is the master critical question because you can order a chaos by means of it. Answering *HDWDWW?* will give you names for *agent* and *action, manner* and *purpose;* if names are not in your chaos for substantiating the terms of the question, then you will know that you need to generate them. You can see how HDWDWW? works to guide the process of ordering chaos if you consider the problem of explaining a snowshoe. If you had nothing to guide you but "What is a snowshoe?" you might have a hard time getting started, but generating a chaos and then asking HDWDWW? gives the snowshoe a setting, makes it part of an activity and thus helps you develop a context so you can substantiate, specify, and define. Let's try it.

First, a little chaos, generated in response to SNOWSHOE:

SNOW: wet, deep, pretty, cold, white, fluffy

SHOE: foot, protection, Massachusetts, support, boots and
    slippers, warmth, protection

SNOWSHOE: An old trapper
           L. L. Bean
           Old-fashioned rug beater
           Bear paw
           Rats gnaw rawhide
           Lacquer
           Leather straps
           Sloan's Liniment
           Sport
           Practical

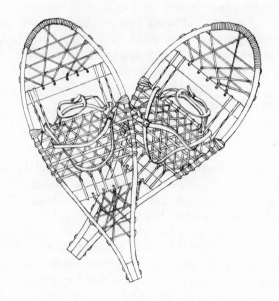

Note how space, time, and causality are represented: there
are words that derive from seeing the snowshoe in *spatial* terms:
old-fashioned rug beater and *bear paw* give us shape. (Do you
have other names for the shape?) There is a *temporal* (seasonal)
term in the name itself. Several names in this chaos have to do
with what snowshoes *cause* (aching muscles); others suggest
effects or what snowshoes bring about or make happen or allow
to happen (*sport* and *practical*). HDWDWW? orders this chaos
by guiding us in asking these questions:

$$\overset{\text{WHO}}{}\qquad\overset{\text{DO}}{}$$

1. How does *the old trapper use* snowshoes?
2. How does *L. L. Bean,* a manufacturer of sporting goods

   and hunting equipment, construct a snowshoe?

Naming an agent (a *do*-er) lets us transform *DO* to *use* and *construct.* We can now ask questions about snowshoes as *something used for something* and as *something made out of something*—and we can then answer those questions.

3. Why does the old trapper *wear* his snowshoes?
   Whenever the snow is deep enough so that walking is difficult, the old trapper wears snowshoes that support him on top of the snow.

4. How do snowshoes support the wearer?
   By distributing the weight over a larger area than a regular shoe would cover.

If you combine those two answers, you get this sentence:

Whenever the snow is deep enough so that walking is difficult, the old trapper wears snowshoes, which support him on top of the snow by distributing his weight.

For the purposes of explanation, you don't need the old trapper, picturesque as he may be, so you can generalize:

Snowshoes are useful in deep snow, since they allow you to walk without sinking by distributing your weight over a larger area.

Snowshoes, which are like expanded shoe soles, enable the wearer to walk on the surface of deep snow without sinking.

Your explanation can continue with descriptions you can develop from a question about construction:

5. How are snowshoes made?
   Snowshoes are made of rawhide strips woven into a network in a frame.
   Snowshoes are made by weaving rawhide strips in a diagonal pattern secured by a frame.

Snowshoes are constructed of rawhide strips woven into a diagonal, open-work pattern anchored to an oblong frame. They have leather straps so they can be tied to moccasins, boots, or shoes.

     ∿ Using HDWDWW? as your guide, write a paragraph on the subject of expressways (superhighways). Proceed as we did in the case of the snowshoe:

1. Generate a chaos of names by considering spatial, temporal, and causal aspects of an expressway from different points of view.
2. Using your chaos, adding to it when necessary, substantiate—give substance to—the terms of HDWDWW? Name the various *who*'s and *what*'s and the *actions;* etc.
3. Make a statement explaining either *agent, action, manner,* or *purpose.* Decide how specific you want your terms (*The old trapper* or *the sportsman-hunter* or *the wearer? Parsnips* or *vegetables* or *produce? Ash tree in winter* or *tree* or *branching system?*).
4. Make other statements until you've substantiated all the terms of HDWDWW? Do you have a paragraph?

Getting started on a composition requires knowing how and when to be specific, deciding how general the names can or should be for the purpose and how particularized they might be. Your grocery list can be in code because you are the user and you can particularize or generalize to suit your needs and purposes. But when you write for a larger audience (or even for yourself at another time), your composition will have to be on its own, so to speak, since you can't staple yourself to the cover sheet or the folder. You have to be sure that when particularization is called for, you will know how to get down to brass tacks and that when the subject needs to be defined in "larger" terms, you will know how to develop the appropriate generalizations.

And who decides what is needed, what is appropriate? You do: the composer does. Those decisions are what keep the composing process going. Of course, your decisions can be wrong: the most difficult thing for any writer to realize is that what is written on the page may not represent what's in his head. You may have written in a code without being aware of it, without properly translating. In conversation, you have feedback that lets you know: "Huh?" "Whaddaya mean?" "How's that?" "What!?" When you're writing, what you have instead of audience feedback is your own inner dialogue, which you can train yourself to hear critically.

That is not entirely different from what a journalist learns to do. A reporter has to have a nose for news, but she must also develop a sense of what needs to be said in order to make things clear. When you write for a newspaper, you judge which names are appropriate to your subject by keeping in mind the context of situation: How much do your readers know already? How much do they need to know? Like all other writers, the journalist has to learn to avoid, on the one hand, writing in a code that doesn't make sense without extensive interpretation and, on the other hand, setting down in great detail what is self-evident.

By guiding you in defining other choices, a method of composing can save you from setting down empty generalizations or parading presuppositions dressed up as propositions. It does that by helping you get the dialectic going, the naming and defining, which provide the means by which you *substantiate*—give substance and content to—generalizations. Deciding how general your statements should be at what point and which names are appropriate for particularizing is at the heart of the composing process and it can be a very interesting challenge if you can develop some skill in listening in on the inner dialogue.

Knowing how to specify means knowing what's relevant. Deciding what's relevant requires, in turn, having criteria by which to judge what's relevant. If you find yourself saying "I know what I mean, but I just can't put it into words," it's a sign that you are trying to compose without the criteria for deciding what's relevant. Of course, when you're getting started in composing, you can't be sure about what is and what is not relevant and you can't be absolutely sure of the criteria—unless, of course, you are writing a paper in which every step has already been spelled out for you. In the snowshoe chaos, for instance, I set down several words that came to mind in responding to "snow." For the purposes of explaining a snowshoe, I was not immediately sure what would be relevant, what I might need to say about snow, but when I came to thinking about when snowshoes would be used—the context of situation—it was clear that *depth* was a relevant particular: How deep the snow is has something to do with the function of snowshoes. That thought occurred because "fluffy" reminded me that sometimes snow packs and thus led me to consider what kind of snow would make wearing snowshoes a feasible idea—or even a necessity. "White" and "pretty" were themselves completely irrelevant from the start, but they helped to generate "fluffy," which in turn led to thinking about kinds of snow and thus to developing a context of situation. Such are the uses of chaos: It affords the materials for thinking with.

Somebody from Maine or Minnesota would not have had to go through all that hassle because images of people wearing snowshoes would have guided her directly to the point, but I've never seen an actual snowshoe—only pictures in the L. L. Bean catalog. I therefore needed to generate a chaos in order to get started on an explanation. Of course, you use whatever you already know in getting started, but the point of having a method of composing is to know what to do when you face the unfamiliar.

Naming generates chaos, which is ordered by a process of renaming. HDWDWW? converts the snowshoe from a thing to an activity and thereby helps you decide what specifications are needed in explaining what snowshoes are for. The same thing with "expressway" or any other term or idea, once you have a chaos on hand: HDWDWW? guides you in naming the *who* (agent), the *what* (action), the *how* (manner), and the *why* (purpose) and in relating them to one another. The way out of chaos is by means of making meaning, which is a matter of seeing relationships. HDWDWW? helps identify what needs to be related or what can be related.

The other means I am suggesting for finding relationships is drawing a line down the middle of the page. This generates *oppositions*, the term which throughout this book refers to relating and relationships. Anything set over against something else is an opposition: word/word; word/thing; thing/thing; member/class; particular/general; name/context; etc. Oppositions are forms that find forms; oppositions are means of making meanings. In responding to Fig. 1 (the bare tree, etc.) you set verbs over against nouns; one word over against those clustered around it; the most general term with the names it gathered. You related the two names that seemed the farthest apart and probably the two meanings that seemed the farthest apart; and you organized the entire chaos in two sets. In all these activities, you formed oppositions. The line down the middle of the page can start this kind of ordering because it allows you to see relationships and to develop context so you can specify and substantiate. In composing, opposing is the way you get from naming to defining.

Like every other aspect of the composing process, opposing goes on all the time. Seeing something with respect to, in terms of, in relation to something else involves oppositions, the forms of relatedness. Here is a checklist you can use in the assisted invitations that follow.

A Checklist of the Forms of Relatedness

1. Is A *the same as* B?
2. Is A *above, beyond, behind, next to, inside, ahead of, before,* etc. B?
3. Is A *the cause of* or *the effect of* B?
4. Is A *a repetition of* or *a duplication of* B?
5. Is A *an example of, the same kind of thing as* B?
6. Is A *comparable in some respects to* B?
7. Is A *a part of* B? Is A *made up of* B?
8. Is A *derived from* B?
9. Is A *the opposite of* (antithesis, antonym) B?
10. Does A *complete* B?
11. Does A *depend on* B?
12. Is A *necessary to the function* of B?

            ∾ If A is a trout fly, how many of these oppositions would be useful in describing it? What Bs would you choose? Write out a few sentences of description.

            ∾ Review your journal of observation: how many of these oppositions—forms of relatedness—were prominent in your composing?

            ∾ Generate a chaos of names in response to the word/idea *education*. Which oppositions are helpful in ordering the chaos?

            ∾ Using the Checklist as a guide to your questioning, see if you can explain the relationship between the two items in each of the pairs listed below. Write a sentence or two about each; you can incorporate the italicized phrases in the Checklist.

a. rubber stamp/ink pad
b. gun/bullet
c. barn/house
d. oars/paddles
e. cellar/attic

f. ping/pong
g. streams/ponds
h. recognition/memory
i. interpretations/war
j. health/sickness

ᐁ Here's an assisted invitation to listen in on the classifying process. In each of the paired words below, use the opposition to help you name the class to which both things or ideas or activities belong. Ask HDWDWW? to generate whatever names you need in order to compose a sentence that says something about both names. Finally, check your sentence over against the dictionary definitions: are there any terms in common?

clarinet/trumpet
harpsichord/piano
men/mice
swimming/flying
deserts/islands
caves/mountains

chanting/dancing
oil drum/thermos bottle
Thanksgiving/Christmas
development/change
first violins/second violins
introduction/finale

ᐁ In the pairs below, the opposition is between a particular thing, idea, or activity and a class to which it could be assigned. Using this opposition to provide a context, name another particular thing, idea, or activity and compose a sentence in which you compare or contrast the given particular and the new particular.

Charlie Chaplin/hero
family/institution
The Great Depression/
    history

automobiles/technology
history/liberal education
technology/human
    achievement

Recapitulation

In getting started, a method of composing should help you keep things tentative so that you don't come to conclusions too quickly and thus lose the chance to explore relationships. You write from the start in order to discover what you mean; naming and opposing are your means of making meanings. As soon as names begin to cluster, chaos is being shaped. Clustering is a kind of classification; it's like gathering fruits and vegetables and laying them out together under a sign that says *"produce."* It's like drawing a circle around certain items on a list, thereby indicating that they go together for some reason or other. Those reasons have to do with your purposes in composing. From naming to defining by way of opposing—relating—is a good way of thinking about the composing process, if you remember that defining leads, dialectically, to further naming, further purposing. You let what you say discover what you mean.

You name and define when you make sense of the world, and in composing you continually name and define, rename and redefine. A method of composing should help you keep that dialectic in progress. You take a general idea and bring it down to earth with lots of naming—examples, comparisons, demonstrations—just as you can convert a generalized figure—a design—to a particular object by looking at it in a certain way, from a certain perspective. And you take a highly particularized event, object, statement, and find out how it is related to other instances and examples. In fact, you can't do one without the other: composing always involves both generalizing and exemplifying; both classifying and specifying. Deciding on the degree of generality is central to the composing process. The more details you develop, the more particular the form becomes; the fewer the details, the more general. That tradeoff is the dialectic in operation. It's not something you decide ahead of time; these are decisions you make in the course of writing.

2. Forming Concepts

Making Statements

Language can express ("Ouch!") and indicate ("There it is."), but its chief function is to give form to feelings and ideas, which it does by representing them, by re-presenting them. The form of language finds the form of thought and feeling; those forms then find further language. By re-presenting our thoughts and feelings, we make meaning.

Thinking is implicit in the very act of naming. Every time you name something *A*, you are simultaneously seeing its relationship to something else; you are differentiating and classifying. If it is *A*, it is therefore not *Not-A*; if it is *A*, then it must be recognized as a *kind* of thing. The most important fact about language is that we identify and classify at the same time. Naming means identifying, which is inconceivable without classifying. You tell what something *is* by seeing what it's *like*, what it goes with. Naming involves, simultaneously, the identification of a thing and the recognition of the *kind* of thing it is. As soon as we say, "This is a tree," we imply, "This is the kind of thing a tree is." A *kind* is a *class*. This is the reason for saying that naming both creates chaos and discovers the way out of chaos. As you figure out how one thing is related to another, how one name is related to another, seeing how things and words can be grouped, you are necessarily comparing and differentiating, deciding in which respects they are similar and in which they are dissimilar.

You don't have to learn to do this: you're born knowing how; it's the way your mind works. But as a student of composition, you have to learn how to put those natural facilities to work in organizing names into sentences and sentences into paragraphs. Here, again, you don't have to invent the means because the structure of language itself is what allows you to get from name to name. It's the discursive character of language —its tendency to "run along," which is what *discursive* means, gathering words to words, attaching groups to groups—which allows you to make meanings and thus to order chaos. When it comes to writing, you compose statements that represent your thinking; in the process, you are making meanings. Both the way you think and the way language works make that possible: language is a form that finds thought, and thought is a form that finds language. That is the dialectic of composing.

You've seen how a chaos of names can be organized by substantiating the terms of the question HDWDWW? and by developing oppositions that represent the relationships you see between various names. The next step out of chaos is developing your specifications and oppositions as statements. A statement predicates, i.e., it says something about something. You make statements by composing sentences about agent, action, manner, and purpose. Unless all of those sentences are to take the form of simple assertions, *This-is-that*, you will need a repertory of syntactical structures—sentence patterns. The reason for having sentence patterns on hand is not to have "variety" but to provide yourself with linguistic forms that can help find conceptual and expressive forms. A repertory of sentence patterns provides you with ways of putting meanings together. Knowing several ways of stating comparisons, for instance, can help you identify comparable ideas; knowing that a semicolon lets you juxtapose a particular name and a general name can help you find such names.

Note that punctuation marks indicate the syntactical relationships—the way the parts of the pattern are put together. They are ways of signaling what kind of relationships to expect. Here, then, are five patterns that can form the core of your repertory:

1. A structure for listing and renaming. (The items listed can be in the form of single words or groups of words.)
   _____, _____, _____: _____.

   Lively, beautiful, sad: Western Ireland is never more inviting than when it seems forbidding.

2. A structure to relate condition and result, cause and effect.
   If _____, then _____.

   If chaos is thought of as a source, then it is less frightening to the composer.

3. A structure for articulating a comparison with a difference.
   Just as _____, so _____;
   but if you consider _____, then _____
   _____.

   Just as soap operas feature stereotypes, so Chekhov in his stories develops types; but if you consider how individualized they are, then you can see that it isn't the types but what you do with them that makes the difference.

   Just as harpsichords have keyboards and a set of strings, so pianos are also keyboard instruments; but if you consider the manner in which the sound is produced, then you can account for the difference in sound.

4. A structure for stating differences with something in common.
   However _____, _____.

   However various the appearances are, the basic pattern can be seen.

5. A structure for restating with a greater degree of specificity or generality.
   _____; _____.

   Some artists don't mind chaos; Paul Klee considers it "a natural place to start."

   Odili ran for office; he decided to accept the political process.

My colleague, Susan Horton, asked her students to compose and collect "workhorse" sentences. She gathered some of the strongest and circulated them, not indicating which were written by students. Here they are; add your own.

1. To satisfy customers, she developed an array of techniques as much psychological as physical, which allowed her to steal, by her accounts, from stores that might well have thought she was a good customer.
2. And older still, he might have divined the true reason: that the element of fire spoke to some deep mainspring of his father's being, as the element of steel or of powder spoke to other men, as the one weapon for the preservation of integrity, else breath were not worth the breathing, and hence to be regarded with respect and used with discretion.
3. I'm being paid to be serious, to tell potential book buyers what the product is about, to analyze the author's intentions, to interpret, if possible, his symbolism, or to criticize his conclusions.
4. She pooh-poohed Mother's taste, snorted at our ignorance of Myers family history, treated us as mere custodians of the Myers furniture, resented alterations, and had the memory of a mastodon for Cousin Cassie's associations with each piece.
5. There are degrees of violence, from the relatively normal shock effect of many forms of modern art, through pornography and obscenity—which achieve their desired reaction through violence to our forms of life—to the extreme pathology of assassinations and the murders of the moors.
6. In Dorothy Parker's short story "Promises, Promises," as the protagonist appeals to God for assistance, for courage, for attention, it becomes evident that the man her heart is buried in and the God she appeals to are interchangeable; both are intermittently faultless and contemptible; both are to blame for her hope and her lack of hope; both are projections of her own insecurities.
7. The experimenter prescribes what the child shall do, not how he shall do it, and the results are enlightening not only because of what they tell us about the potential range of the children's ability, but also by what they refuse to do and cannot do.
8. Rather than wasting time constructing long-winded sentences that circle unendingly, never reaching the point, never saying anything, a writer should take his reader by

the mind, lead him down no dark alleys, honor him with clarity: inform rather than perform.

If you try to use these or any other patterns without having on hand a chaos of names, they will simply remain slots to be filled, but if you have a chaos that can provide the materials and you have done some preliminary opposing, then you can use them as forms to find forms, linguistic structures to help you discover and formulate relationships and thus to make meanings in making statements.

           Review the composing you've done in the previous section (*Listing and Classifying*). Practice using this repertory of sentence patterns to convert "X is Y" sentences.

Generalizing and Interpreting

As you make statements, you soon leave chaos far behind. The classifying implicit in naming becomes explicit; the oppositions generated from a chaos of names become sentences. The composing process of naming, opposing, defining involves you in *forming concepts*. A concept is a supername: logicians define a class as "the field of a concept's application." You can think of a concept as the name of a class. Forming concepts is a dialectical operation: concepts don't just "have" meanings; they are our means of making meaning. Forming concepts is not something you do before you write. ("How are you coming with your paper, Abner?" "Oh fine. I've thought it all out and tomorrow I'm going to put in the words.") A concept is like a hand that gathers; it is also the handful. Here's how it works:

- What's that?
- A boomerang.
- What's it for?
- Fun. It's for fun. You throw it and it comes back.
- Well, how does it work?
- It's like a foil. It's a wind foil.
- Like an airplane wing, sort of?
- Yeh, except it's all wing. The curve, the way it's made, determines the flight path so that it doesn't just keep going; it curves back.
- I'll bet you can't throw it around in your backyard.
- No way. This old football field is the only place. On the beach, it might hit somebody.
- You could hit me!

The inventors of the boomerang were the Australian aborigines. If HDWDWW? were directed toward an Australian bushman, the answer might be in narrative form, a telling rather than a definition. Or it might be wordless: a demonstration would serve. From a different perspective, HDWDWW? would generate different answers, but the appearance of the boomerang, its shape and construction, would obviously not be changed by one description or another.

But now consider what happens if *boomerang* is taken to refer not to the object but to what it does. Not just boomerangs boomerang. As a verb, *boomerang* refers not to shape but to the kind of action in which something is thrown out, only to come back at the thrower in a surprising and generally sinister way. Remarks and good deeds and a solution to a problem can be classified as things that boomerang. Boomeranging gives a name to the action of going-out-and-coming-back-towards-you-on-its-own; and it gathers up examples of that action. Boomeranging is a concept because it provides the limits that guide you in classifying and exemplifying. A concept provides the criteria by which you can judge how something resembles something else; it provides a form that can help you find further instances that represent it.

Here is a philosopher's explanation of how we form a concept:

> Consider . . . how many motions follow the general pattern called "oscillation." The swing of a pendulum, the swaying of a skyscraper, the vibration of a violin string over which the bow is passing, the chatter of our teeth on a cold day— all these are examples of the type-form called "oscillation." Now, if we were to define this type-form, we would omit all reference to skyscrapers and fiddle-strings and teeth, and describe it, probably, as "rhythmic motion to and fro," or in some such terms that would connote only the *sort of motion* we are talking about and not the *sort of thing that moves.* Probably each of us has learned the meaning of oscillation through a different medium; but whether we gathered our first idea of it from the shaking of Grandpa's palsied hands —or from the quiver of a tuning fork—or from the vibration of a parked automobile with the motor running—however our *mental pictures* may differ from each other, they have one thing in common: they are all derived from some rhythmic motion to and fro. The things exemplifying this *type* of motion are not necessarily alike in other respects;

the swaying skyscraper and the vibrating violin-string are certainly not alike in appearance, origin or purpose. But their motions have the common property of going rhythmically to and fro. This property is the *logical form* of their motions, and so we may call all these motions diverse instances of the same form.

When we consider the common form of various things, or various events, and call it by a name that does not suggest any particular thing or event, or commit us to any mental picture—for instance, when we consider this common form of various movements, and call it by a name such as "oscillation"—we are consciously, deliberately abstracting the form from all things which have it. Such an abstracted form is called a *concept.* From our concrete experiences we form the *concept of oscillation.*

Susanne K. Langer, *Introduction to Symbolic Logic*

The organized comparing by which you discover "the common form of various things" is called *generalization:* When you use the abstracted form to identify further examples of the concept, this is called *interpretation.* You can go "up" from individual events, objects, activities to the idea that they could be said to represent—or you can go "down" from the abstracted form to the particular instances. Forming concepts involves moving in both directions. You can't form a concept until you know how it might apply, nor can you gather up examples and instances unless you know what they might be examples of. The composing process is dialectical: how can you know what you think until you hear what you say? How can you know what things belong together until you have an idea of what they have in common? How could you know what might be the common characteristics unless you had an idea of their commonality? Forming concepts is a circle all right, but not a vicious circle; it's a methodical circle:

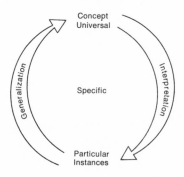

Here's how generalizing and interpreting work together to form the concept of *city:* When you note that everywhere you go in a certain kind of place there are streets, you are generalizing, since any one street might look very different from the others. In generalizing, you note what is similar in a number of streets—forms that you recognize as being *different* from, say, open spaces. You note a general character as represented in particular streets. Then if you note that in other places there are also many streets, you can conclude that places-with-many-streets form a class that has the conventional name of *city.* As you discover that there are several such characteristics notable in every city you visit, that there are several general statements that hold true for the class of places named *city,* then by this organized comparing you are forming the concept of *city.*

Now then, suppose you have limited the field of application of the concept *city* by listing ten characteristics and that you begin to study the cities of China and India: what if only five of your general statements hold true for these new examples? By generalizing, you have formed a class, but in using this class-concept (the concept is the name of the class) to guide your investigation of other possible members of the class, you see that the membership "rules" don't apply. You have two choices: either you deny membership to the new samples or you change the rules to allow entry. You could decide that in order to be classified as a city, a place need have only five specified characteristics, thus changing the criteria for membership in that class; or you could keep the specifications and decide that the conglomerations you've been studying aren't eligible for membership in the class "city."

Forming concepts requires not just one such adjustment of class-name and specifications, but a continuing operation of naming and defining, renaming and redefining. One of the most interesting things about composition is that in learning to write you are learning to exercise choice by recognizing and using limits that are, of course, forms that find forms. But limits are not laid down in Heaven: they are subject to change according to the composer's needs. Limits are recognized, but they are also modified and adapted, discarded and reestablished. That process—which is essential to the forming of concepts—is carried on by means of stating and restating. Paraphrasing—restating—is the best way of converting "What do I mean?" to a critical question: "If I say it this way, how does that make it different from what it is when I say it that way?" By paraphrasing, you draw out the implications of your statement: You "spell out" what you mean.

Along with paraphrases that restate, one of the chief means of forming a concept is to state the opposite case. We have noted that naming something *A* implies that it is not *Not-A*. When you state the opposite case, you name *Not-A* and in the process you more clearly differentiate *A*, thus establishing limits that will help you in interpreting, deciding just what is to be classified as *A*. Like all other kinds of opposition, "the opposite case" helps you discover what you want to say; it helps you form the concept you intend to explain or discuss. Saying what something is *not* is one way of determining what it *is*.

Here's how a master explainer uses the opposite case to characterize and define the language of epic poetry.

> The language . . . must be *familiar* in the sense of being expected. But in Epic, which is the highest species of oral court poetry, it must not be *familiar* in the sense of being colloquial or commonplace. The desire for simplicity is a late and sophisticated one. We moderns may like dances which are hardly distinguishable from walking and poetry which sounds as if it might be uttered *ex tempore*. Our ancestors did not. They liked a dance which *was* a dance, and fine clothes which no one could mistake for working clothes, and feasts that no one could mistake for ordinary dinners, and poetry that unblushingly proclaimed itself to be poetry. What is the point of having a poet, inspired by the Muse, if he tells stories just as you or I would have told them? It will be seen that these two demands, taken together, absolutely necessitate a Poetic Diction; that is, a language which is familiar because it is used in every part of every poem, but unfamiliar because it is not used outside poetry. A parallel, from a different sphere, would be turkey and plum pudding on Christmas day; no one is surprised at the menu, but every one recognizes that it is not *ordinary* fare. Another parallel would be the language of a liturgy. Regular church-goers are not surprised by the service—indeed, they know a great deal of it by rote, but it is a language apart. Epic diction, Christmas fare, and the liturgy, are all examples of ritual—that is, of something set deliberately apart from daily usage, but wholly familiar within its own sphere.
>
> C. S. Lewis, *A Preface to "Paradise Lost"*

In a critical reading of C. S. Lewis's explanation of the character of epic diction, you can see that he *classifies:* he tells us that epic diction has a kind of familiarity that he explains by *stating the opposite case.* He then *interprets* this concept by *exemplifying,* by presenting *particular* examples of activities that are like the language of epic poetry and thus can be grouped as members of the same class. He thus *establishes the field of the concept's application.* Lewis ends the paragraph by renaming this class of the familiar-which-is-expectable-but-not-commonplace; he has *formed the concept* of ritual which dialectically has enabled him to explain epic diction.

Forming concepts is the way you see/explain relationships; as you form concepts, you are making meanings, and that is the purpose of language and the purpose of composition. Everything Lewis does in forming the concept of ritual in order to explain epic diction—I have italicized above the acts of mind involved —could be described in much more complex logical language, but no such analysis could help you learn from reading him how to compose your own definitions. For that to happen, I believe you have to think about his thinking and thus learn ways of thinking about your own thinking.

ꙮ Here is how Astrid Oosterman used the opposite case to guide her description of a building. Read her paragraph (and reread Lewis's) and then compose your own paragraph(s) describing a person or place, using the opposite case.

The Boston Public Library is a classically designed, symmetrically balanced edifice intended to be a lasting monument to wisdom and learning. It has a magnificent setting and facade facing Copley Square. One walks between the two symbolic Greek statues to the center entrance flanked by a series of identical round-headed windows. From the small main lobby, a grand divided staircase leads to the second floor and the main reading room, a spacious hall with a high vaulted ceiling supported by heavy pilasters. The decorations, both inside and out, are many and ornate: the well-known wrought-iron gates and lamps at the entrance and the murals, decorated ceilings, and imported marble and tile used on the floors and staircase.

On the other hand, one is less impressed with the University of Massachusetts library as an individual edifice because it was designed to be a functional part of the whole university. This functional use of space is what sets modern architecture apart from the classical style. The building has no obvious facade or entrance. In fact it can only be entered from the underground garage or the glass catwalk that connects the university buildings. The use of steel beams presents the opportunity for cantilevered construction. This means that portions of the building can project or jut out over the perpendicular supports, using space that otherwise would not be available. The lines are simple, severe and clean; in effect, the building speaks for itself; any exterior decoration would detract from, not add to, its functional appearance. Inside, the poured concrete walls and severe geometrical shapes are softened by the use of carpeting, bright paint, and soft, inviting couches. This modern style is conclusively demanded by its use as a multi-media center.

Here are some assisted invitations to see how forming concepts is a process that guides composing. First, a brief recapitulation of the procedure as we've discussed it so far.

1. Generate chaos by naming in response to a word/thing/example/concept.
2. Substantiate the terms of HDWDWW? (Name the *who*'s and *what*'s, the *how*'s and *why*'s.)
3. Develop oppositions to represent the relationships between agent, action, manner, purpose; between particular examples and generalization; between generalization and generalization. (Draw a line down the middle of the page to get started.)
4. Make statements by developing oppositions in sentence form.
5. State the opposite case.

          ❧ Form a concept by means of which you can explain *academic grading*. Some of the steps listed above will be more helpful than others. You can discover the concept by comparing academic grading to other kinds of grading and then to other kinds of academic activity. Developing the opposite case can help you form the class, the field of application of the concept. Use Lewis's paragraph as a model for organizing your statements.

𑀂 Form the concept of *matur-ity* by describing examples of mature behavior, mature decisions, mature attitudes—or any examples of acts and manners you can think of. You can discover such examples by answering HDWDWW? Compose statements in which you interpret and generalize until you have established the concept's field of application.

𑀂 Form the concept of *the country*. When you come to the opposite case, develop three: *city, suburbs, wilderness*. Which one best helps you to establish the field of application of the concept of the country? Organize your statements in order to explain the character of the country.

𑀂 Form the concept of *welfare* in such a way as to gather up the following two statements:

1. "We the People of the United States, in Order to form a more perfect Union, establish Justice, insure domestic Tranquility, provide for the common defence, promote the general Welfare, and secure the blessings of Liberty to ourselves and our Posterity, do ordain and establish this Constitution for the United States of America."
2. The reason our taxes are so high is that we are paying for people on welfare who don't want to work.

𑀂 Here is an assisted invitation first to see how the concept of the West of Ireland emerges from three passages, and then to compose a paragraph in which you form the concept of a particular place.

1. V. S. Pritchett, in this first passage, manages just about everything a writer ever does: he describes and generalizes, interprets and defines, setting forth a point of view that he then supports with facts and explains with his own interpretations. He names and develops oppositions, expressing personal opinions and general truths. By the end, he has established limits so that he can continue his

interpretations and generalizations. In short, he has formed a concept.

> In these western solitudes, where the sky puts on an even wilder show than it does over the Irish Sea, where the long twilight is like an evening in the theatre, the people have several kinds of foreignness, for Ireland is more Irish, less Cromwellian,* less genteel. People still talk of Cork men, Galway men, Limerick men, with a certain note of tribal mockery and touchiness in their voices. "Cork men hang together," says a Galway man in the voice of one preparing a cattle raid.† Another foreignness is an almost morbid quickness of mind: they listen to half your sentence, guess the rest and cap it, getting their blow in first. I call it morbid because of its mixed source in the desire to ingratiate and to flatter with an apparent sympathy and yet to be sure to win and give nothing of themselves. Unlike the English, the Irish do not wear their heart upon their sleeves. They prefer comedy: it hides the self from vulgar definition. And there is the final foreignness of having known what it is to be foreign in another country. Most of them have. Tragically, inevitably, Ireland has always been the country of goodbyes. That is what nearly all the ballads are about, the ballads you hear at Howth, at Bray, in Galway, in some of the Dublin pubs. Perhaps the real foreignness of Ireland in the modern world is nothing to do with race, history or climate, but is created by its empti-

---

* In the seventeenth century, some of those who had supported the rebellion against the English monarchy were rewarded by Oliver Cromwell, the ruler of republican Britain, with estates in the east of Ireland. Their descendants are Protestant and, in many cases, are more "English" than "Irish" in their temperament and sympathy.

† Cattle raids are important subjects in Irish epic and folklore. Pritchett's observation suggests that whatever is represented in the character of those heroic thieves is still alive in the modern Irishman, at least in the West of Ireland.

ness, the only emptiness in Europe, a spacious-
ness tragically made by all those goodbyes,
but which we, in the crowded corner of Europe, look at with envy and with covetousness.
There is a discreet immigration from abroad
but whether the outsiders can ever join the
secret society is another matter.

2. John Millington Synge, whose play "The Playboy
of the Western World" was driven off the stage
in Dublin and elsewhere at the turn of the century
because it dealt with Irish life in a way considered
scandalous, wrote personal narratives of his travels in the West of Ireland among the peasants,
whose imagination he admired and with whose
struggles he sympathized. In this passage (from
"In West Kerry," 1907) he describes a scene and
his experience at the time in the manner of a
letter.

> . . . I went on towards Dunquin, and lay for a
> long time on the side of a magnificently wild
> road under Croagh Martin, where I could see
> the Blasket Islands and the end of Dunmore
> Head, the most westerly point of Europe. It
> was a grey day with a curious silence on the
> sea and sky and no sign of life anywhere, ex-
> cept the sail of one curagh—or niavogue, as
> they are called here—and that was sailing in
> from the islands. Now and then a cart passed
> me filled with old people and children, who
> saluted me in Irish; then I turned back my-
> self. I got on a long road running through a
> bog, with a smooth mountain on one side and
> the sea on the other, and Brandon in front of
> me, partly covered with clouds. As far as I
> could see there were little groups of people
> on their way to the chapel in Ballyferriter, the
> men in homespun and the women wearing
> blue cloaks, or, more often, black shawls
> twisted over their heads. This procession
> along the olive bogs, between the mountains
> and the sea, on this grey day of autumn
> seemed to wring me with the pang of emotion

one meets everywhere in Ireland—an emotion that is partly local and patriotic, and partly a share of the desolation that is mixed everywhere with the supreme beauty of the world.

3. Thomas H. Mason has no claim to fame; he was an optician from Dublin, an antiquarian and a photographer of birds, who loved islands and wrote about his travels in an unpretentious little book called *The Islands of Ireland* (1936). Here he tells a story he heard on Clare Island, off the coast of County Clare in the West of Ireland.

There are no police on the island, but before the Free State regime they occupied Granuaile's Castle, often having to keep their prisoners for a considerable time until it was possible to make the crossing to the mainland, for there was no magistrate on the island. The social center is the kitchen of the hotel where, in the evening, one will always find some men sitting on forms [benches] placed against the walls. I heard many stories of the agitation before the island was "taken over" by the Land Commission. During the "Land War" the entire population gathered together one evening with all the horses and donkeys on the island; they spent the night singing and dancing and turned the animals loose among the crops raised by the bailiff on a "seized" farm. Needless to say, the crops were ruined; the police were powerless, but when the excitement had somewhat died down a few of the supposed ringleaders were arrested and brought for trial to the mainland.

The country Irishman is a very astute witness in the courts and often scores at the expense of the lawyers. On this occasion the principal prisoner was asked on his oath had he not got his horse with him on the night in question. His reply, "On my oath, I never had a horse," was greeted with cheers and laughter by the islanders who thronged the court. They saw the point which the Crown Prosecutor failed to perceive: the prisoner had no horse, but he certainly had a mare. He was acquitted.

He boasts that he has done more for his country than any of the politicians, because he was arrested later for throwing stones at the bailiff's son and spent a month in jail. He is now an old man clad in homespuns, with a white beard and of venerable appearance. Although almost eighty years of age he is out before daybreak working on his farm, and his one great regret is that he paid his land annuities [taxes] when others on the island had already ceased to do so.

        ∾ Form the concept of the West of Ireland as it emerges from these three passages. (You will be explaining what *kind* of place it seems to be.)

        ∾ Consider a part of the country you know well and, following the procedural guide, develop a concept of this region, large or small. Then compose a paragraph or two in one or another of the following modes: (a) a personal letter or a passage from such a letter; (b) a guidebook description; (c) an editorial. (Editorials are differentiated from features and news stories by explicitly setting forth opinion on public matters, urging one course of action or another, or thinking out loud about ideas, what's happening, etc. In an editorial you could, for instance, consider a region from an ecological point of view.)

Defining

You form a concept by generalizing from particular examples and by interpreting those examples and others in the light of the class-concept you have formed. This process of forming should be kept dialectical because if you decide too quickly or too absolutely what belongs in the class, you lose the chance to discover ways in which the class itself could be changed in order to accumulate further interesting and important examples. It isn't a tick-tock, tick-tock operation: Each time you examine another instance and decide about where it goes or if it goes, you are evaluating both the class-concept and the particular object, event, thing, or word you are trying to place.

This dynamic character of concept formation means that you can't expect the dictionary to do much more than establish the outer limits. If you're writing a paper on revolution or urban renewal or on the allegation that women have been subjugated by religion, the dictionary can't offer much help in deciding what contexts are appropriate or what happens when one word is juxtaposed with another. The dictionary could tell you what the word *subjugate* means, but the concept of *subjugation* has to be critically analyzed in context: Who is using the word? About what? With what purposes? Using which examples? And so forth. "Webster tells us . . ." is an opening that can't help you know what to develop next, and it certainly doesn't engage your reader in the kind of dialogue that makes your composition interesting or persuasive. A dictionary definition can help you determine the presuppositions; it can encourage you to look at the history of the word in considering the range of its meanings; the listed antonyms can help you decide what it is you are not talking about so that you can build the opposite case. A dictionary definition of a concept describes the field of its application, but it's only by a process of organized comparing that you can explore that field. You can't make meanings unless you form concepts, and that involves you in generalizing and interpreting; in gathering examples and seeing how they are related to one another and to the class to which you are tentatively assigning them; in moving from the conceptual term to the field of its application and back again.

Defining the term *aircraft* is something the dictionary does by setting the limits of what the word can mean, but seeing how the limits apply—interpreting those meanings—is something else. It requires that sorting and gathering that we've been calling concept formation. Watch how it works with *aircraft*. With that term you can gather up a Piper Cub, a Boeing 747, a DC-10, and a Messerschmitt. You can then use *aircraft* to help you find other examples of a somewhat different kind: balloons and zeppelins form a subclass of the class *aircraft: wingless aircraft*. But then there is the problem of how to classify something that has wings but no motor: would gliders go with balloons and zeppelins or with the 747 and the bomber? It depends on you; that is to say, it depends on how you are limiting the subclass, whether it is to include only things that fly, with or without a motor, and do not have wings or if it is to include things that can have motors and which may or may not be winged.

In classifying and in developing subclasses, it's the criteria of the one doing the classifying that determine how the items are to be sorted and grouped and gathered. There are constraints, of course. If you decided to classify as aircraft flying things that have wings and feathers and feet and that utter loud squawks, you would either be setting up as a cartoonist—a plane can be made to resemble a sea gull—or you would have to be considered as an inhabitant of Wonderland where meanings are determined solely by individual decisions: the usually accepted criteria for defining aircraft include the fact of the object being man-made, mechanical, and nonnatural. You could include a herring gull with the 747 and the balloon, if you broadened the field to include *flying objects*. But you might be surprised to discover, then, that that class could include rolling pins, baseballs, UFO's, and Superman, as well as herons and plovers. Your choice would then be either to modify *flying objects* by adding an adjective and thus restricting the limits of the application of the concept or to abandon *flying objects* as too wide-ranging.

This schema represents the stage we've reached:

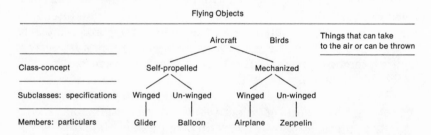

Checking particulars by specifications and specifications by classifications reveals some illogical relationships here. First of all, gliders and balloons are correctly differentiated—one has wings, the other doesn't—but gathering them both under "self-propelled" creates a difficulty, since a balloon, although it doesn't have a motor, does have either hot air or gas and therefore is not "self-propelled" in the same way as a glider, which does not depend on anything but air currents. Gathering both glider and balloon under "self-propelled" makes it possible to see that that subclass is not well-defined. There are also difficulties with the classes: some birds are flightless, and "things that can take to the air or be thrown" includes so much that it can't be considered the same kind of class as Aircraft and Birds; indeed, it is simply another way of saying "flying objects." It doesn't limit "flying objects," and if it doesn't set limits, it can neither classify nor define. We can extend definitions to accommodate what we think we want to classify (the phrase used is "by extension"), but unless there is a limit, a definition can't function.

Aircraft is not the kind of concept that will give you trouble in writing papers, but if you can learn to listen in on the inner dialogue in progress when you are figuring out how such a simple word is defined, you will be learning something about the operations involved when you're defining classes, which is what we've been calling concept formation. Sometimes a word or phrase will look fairly simple; take *antiballistic missile*. You can look up *ballistic* and *missile* and by reading *anti-* as *against*, you can develop a sound definition of an antiballistic missile as a defensive weapon used to defend against offensive missiles. But when you come to explain the antiballistic missile, you will need to go farther in exploring this concept of a defensive weapon. You will discover that if a government decides to build a great many antiballistic missiles (ABM's), that act can be interpreted as a development of offensive strength because it could signal a change from the *strategy of deterrence*—neither side will use thermonuclear weapons because each would suffer *unacceptable casualties*—to a strategy in which one side might plan on a *first strike capability* with an ABM defense system to protect against *the enemy's retaliatory response*. Each of these italicized words names a concept that has a complex field of application. After further analysis, you could well conclude that, in strategic terms, an ABM can be interpreted as an *offensive* weapon.

In defining words and in defining classes, you are establishing limits and interpreting by their means. It is useful to remember that the root of de*fin*ition derives from the Latin word for *boundary*. Further definition of definition you can leave to the linguists and logicians, once you grasp the fact of its oppositional character, which is explained in terms of body and soul by Andrew Marvell, a writer of the seventeenth century:

> Definition always consists, as being a dialectical animal, of a body which is the genus, and a difference, which is the soul of the thing defined.

A definition must do two things: It names the class and it specifies so that one member of the class can be differentiated from another. To say that a chair is an article of furniture classifies but it doesn't define; to define, you need a further limit: A chair is an article of furniture to be sat upon. That satisfies the requirements because it gives us both the body ("article of furniture") and soul ("to be sat upon").

Defining objects is a lot easier than defining classes. If you try to define *furniture,* for instance, you can list the various items that are designated by that term—neckties and mittens as well as marine hardware and linens—but when you generalize about those items, it's quite possible to end right back where you started. What the items have in common is that they furnish and "furniture furnishes" is clearly not a useful definition. It only creates the problem of defining "furnishes." It's what logicians call a tautology. (*Tautology* derives from the Greek for "the same saying.")

The easiest way to break out of this dizzying circle is to rename the activity: How does furniture furnish? Furniture *supplies* and *decorates* and *equips.* Those words are generated by asking HDWDWW? about particular items. This statement classifies by telling us what furniture is for, what it does. But as a definition, it lacks "soul": we know what furniture does, but we do not know how to differentiate it from other things that might be said to "supply and decorate and equip."

Our procedural guide for forming concepts provides the method for breaking out of the tautological circle and moving toward definition. Paraphrase has generated new terms; if we use one of them for a class name and the others as specifications, we can create a dialectical animal:

> Furniture is a kind of *equipment* used to *decorate* or to *supply.*

If you can develop the "opposite case," you can be "more specific." We speak of office *supplies,* and it's clear that they are not *furniture;* cake icing *decorates,* but doesn't *furnish.* What do paper and typewriter ribbons have in common with cake icing? They are used to supply or decorate—and they are *used up.* In opposition to supplies and decoration, furniture is not used up.

> Furniture is a kind of equipment used more or less permanently for decorative or practical purposes.

ᐁ Practice breaking out of the tautological circles below by following this procedure for creating a "dialectical animal":

1. Paraphrase by renaming the activity (HDW-DWW?).
2. Develop specifications by stating the opposite case.
3. Classify and specify in a single sentence using a *which* or *who* clause.
   - Warriors make war.
   - Fences fence.
   - Writers write.
   - Papermakers make paper.

Of course, most tautologies are not so obvious. Here is an example: "In a universe divested of illusions and lights, man feels an alien, a stranger." If you are on the lookout, you will come across other examples from textbooks, newspapers, etc. "When many people are out of work, unemployment results." Correcting other people's tautologies is easier than spotting your own, but it's good training in any case.

ᐁ Break out of those two tautological circles above.

In defining both words and concepts, you indicate where the boundaries are and what meanings are possible within those limits. Setting the limits is up to you—up to a point. Defining words and concepts is not something you can do all on your own, or if you do, the judgment will be that you are mad.

When Humpty Dumpty explains to Alice that there's only one day a year when you can get a birthday present but 364 when you can get unbirthday presents, he says, "There's glory for you!"

"I don't know what you mean by 'glory'," Alice said. Humpty Dumpty smiled contemptuously. "Of course you don't—till I tell you. I meant, 'There's a nice knock-down argument for you'!"

"But 'glory' doesn't mean 'a nice knock-down argument'," Alice objected.

"When *I* use a word," Humpty Dumpty said, in rather a scornful tone, "it means just what I choose it to mean—neither more nor less."

"The question is," said Alice, "whether you *can* make words mean so many things."

"The question is," said Humpty Dumpty, "which is to be master—that's all."

The author of *Alice in Wonderland* and *Through the Looking Glass,* the sequel to *Alice in Wonderland,* Lewis Carroll (Charles Dodgson was his real name), was a mathematician who delighted in the puzzles and paradoxes of the language of signs employed in algebra and other branches of math. In this exchange, he is probably having fun with the notion of declaring "Let $x = 500$. . . ." But what the mathematicians do necessarily, all of us do unconsciously every time we say a single word: A presupposition of every utterance is the comparable notion, "Let the following little squeaks and breathy rumbles represent certain syntactical structures according to the conventions of one language or another." Those linguistic conventions act as constraints when we establish criteria for classifying and specifying in order to define.

Once we're out of Wonderland, the dictionary is, in a sense, "the master": It gives us the conventions in generally accepted forms. But, of course, that's only the beginning. Dictionaries don't grow naturally; they are composed and the definitions that lexicographers list are as open to question as any set of facts is. A lexical definition, at best, gives you only the conventional range of meaning; it can't locate any particular meaning within the range without developing a context. The king of dictionaries, the Oxford English Dictionary, does just that: it cites sentences in which the word being defined occurs, sentences from over 1,000 years of English usage. (The OED is in 12 volumes, each over 1,200 pages.) The only way to understand the meaning of a particular word in a particular sentence is to supplement the lexical definition with a contextual definition.

Every student of composition should understand the structure of a formal (lexical) definition in order to realize its uses and limitations. All formal definitions classify and specify: they assign the object/word to a class and they differentiate the object/word from other members of the class:

The Volvo is a Swedish automobile.
Classification: genus: "body" = *automobile*
Specification: differentia: "soul" = *Swedish*

A definition sets up the limits by means of which the name can mean; it indicates both what kind of thing is named by the word being defined and how this particular thing is different from others of the same kind.

Now this is all quite simple as long as we're working with definitions for Volvos and Blackburnians, because the next degree of generality is already known; if we know the name of the particular item, we probably can name the class as well. The trouble for the student of composition (and occasionally for practiced writers as well: ask them!) arises not from trying to name the particular example and the class to which it self-evidently belongs, but in going on from there to the next degree of generality. You name and classify, classify and name, but the naming gets more difficult as the degree of generality increases. The result is that we are all tempted to write "thing."

The main reason for learning something about the formal character of definition is to understand how classifying and specifying provide limits that can help you discover and develop "what you want to say," first of all by guiding you in identifying the concept and then in using it as a form to find form. Remembering that classification and specification operate dialectically can help you resist that temptation to depend on *thing* or to grab at the first word that offers itself as a substitute, without regard for the specifications that are to follow.

A radio is a thing you use to communicate with.

This provides neither class nor specifications. But when you substitute a less general term for *thing*, that class name should match what it is you want to specify. Here, for instance, is an illogical definition:

A radio is a commodity that receives and transmits signals.

The fact that radios can be bought and sold (a *commodity* is such an item) is not an appropriate classification, given the specifications that follow. If you want to specify in terms of function and structure (*how? why?*), then you need a class name that is appropriate to those names. In this case, you could write:

A radio is a device that receives and transmits signals.

On the other hand, if you wanted to classify the radio as a commodity, then you would need to specify accordingly:

A radio is a commodity that was considered essential in American households of the 1930s.

Sometimes class names and specifications are deliberately mismatched as a means of emphasizing a freshly perceived/conceived relationship. By defining a *chair* as a *machine for sitting in,* the architect-designer LeCorbusier called attention to the fact that sitting can be described as a mechanical operation to which a chair should be mechanically adapted. He thus formed a new concept of a chair and set about designing one to those specifications. You can be deliberately illogical, but you should know that you're doing so.

∾ See if you can repair the following faulty definitions by readjusting the class and the specifications until you have a "dialectical animal."

1. A knife is a utensil used for eating.
2. Barns are houses for cows.
3. School is a place where instruction is given.
4. Necessity is when you have to act.
5. Ambition is the driving force that leads to one's goals.

∾ What class-names would you choose for the name being defined if you use the specifications listed?

Name to be defined	Specifications	Class-name
orange juice	sold all over the U.S. in different forms	?
street light	essential to street safety	?
faucet	expensive to repair easy to repair	?
bone	porous, light, strong	?

Compose definitions for each item.

∾ What specifications would you need in order to make the following class-names appropriate to the items with which they are paired? Compose the definitions.

Name to be defined	Specifications	Class-name
Horse	?	Luxury
Horse	?	Necessity
Wood	?	Energy
Bicycle	?	Convenience
Man	?	Animal

When you ask HDWDWW? in working out a definition, you will often be able to develop verbs that can help classify and specify. The student of composition who has discovered that there are ways of making statements other than saying *X is Y* often decides that "contains" can do the work that used to be done by "is."

     ❧ Review your definitions in the assisted invitations above and analyze the verbs used in defining.

     ❧ Here is a famous definition. Work out a schema to represent the generalizations and specifications.

Let us define a plot. We have defined a story as a narrative of events arranged in their time-sequence. A plot is also a narrative of events, the emphasis falling on causality. "The king died and then the queen died" is a story. "The king died, and then the queen died of grief" is a plot. The time-sequence is preserved, but the sense of causality overshadows it. Or again: "The queen died, no one knew why, until it was discovered that it was through grief at the death of the king." This is a plot with a mystery in it, a form capable of high development. It suspends the time-sequence, it moves as far away from the story as its limitations will allow. Consider the death of the queen. If it is in a story, we say "and then?" If it is in a plot we ask. "why?" That is the fundamental difference between these two aspects of the novel. A plot cannot be told to a gaping audience of cave men or to a tyrannical sultan or to their modern descendant, the movie public. They can only be kept awake by "and then—and then—"; they can only supply curiosity. But a plot demands intelligence and memory also.

E. M. Forster, *Aspects of the Novel*

Studying the dictionary is an old-fashioned way of developing a facility in matching specifications to the class-name and, conversely, choosing the appropriate specifications for a given class. ("Finding the produce level" is what my students call it.)

            ❧ Study the entries on any two pages of a desk dictionary. List the terms used for classifying the references of all nouns. For example:

knacker—*one who*
knapsack—*a case*
knapweed—*a plant*
knick-knack—*an article*
knife—*an instrument*

Then choose another double page and, covering up the definitions, see if you can anticipate the class-name for each noun.

Composing involves you in an inner dialogue that can be like carrying on a conversation in a foreign language: You know what the answer is, but you can't frame the question, or you have the details, but you don't know where they belong. It can be a kind of game, matching specifications to classes and classes to specifications; *renaming* is the name of the game. Finding class-names or inventing them when they don't exist is common to some of the procedures of scientific discovery, to charades and to riddles, which are questions in which the class names are empty or disguised. The Riddle of the Sphinx is the most famous: "What animal is that which in the morning goes on four feet, at noon on two, and in the evening upon three?" When Oedipus answered, "Man, who in childhood creeps on hands and knees, in manhood walks erect, and in old age with the aid of a staff," the Sphinx in a fit of despair threw herself over a cliff. Five year olds feel the same.

    You don't *write* in riddles, but you compose by formulating them: knowing the kind of class you need to form without quite knowing how to name it; recognizing the kind of specifications that seem pertinent, without quite knowing what they are pertinent *to*. This is the dialectic of composition. Tolerating chaos is the principal thing to learn in getting started; tolerating riddles is what you learn in forming concepts.

    In thinking, classification is the way of seeing relationships; in writing, you sometimes announce explicitly that you are *classifying:*

> A sampan belongs to that class of flat-bottomed boats that can be managed in very shallow waters by means of punt poles.

Or you can explicitly announce that you are *specifying:*

> This cortisone ointment is prescribed specifically for iritis.

Or you can do both:

> This is the kind of order for which we will need further specifications.
> ("You're talking about a class of penalties we gotta get into the specifics of.")

But, of course, no such words as *sort, class, kind, belongs to* need appear: whether or not it announces that it is doing so, every statement classifies in the very act of predicating. We can use the terms *implicit* and *explicit* to name the different modes of statement. "The cat is on the mat" *implies* a classification. Here's a version that makes the classification and specification explicit:

> That object, which we name "cat" and which belongs to the class of all cats, is sitting on that thing, which we name "mat" and which belongs to the class of all mats."

As you can see from this example, you don't have to be explicit to be "clear" and, indeed, being explicit sometimes involves you in statements that are very unclear. Part of the job of composing is to recognize the hazards both of too much explicitness and of letting implications do the work of argument and explanation. This matter of being sure of your implications and of deciding on the degree of explicitness necessary to clear exposition is discussed in the next two sections; for now, what needs to be said is that you don't need to say "class" in order to classify, any more than you have to say "Webster tells us . . ." in order to develop a definition. But it's important for the writer to understand what's going on in the process of making statements in order to be able to control the making of meanings.

An *implication* is unstated but intended; it is "wound into" or "bound up with" what is said. *Implicit* can refer not only to classification but to the judgment and evaluation classification *entails*. Making the statement—naming and relating the names— entails classification. This is also true of perception: if you couldn't see the cat as a *kind* of something, you couldn't recognize it at all. (Do you remember Barfield's house? See Part I, p. 34.)

There is a continuum of classifying: every time we see an object, we see it as a *kind* of object; every time we name something, we imply that it is a *kind* of thing; every time we make a statement about something, we are seeing it—placing it—in relation to something else that it is like or unlike. Whether you want to consider it a linguistic or a psychological or a philosophical matter—and it is all three—the fact is that when we make sense of the world, we are classifying.

Every "is" implies "is a. . . ." Thus "The cat is on the mat" can be restated in ways that make explicit the classification implicit in the naming of "cat."

It looks like a cat, an animal that belongs to the class of household pets.
On the mat is something that looks like the kind of thing I call a cat.
The general appearance of that ball of fur on the mat suggests that it is a member of the genus *Felis catus*.

The furry thing on the mat, which ⎰ looks like others of the same / belongs to the

⎰ kind / class / sort ⎱ of ⎰ animal / creature / household pet ⎱ with ⎰ small round head / pointed ears / tail curled alongside / paws tucked up under the body ⎱

⎰ seems to be / is / must be / appears to be ⎱ a cat.

The conventions of English grammar allow us to use a single word to represent both "that cat" and "that thing that is a member of the class *cat*." Sometimes, a particular cat may be our primary reference, but we can also say "a cat" referring not to one cat in particular, but to all cats or all female cats:

A cat likes fish.
A cat can have kittens by the time she is 8 months old.

You can see this kind of reference used as a class in the following passage, a description of how the world appears to "the man habitually on horseback."

Everything appears differently to the man habitually on horseback. It raises him up, makes him wear different clothes, makes him a centaur. In the *Politics,* Aristotle attributes the strong oligarchy that always ruled in Thessaly to the horses, to the advantage, moral and physical, they gave to richer people. The continual use of horses is a barbaric splendor—in the Greek sense of barbaric—a meaning which suggests extravagant or miasmic horizons as if Space moved, or, instead of being the medium in which things stand, could be devoured like Time. Certainly the horseman feels that he devours Space. The ground totters past him. He is an upstart creature, the lover of princes and gaunt ceremony. The poor man is, to him, a biped, a dust-treader. The horseman takes his nobility from the horse. The mountains rear for him, they do not stand. He scatters the stones or curses them.

Adrian Stokes, The Stones of Rimini

These descriptive statements do not use such words as "kind" or "class" but they classify by naming "the horseman." The purpose of the statements, when they are taken as a whole, is to characterize the attitudes of that class of men who are "habitually on horseback." Reference to "the horseman" is not to one particular man riding a horse; in the context of these statements, "the horseman" doesn't indicate "the horseman depicted in that antique frieze" or "that cowboy in the cigarette ad." "The horseman" in this passage means "the kind of man habitually on horseback."

When you know the kind of thing you mean but are not interested in naming it, you simply say "He's sort of lazy." That is an informal idiom for "He is the sort of person who is lazy." (Or you say "He's kinda lazy," shorthand for "He's of the kind of person who is lazy.") The important thing to remember is that every time you make a statement, you are classifying, whether or not you announce that you are doing so, whether or not you have named the class.

                                                             ∾ Compose three statements in which three different singular nouns (such as *a cat, the horseman*) are used as class-names.

Restate, announcing classification by one or another of these phrases: "the sort of," "that belongs to," "a kind of," "that can be grouped with."

Paraphrasing is a way to make explicit the classification that every statement makes. The best way to get started again when your composition comes to a full stop is to return to your original statement and to identify the classification that is implicit or explicit and then to restate, to paraphrase. Recognizing the classification a statement makes is as essential to critical reading as it is to the critical review of your own writing: you are your own first reader. You can learn to locate and make more emphatic the classifications in your own statements by practicing recognizing them when you read. Begin with this passage from Aleksandr Solzhenitsyn's *The Gulag Archipelago:*

> In 1949 some friends and I came upon a news item in the magazine *Priroda* [*Nature*] of the Academy of Sciences. It reported in fine print that in the course of excavations on the Kolyma River a subterranean ice lens, actually a frozen stream, had been discovered—and in it were found frozen specimens of prehistoric fauna some tens of thousands of years old. Whether fish or lizard these were preserved in so fresh a state that those present immediately broke open the ice and devoured them on the spot.
>
> As for us, we understood instantly. We could picture the entire scene down to the smallest detail: how those present broke the ice with tense haste; how, flouting the lofty interests of ichthyology and elbowing each other to be first, they tore off pieces of the prehistoric flesh and dragged it over to the bonfire to thaw it and bolt it down.
>
> We understood instantly because we ourselves were the same kind of people as *those present* at the event. We, too, were from that powerful tribe of "zeks" [prison camp inmates], unique on the face of the earth, the only kind of people who could devour prehistoric lizard *with pleasure.*

❧ Does Solzhenitsyn classify implicitly or explicitly? Write a few sentences explaining the classification. Then check your reading against these attempts to answer that question:

1. Solzhenitsyn feels that because of his internment in a prison camp he is capable of a complete understanding of how persons coming upon a valuable and extraordinary find are able to act as savages and eat the same without showing and sharing with the rest of the world.

2. . . . A rare find is an experience most people find exciting and the excitement generated is infectious.
3. Solzhenitsyn is demonstrating the similarities between inmates at a prison camp and desperate men on a nearly suicidal expedition.
4. The author and his friends are relating the article to an experience they had at a prison camp. They had once been so hungry they knew what the feeling was like. The prehistoric fauna could be the old ways and by devouring it they could get rid of these old laws.
5. The members of the excavation were starving in the freezing environment of the Kolyma River. Upon finding frozen fish and lizards preserved in the ice, they scrambled savagely to eat it. Forced to for survival, blinded against all else, we are all creatures subject to the cages of reality, capable of stretching our capacities back to that of uncivilized man.

Which of these students misread Solzhenitsyn's account because they disregarded the class-announcer, "the same kind of"?

                 ∾ Here is a passage in which the classification is implicit; that is to say, there are no phrases like "the sort of," "the kind of," or "belongs to." Locate in each passage any singular nouns (*a cat, the* horseman) that name classes; that means finding the words that name the *kind* of person, people, problem, situation, etc. being described. Then compose a sentence in which you make the classification explicit, using in your sentence such a phrase as "the kind of," "can be classified as," etc.

Our interest in history is, however, inseparable from books. It is very remarkable that our dependence upon books is so little realized, even by teachers and writers, who live by books. An illiterate person, if he were interested in history, could learn it only from the lips of a historian, or from a person who could read a history book to him and if he forgot a fact he could regain it only by having recourse to his teacher. The amount of historical knowledge that he could acquire would be limited by the fact that he would have no means of tabulating or classifying it, and could therefore have no idea of chronology outside the very limited range of his own experience. All history depends upon chronology, and no real idea of chronology can be obtained except by seeing facts tabulated in chronological sequences. . . . It would be almost impossible to make an illiterate person realize that the date A.D. 1600 had any meaning at all. Calendar sticks are used by tribes of both Africa and America to keep a record of events within living memory, but there is no means by which such a record could be preserved longer. Bundles of sticks convey nothing except to those who tie them together, and if you were to tell your illiterate that a stick represented a year, and then count out 335 sticks, he would be little the wiser. And if you were to tell him that Queen Elizabeth and Shakespeare both lived then, he would find it difficult to believe, since if Shakespeare were really connected with some ancient monarch, which since a play of his was performed quite recently seems highly improbable, it should be King Lear, whom he tells us all about, rather than Queen Elizabeth, whom he hardly mentions.

Lord Raglan, The Hero

∿ Make two statements about each of the following concepts, one of which explicitly classifies and one of which implicitly classifies: *Housekeeping, Childbearing, Diplomacy, Music, Religion, Engineering.*

Recapitulation

If you remember *classifying* the parsnip as produce; *renaming* the bare tree as a branching system; *specifying and generalizing* in order to describe and define a snowshoe, you will be *forming a concept* of forming concepts. *Interpreting* and *generalizing* work together as you specify: Being specific is the way you classify and thus form concepts. Very often on exams you are directed to "Be specific." This sometimes should really read "Be particular; give particular examples." Or it could— and it generally does—mean "Explain how certain particular details that you can furnish on the basis of the X document and the Y study are related to the general statement you can make about such and such a topic." In the terms we've been using, "Be specific" means "Form the concept."

For the student of composition, the important point is not to be able to define "specification," but to be able to recognize specifications and to compose them. Learn whatever terms can help you think, and to remember that every phase of the composing process—naming, opposing, defining—is implicit in the other and that none is a one-shot affair. In composing, you name and re-name; you oppose (specifying, classifying, defining are all ways of opposing) and re-compose your oppositions; you state and re-state by way of defining. Those "re-"s are vital to the composing process: everything has to be kept tentative so that you can be free to re-cognize the emergent classes and thus form new concepts. You don't "have" a fully formed concept, which you then "put into words." It's making the statement—putting down the words—that guides you in forming the concept. You discover what you mean by responding critically to what you have said. *Learning to use statements to form concepts and concepts to direct the revision and sequence of statements is learning to compose.* You compose by the dialectic of seeing and knowing, naming and defining, saying and meaning, stating and forming concepts.

"*Young man, at table you either particularize or generalize, but not both.*"

Drawing by Koren: © 1976 The New Yorker Magazine, Inc.

Compose an answer for the poor kid.

3. Developing Concepts

Naming the Classes

As you compose statements, what you want to say and why you want to say it determine how you name the classifications you are developing in the process of forming concepts. The names you give the classes—a class is the field of a concept's application—represent the way you see the relationships, your judgment of them. Solzhenitsyn could have said that zeks are *people who are starving to death in labor camps.* Naming the class that way would not change the reference; the people are the same as *those who could devour prehistoric lizards with pleasure.* What Solzhenitsyn's naming does is to express his feelings and to represent his judgment of the state of affairs. The way a writer names the classes is one of his or her chief means of expressing judgment, of implying evaluation; the naming of classes is an essential phase in the making of meaning.

Suppose you are to make a statement about a *marsh.* If you are seeking the legal right to drain the marsh in order to build a shopping center, it will be to your advantage to classify the marsh as a valueless, worthless, entirely useless tract of land for which you have discovered redeeming purposes. In your statements, it will be useful to name the marsh a *swamp,* which obviously belongs to the class of things named *useless ground.* Since *swamp* brings to mind yellow fever, rattlesnakes, cold feet, Bad Indians, scum, stinky water, etc., that term furthers your purposes by establishing a context in which your scheme for a parking lot will be easy to classify as a "worthwhile project." If, on the other hand, you are a birdwatcher or a citizen interested in land use, it will suit your legal or moral purposes to refer to the marsh as *wetlands.* Indeed, that word has recently been invented by amalgamating *wet* and *land* to serve the needs of people who oppose draining marshes. A marsh is a marsh is a marsh: it can be defined as a member of that class of topographical areas that are subject to periodic flooding, have a very high water table, are perpetually wet, etc., but how you name the marsh—how you "call" it—will be determined by how you want it to be interpreted; your choice of a name for *marsh* will help to determine the opinions of your audience or readers. The name you give the marsh doesn't change the marsh itself, but it powerfully controls the concept of marsh that you want your audience to form.

Speaker	Interest of speaker (*from his/her view-point*)	Concept	Class-name
Businessman	Progress	Completely worthless land, in current condition	Swamp
Birdwatcher	Conservation	Area vitally important to the ecological system	Wetlands

Using the schema above, develop two different class-names for the following (particulars):

- A cross-town expressway
- An oral contraceptive developed under the auspices of the United Nations
- A public university admitting all high school graduates
- Guaranteed annual income

    ~ Compose a 100-word statement to be printed on a flyer in support of or in opposition to one of the above.

You don't have to introduce a statement with a phrase like "In my judgment . . ." in order to pass judgment any more than you have to announce that you are classifying: naming classes entails evaluation. For that reason, when it is to the advantage of the speaker/writer not to reveal just what his evaluation is, class-names are often opaque or neutral. One of the chief uses of jargon is to provide all-purpose class-names: *area, problem, problem-area, situation, parameters, trouble, matter, decision-making process, system*. With a little help from such noises as "in my judgment," "really," "in terms of," you can handle almost any question:

Well, that's a very important problem area. How we handle that situation, just what parameters we work with, should be, in my judgment, a matter for an open decision-making process. The American people deserve nothing less.

When this process serves the purpose of deception, language is corrupted. In one of the most famous passages of modern journalism, George Orwell comments on the relationship of political attitudes and the corruption of language.

In our time, political speech and writing are largely the defense of the indefensible. Things like the continuance of British rule in India, the Russian purges and deportations, the dropping of the atom bombs on Japan, can indeed be defended, but only by arguments which are too brutal for most people to face, and which do not square with the professed aims of political parties. Thus political language has to consist largely of euphemism, question-begging and sheer cloudy vagueness. Defenseless villages are bombarded from the air, the inhabitants driven out into the countryside, the cattle machine-gunned, the huts set on fire with incendiary bullets: this is called *pacification*. Millions of peasants are robbed of their farms and sent trudging along the roads with no more than they can carry: this is called *transfer of population* or *rectification of frontiers*. People are imprisoned for years without trial, or shot in the back of the neck or sent to die of scurvy in Arctic lumber camps: this is called *elimination of unreliable elements*. Such phraseology is needed if one wants to name things without calling up mental pictures of them. Consider for instance some comfortable English professor defending Russian totalitarianism. He cannot say outright, "I believe in killing off your opponents when you can get good results by doing so." Probably, therefore, he will say something like this:

"While freely conceding that the Soviet régime exhibits certain features which the humanitarian may be inclined to deplore, we must, I think, agree that a certain curtailment of the right to political opposition is an unavoidable concomitant of transitional periods, and that the rigors which the Russian people have been called upon to undergo have been amply justified in the sphere of concrete achievement."

Orwell's analysis of the relationship of political attitudes and the use of language to camouflage or promote them has not been surpassed. "Politics and the English Language" is very widely quoted and not infrequently by people whose writing seems to exemplify the very manipulations of language Orwell excoriates. This suggests that, though we might all agree that the examples Orwell presents are indeed contemptible and although we can easily find comparable examples in the rhetoric of others, we cannot always recognize those manipulations and evasions when we ourselves are speaking or writing about issues or experiences that we are involved with, especially when we are out to persuade others of our view.

It's true that politicians—as Orwell implies, the chief sinners—twist and stretch language; they don't say what they mean; they are deliberately obscure; they mislead, on purpose —but what if we agree with the purpose? If a politician, goaded by journalists, holds his ground but keeps them guessing just what it is, do we never applaud? Naming the classes so that some people can see things one way and others can think of them another way is using the resources of language for purposes that may or may not be honorable. *Equivocation*—literally, "speaking in two voices" or, as movie Indians say, "with forked tongue"—is no less necessary to lawyers, preachers, editorialists, lovers, parents, children, teachers than it is to the politician: we are all equivocators. *Casuistry* is the art of stretching language to cover more than it ordinarily would or narrowing it so that it covers less than it is expected to. The casuist tries to keep a conflict alive—or to smother it—by renaming, restating, redefining. Or he may attempt to resolve a conflict by letting one client/interest group/constituency think that he means X, another that he means Y; he tries to satisfy one without exactly betraying the other; he protects and defends without, perhaps, acknowledging danger or guilt. If we do not gain from the maneuver, we tend to sneer at the casuist or condemn him as a liar; when he's one of us, we may smile at his cleverness and salute his brilliance.

Casuistry is cognate with *case*, which in medicine, law, and logic is a falling—"the way things fell out"—a situation, or happening. Addressing oneself to a case is the fundamental meaning of casuistry, which from the first carried with it the notion of arguing by means of exploiting the resources of language. The first casuists were moral counselors who were charged with resolving conflicts in cases where the choice between two duties was complex. This frequently meant protecting certain values from the attacks of those whose motives were not above suspicion.

Then went the Pharisees, and took counsel how they might entangle him in his talk.

And they sent out unto him their disciples with the Herodians, saying, Master, we know that thou art true, and teachest the way of God in truth, neither carest thou for any man: for thou regardest not the person of man.

Tell us therefore, What thinkest thou? Is it lawful to give tribute unto Caesar, or not?

But Jesus perceived their wickedness, and said, Why tempt ye me, ye hypocrites?

Shew me the tribute money. And they brought unto him a penny.

And he saith unto them, Whose is this image and this superscription?

They say unto him, Caesar's. Then saith he unto them, Render therefore unto Caesar the things which are Caesar's; and unto God the things that are God's.

When they had heard these words, they marvelled, and left him, and went their way.

Matthew XXII, 15–22

You can contrast this casuistry with another example in which one politician draws a distinction only to have another politician try to obscure the line being drawn.

At one point in a public hearing last week, Senator Frank Church of Idaho, the Democratic chairman of the intelligence committee, posed one position:

"I think we should recognize the distinction between war and peace, and it poses the question whether this country in peacetime wants to live always under the customs of war."

Senator John G. Tower of Texas, the Republican vice chairman, quickly responded with the other side:

"I think to make a fine distinction on a matter of war and peace ignores the fact that we are confronted in this world by a very powerful adversary that would not hesitate to resort to military means to achieve its political objectives, a powerful adversary that itself through its clandestine activities and overt activities generates military activity all over the world to accomplish political ends. . . . So I think that we cannot draw this in strict terms of war and peace, in terms of whether or not the United States is actually at war. We are in effect in a war of sorts. That is a war of preservation of the climate in this world where national integrity will be respected."

The New York Times, November 11, 1975

What a student of composition can learn in studying equivocation and casuistry is that ambiguities can be good or bad. In an ambiguous statement, the possibility of more than one interpretation is more apparent than it usually is. When we judge ambiguities, interpreting them one way or another, we are judging the speaker's (or writer's) purpose. When you are composing, you are the speaker and the audience; studying ambiguities is one of the best ways to learn to listen in on the inner dialogue. Judging the speaker's purpose—what he intended to say—is a philosophical matter, since it involves us in judgments of meaning: *purpose* and *intention* are two of the principal meanings of *meaning*. And, of course, getting lost in that thicket is very easy. Sometimes, in order to find our way out (or to lose someone else) we dismiss arguments over meaning as being themselves meaningless: "Oh, it's just a matter of semantics." And, of course, "it" is—whatever "it" is: all linguistic forms are by nature and function dependent on meaning (*semantics* is the study of meaning), which is in turn created by a speaker's purpose, a context, an interpreter's need and expectation, the kind of language being spoken, and the speech community in which the communication is going on. Nevertheless, some questions are "merely verbal": one good test of whether or not the problem in an argument is a "matter of words" or "just semantics" is the ease with which a compromise is accepted. If a third term is quickly and happily agreed upon by the arguers, then it probably was a *quibble*. (A *quibble* is a confusion of words, sometimes for purposes of evading an issue, sometimes for the sake of humor, in which case it is called a *pun*.) But more often than not, what someone wants to dismiss as "a question of semantics" will turn out to be the heart of the matter.

A philosopher named Mortimer J. Adler once wrote a book called *How to Read a Book;* another philosopher named I. A. Richards responded with a book called *How to Read a Page*. Here is a passage in which Richards discusses the matter of ambiguity:

> . . . The *systematic* ambiguity of all our most important words is a first cardinal point to note. But "ambiguity" is a sinister-looking word and it is better to say "resourcefulness." They are the most important words for two reasons:

1. They cover the ideas we can least avoid using, those which are concerned in all that we do as thinking beings. 2. They are words we are forced to use in explaining other words because it is in terms of the ideas they cover that the meanings of other words must be given. A short list of a hundred such words will help make these reasons for their importance clearer. . . . I have, in fact, left 103 words in this list—to incite the reader to the task of cutting out those he sees no point in and adding any he pleases, and to discourage the notion that there is anything sacrosanct about a hundred, or any other number.

AMOUNT ARGUMENT ART BE BEAUTIFUL BELIEF
CAUSE CERTAIN CHANCE CHANGE CLEAR COMMON
COMPARISON CONDITION CONNECTION COPY DECISION
DEGREE DESIRE DEVELOPMENT DIFFERENT DO
EDUCATION END EVENT EXAMPLE EXISTENCE
EXPERIENCE FACT FEAR FEELING FICTION FORCE
FORM FREE GENERAL GET GIVE GOOD GOVERNMENT
HAPPY HAVE HISTORY IDEA IMPORTANT INTEREST
KNOWLEDGE LAW LET LEVEL LIVING LOVE MAKE
MATERIAL MEASURE MIND NAME NATION NATURAL
NECESSARY NORMAL NOTION NUMBER OBSERVATION
OPPOSITE ORDER ORGANIZATION PART PLACE PLEASURE
POSSIBLE POWER PROBABLE PROPERTY PURPOSE
QUALITY QUESTION REASON RELATION REPRESENTATIVE
RESPECT RESPONSIBLE RIGHT SAME SAY SCIENCE
SEE SEEM SENSE SIGN SOCIETY SORT SPECIAL
SUBSTANCE THING THOUGHT TRUE USE WAY WISE
WORD WORK

You can use this list as a reminder that all conceptual terms are problematic—open to question—since they cover a field. Differentiating ambiguity from quibbling is an important philosophical challenge for the writer.

          ∾ Read #1b in Paragraph Sequence III, Jonathan Swift's famous satire on one solution to the problem of ambiguity (p. 240).

          ∾ Writing instructions generally urge that a writer make himself "clear." What does that mean?

∾ Consider Jules Feiffer's cartoon about the old man (or is he a Senior Citizen?). What is his complaint? Would he have Orwell's sympathy?

∾ In Zimbabwe (Rhodesia), use of the word "native" is considered by the black people to be profoundly offensive; in the United States, some "Indians" now prefer to be called "Native Americans." Look up "native" and discuss the ambiguities of its use.

∾ Read the following passage by the young German writer Peter Handke. Consider his analysis of the class-name "poverty" and then do the same sort of analysis, choosing two words that refer to to the same situation or event but that name different concepts, e.g., *barber/hair stylist; invasion/cross-border operation; juvenile delinquent/young hood.* Explain how these words are used and by whom.

The word "poverty" was a fine, somehow noble word. It evoked an image out of old schoolbooks: poor but clean. Cleanliness made the poor socially acceptable. Social progress meant teaching people to be clean; once the indigent had been cleaned up, "poverty" became a title of honor. Even in the eyes of the poor, the squalor of destitution applied only to the filthy riffraff of foreign countries.

"The tenant's visiting card is his windowpane." And so the have-nots obediently bought soap with the money provided for that purpose by the progressive authorities. As paupers, they had shocked the official mind with repulsive, but for that reason palpable, images; now, as a reclaimed and cleansed "poorer class," their life became so unimaginably abstract that they could be forgotten. Squalid misery can be described in concrete terms; poverty can only be intimated in symbols.

Peter Handke, *A Sorrow Beyond Dreams*

Details, Examples, Facts, Images

In naming the classes that emerge as you form concepts, you choose one word rather than another—*swamp* rather than

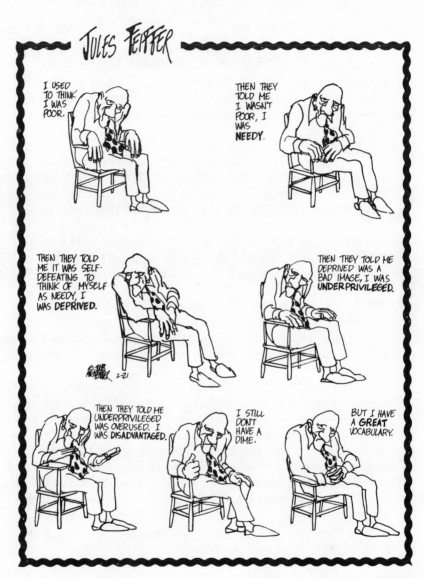

wetlands—and thus express your opinion of the facts. In the same way, the kinds of examples you choose, the number of details you develop, will also help to determine what you want to get across. Composition requires a careful balancing of generalization and particularization. Too many particular examples without generalization will result in obscurity: nobody will be sure of what you are talking about. On the other hand, too many generalizations without examples of what you mean will make it difficult for your readers or your audience to understand the implications of or "to relate to" your view of the subject.

Suppose that you describe in very careful, highly particularized detail one teacher or supervisor you have known. You can list details of dress and manner, appearance and behavior; you can set down examples of how this person sees the world and so forth until we have a very clear picture—of one teacher or supervisor. If you wanted to define a typical teacher, even in so limited a context as your school, these details would stand in the way of any generalizing your reader could attempt. To typify— to provide a "profile"—you would have to choose details that would be representative of more than just one teacher's habits and attitudes. Particularization and classification—describing the individual and characterizing the type—are both essential to almost any kind of writing.

That will seem obvious to anyone lucky enough to have avoided two directives that are great favorites with English teachers—almost as sacred as, "What is the author trying to say?" They are the admonitions "Show, don't tell!" and "Don't generalize!" Both are nonsensical. *Showing*—and there is no more problematic term in the language *—is a way of *telling*. What is generally meant by "Show, don't tell" is something like this: "Don't go on and on writing statements that are all conceptual; don't depend on dictionary definitions; show your reader the examples from which you have generalized." But "Show, don't tell" does not make any of that clear and indeed is sometimes meant to warn students away from concepts altogether. "Don't generalize" is equally absurd, since if you don't generalize, you will have to be contented with pointing. If you couldn't generalize, you couldn't think, since generalizing is

---

* Richards lists the main meanings as follows: "to look at (obsolete); to put in view, to let be seen; to make see, to point out; to be, or give, signs of; to prove, or make certain by argument. . . ." See *How to Read a Page* (Boston: Beacon, 1959), pp. 139–141 for his analysis of this word whose "trickiness derives from our own lack of competence and candor in certain situations."

necessary to the forming of concepts. The point is that you have to learn how to generalize critically, with an understanding of the role of supporting detail and the need for a balance of classification and exemplification. Hidden in these misleading directives—"Show, don't tell" and "Don't generalize"—is the notion that since concepts aren't "real" (they don't take up space, they can't be measured), they should be avoided by everyone except philosophers and critics, who are unaccountably attracted to them. Collecting examples without generalizing carefully to show what it is they exemplify characterizes the writing of students who have been taught that the "life" of writing is in the detail. But, of course, detail is meaningless unless it is a "telling" detail—and you can't tell without having something to tell.

In composing, you have to decide continually how much detail you need in order to explain your argument, what kind of examples can best support your argument or what kind of particular detail can tell your story. As you get more and more general, you give up the freedom to dwell on the particulars; the more your conceptual terms can gather, the less precisely they will characterize any one instance. Conversely, the more you concentrate on what's "in front of you," the less able you will be to make those particular "particulars" representative. When you're close to certain experiences, it's hard to believe that anyone else has ever been through anything quite like it; if you're not involved in certain experiences, no matter how "dramatic" they can seem commonplace.

          ☙ Describe an automobile accident from the following points of view (the same accident):

- Victim or someone at fault
- Relative of victim or someone allegedly at fault
- Traffic policeman
- Newspaper reporter
- Statistician for insurance company

The way you compose is up to you, but the context of situation should guide you in deciding whether to "talk it out" or to "write it up," and thus to choose the kind of detail you need.

          ☙ Compose the specifications for a "Wanted" flyer of yourself, the kind that the FBI posts in federal buildings.

❧ In short stories especially, the balance of particularization and generalization is important because there is no space to develop individual character through many incidents, as there would be in a novel. Description, in the "classical" short story, gives you a particular individual who is a type, a person who is not only himself/herself but representative of a kind of person. In the following descriptions, see if you can give a name to the type represented by the character. Then write your own description of an individual person who could also represent the type. You can present the character in a certain setting, as in the first two selections, or you can have the character speak for herself (himself), as in the third selection.

Little Chandler's thoughts ever since lunch-time had been of his meeting with Gallaher, of Gallaher's invitation and of the great city of London where Gallaher lived. He was called Little Chandler because, though he was but slightly under the average stature, he gave the idea of being a little man. His hands were white and small, his frame was fragile, his voice was quiet and his manners were refined. He took the greatest care of his fair silken hair and moustache and used perfume discreetly on his handkerchief. The half-moons of his nails were perfect and when he smiled you caught a glimpse of a row of childish white teeth.

James Joyce, "A Little Cloud"

While they were in the lake, for the dip or five-o'clock swimming period in the afternoon, he stood against a tree with his arms folded, jacked up one-legged, sitting on his heel, as absolutely tolerant as an old fellow waiting for the store to open, being held up by the wall. Waiting for the girls to get out, he gazed upon some undisturbed part of the water. He despised their predicaments, most of all their not being able to swim. Sometimes he would take aim and from his right cheek shoot an imaginary gun at something far out, where they never were. Then he resumed his pose. He had been roped into this by his mother.

Eudora Welty, "Moon Lake"

You would certainly be glad to meet me. I was the lady who appreciated youth. Yes, all that happy time, I was not like some. It did not go by me like a flitting dream. Tuesdays and

Wednesdays was as gay as Saturday nights. Have I suffered since? No sir, we've had as good times as this country gives: cars, renting in Jersey summers, TV the minute it first came out, everything grand for the kitchen. I have no complaints worth troubling the manager about. Still, it is like a long hopeless homesickness my missing those young days. To me, they're like my own place that I have gone away from forever, and I have lived all the time since among great pleasures but in a foreign town. Well, O.K. Farewell, certain years.

Grace Paley, "Distance"

In many different kinds of writing—not just police reports —the purpose is to establish that a state of affairs is thus and so, to show that such and such is the case. This kind of writing requires "on the spot" investigation, interviewing, various sorts of measurement such as polls and statistical studies; in short, it involves "getting the facts." But as you know, if you've ever tried to report on controversial issues, "getting the facts" may be impossible and even if you manage to establish what the facts of the case are, you still have to interpret them.

At the heart of any controversial issue there is the question of what the facts "really" are. People on opposing sides of the abortion issue, for instance, will never agree about what the facts are, much less about how they are to be interpreted. The doctor who defines viability on the basis of one set of facts will judge a fetus differently—he may even call it a "baby"—from another who proceeds from different facts. The person who speaks of a "baby" has judged the facts one way or has selected one set of facts, disregarding another; the person who speaks of "the products of conception" has made a different judgment by leaving out of account certain facts or by proceeding from different assumptions about their significance. Getting the facts of the matter or of the case is not a skill like learning to use a linoleum cutter, because a fact is not a thing. Writers, like doctors, lawyers, housewives, and detectives, have to know how to "handle" the facts, but that doesn't mean that facts are thing-y: "handling the facts" is a way of describing the process of seeing relationships, making sense of experience and interpreting how the world goes.

The word "fact" is not hard to define, but it is difficult to explain what you mean by it when you use it. If you declare that a fact is "something known to be true," you land right away in a philosophical swamp, since the meanings of *known, to be,* and *true* are all problematic: *knowledge, being,* and *truth* are all concepts, and they can't be explained with dictionary definitions. The history of ideas concerns changes in such concepts, including the concept of *fact* itself. What one era takes as fact is likely to be what the next sees as highly questionable. Here is the art historian Kenneth Clark commenting on this subject:

> Pilgrimages were undertaken in hope of heavenly rewards: in fact they were often used by the Church as a penitence or a spiritualized form of extradition. The point of a pilgrimage was to look at relics. Here again we like to rationalize in modern terms and compare the pilgrim looking at a large fragment of the True Cross in Constantinople with the tourist cricking his neck in the Sistine Chapel. But this is quite unhistorical. The medieval pilgrim really believed that by contemplating a reliquary containing the head or even the fingers of a saint he would persuade that particular saint to intercede on his behalf with God. How can one hope to share this belief which played so great a part in medieval civilization? Perhaps by visiting a famous place of pilgrimage—the little town of Conques, dedicated to the cult of St. Foy. She was a little girl who in late Roman times refused to worship idols. She was obstinate in the face of reasonable persuasion—a Christian Antigone; and so she was martyred. Her relics began to work miracles, and in the eleventh century one of them was so famous that it aroused much jealousy and Bernard of Angers was sent to investigate it and report to the Bishop of Chartres. It seemed that a man had had his eyes put out by a jealous priest. He had become a *jongleur,* a blind acrobat. After a year he went to the shrine of St. Foy and his eyes were restored. The man was still alive. He said at first he suffered terrible headaches, but now they had passed and he could see perfectly. There *was* a difficulty: witnesses said that after his eyes had been put out they had been taken up to heaven, some said by a dove, others by a magpie. That was the only point of doubt. However, the report was favorable, a fine Romanesque church was built at Conques, and in it was placed a strange eastern-looking figure to contain the relics of St. Foy. A golden idol! The face is perhaps the golden mask of some late Roman emperor. How ironical that this little girl, who was put to death for refusing to worship idols, should have

been turned into one herself. Well, that's the medieval mind. They cared passionately about the truth, but their sense of evidence differed from ours. From our point of view nearly all the relics in the world depend on unhistorical assertions; and yet they, as much as any factor, led to that movement and diffusion of ideas from which western civilization derives part of its momentum.

Kenneth Clark, Civilisation

Sorting out questions of fact from concepts can be difficult because the principles by which the facts of a case are defined and recognized are themselves conceptual. What you take as a fact will depend on your experience, your memory, your own power of reason—the capacity to figure out relationships—as well as on your willingness to accept the judgment of others. If we never accepted the authority of tradition or science or witnesses or the community whose principles we affirm as our own, if we never took anyone else's word for anything, we would spend our days formulating and verifying such facts as that fire burns, that the last bus does indeed leave at 9:03, and that it is unlawful to spit in the subway. On the other hand, uncritical acceptance of authority can lead to an abdication of personal responsibility, which is dangerous psychologically and politically.

All of us, especially bureaucrats, take advantage of uncritical attitudes about what is fact and what is a matter for conjecture. One of the chief things we do with language is to lie—to try to convert factual matters to conceptual problems and to make concepts and problematic terms seem matters of fact. Here are examples of each tactic.

> Making facts seem a matter of conjecture:
> *Reporter:* Are we bombing Hanoi?
> *Pentagon spokesman:* No. Well—what do you mean "Hanoi"?

> Making concepts seem matters of fact:
> *Interviewer:* But how could you be sure that Bosch's supporters were Communists?
> *American diplomat:* Well, if they *look* like Communists, and they *act* like Communists, and they *smell* like Communists, then they must *be* Communists.

Trying to isolate matters of fact from concepts is a good way to discover the concepts themselves. Concepts aren't objects; they are ideas that you bring into being by naming. You can ask, "What concept would this fact support?" or you can ask, "What are some facts that could fill out this concept?" Try it.

             ❧ Concerning each of the following concepts, write out a statement of fact. As a working definition of fact, you can think of an aspect of a state of affairs or of a situation that you could point to, measure, or name, without being readily disputed.

- national security
- the right to life
- women's liberation
- mass transportation
- rehabilitation

             ❧ For each of the following statements of fact, name two concepts towards a definition of which they might be relevant. In other words, for which concepts could these statements be "for instances"?

- Twenty dogs and cats per week were treated at the Spay and Neuter Clinic in Boston in 1975.
- The membership of the Glassworkers Union as of July 1976 was 35,000.
- The composition of the five-cent coin continues to be 75% copper, 25% nickel, while the one-cent coins are 95% copper and 5% zinc.
- Mean annual snowfall for Boston, Massachusetts, based on records through 1972, is 42.8 inches.
- Retired and disabled workers and their families and survivors of deceased workers received 70.8 billion dollars in social security cash benefits in the 12 months ending June 1976.
- Surveys have determined that nonpoint sources (runoff from farm chemicals, mines, urban areas) account for 50% of water pollution.
- The Gulf Intracoastal Waterway, 1,137 miles long, extends from Apalachee Bay, Florida, to the Mexican border.

The terms *subjective* and *objective* should be avoided in discussing the roles of facts in composition, since depending on them encourages us in the notion that facts are "out there" where "it" is happening and that concepts are all "relative," merely personal, merely verbal. Insofar as they are formulated, talked about, named, written about, facts too are "verbal." We live in a world built by language; there is no "reality" that can be known or conceived without the mediation of our senses and the forms of thought and feeling the human mind provides. To be "meaningful"—bearers of meaning—facts must be seen in context, related to other facts, seen as being in support of one concept or another. We build up such relationships by means of language, which is not a veil between us and some ultimate reality but our chief means of making meaning and thereby conceiving reality.

A detail or a fact or an example can be brought to life if it is given a form that we can *imagine*, bring to the mind's eye. Such a form is called an *image* and though it generally is visual —a form that could be seen—an image can also be auditory or kinetic, a form that brings to mind something heard or perceived as being in motion. Some kinds of poetry depend on imagery for their very being, though other kinds may have little or none. A poetic image pictures not just a particular thing; it also *re*-presents a conception of that thing and the poet's feelings about it. But using imagery is not limited to poets; you can learn to realize a concept—to make it real—by giving it a shape. We say that an image *embodies* a concept; that's an image of an image. You can't visualize freedom, but you can imagine something that can represent it.

An image must have a context in order to be meaningful, just as a word or an object or anything else we respond to must have a setting, and the meaning changes or shifts as the context changes. An Afro-American storyteller who calls himself Brother Blue accompanies his songs and tales with the clinking and clanging of a chain meant to symbolize the continuing struggle of his people for liberation. A chain in the dark corner of a garage shelf is just a chain; a tire chain shaken with a certain intent, which can be interpreted by an audience, becomes an image. A tiny Chinese shoe that now belongs to me means one thing if I consider it in the context of my childhood: a souvenir brought back by a missionary who had been sent out to convert the heathen; a rather pretty little thing, like a baby's slipper, with a quilted sole and green and pink uppers trimmed with black tape; its place on the parlor table, next to the brass bell from India. But if I look at the little shoe in the context of accounts of the Chinese revolution, it has quite a different meaning; if I see it not as a colorful trinket but as a real shoe for an actual foot, the feeling I have is of disgust or even horror, since this shoe could not possibly fit on a normal foot. (In prerevolutionary China, the feet of young girls were, in some cases, turned backwards, toes towards heel, and bound day and night to prevent normal growth. The resultant malformation necessitated a kind of walk that was thought beautiful and womanly.) Seen in the context of the custom of footbinding, the decorative shoe becomes an image of the oppression of women. Having read that the slogans of the Red Army in organizing the peasants throughout the 1930s and 1940s were "Land to the tiller!" and "Free the feet!", I came to see the shoe as an image of the oppression of a whole people enslaved by traditions that, in turn, helped maintain a certain social and economic order.

Visualizing images that can represent concepts is a skill of fundamental importance to anyone who has to explain, argue, persuade—all of us. Even scientists, some would claim, are dependent on imagery, once they forsake mathematical formulations. For any writer, exploring the relationships between images and concepts can be useful in getting the dialectic started and in forming a concept. The relationship of an *image* to what it represents or expresses is as complex as the relationship of a name and an idea, a word and a thing. (The word *image* has collected as many meanings as the word *form*. It derives from the Latin *imago*, which means *conception, thought, idea,* as well as *likeness*. *Image* is cognate with *imitation*.) You can think of an image as a visual name: it can help you "shape" your ideas by thinking of them as things that take up space. The most common error in thinking comes from confusing the image with what it represents, but that error is not avoided by staying away from imagery.

Like all other forms, an image is a way of seeing relationships. *Imagine* a person, a place, a landscape, an animal, or a thing—singly or in combination—that could represent a concept; that *image* will, at the same time, represent an attitude towards the concept. Imagery is part of the adman's repertory ("Come to Marlboro Country!" "Join the Pepsi Generation!"), but, as I have noted, it is also central in many kinds of poetry. Symbolic gardens, caves, islands, cities, deserts, valleys abound in epic, narrative, and lyric poems and also in some kinds of novels. Here is an account of how a real place became an image for the poet W. B. Yeats. The poem he mentions follows immediately after this passage from *Autobiographies*.

I was in my Galway house during the first months of civil war, the railway bridges blown up and the roads blocked with stones and trees. For the first week there were no newspapers, no reliable news, we did not know who had won nor who had lost, and even after newspapers came one never knew what was happening on the other side of the hill or of the line of trees. Ford cars passed the house from time to time with coffins standing on end between the seats, and sometimes at night we heard an explosion, and once by day saw the smoke made by the burning of a great neighboring house. Men must have lived so through many tumultuous centuries. One felt an overmastering desire not to grow unhappy or embittered, not to lose all sense of the beauty of nature. A stare (our West of Ireland name for a starling) had built in a hole beside my window and I made these verses out of the feeling of the moment—"The Stare's Nest by My Window."

"The Stare's Nest by My Window"

The bees build in the crevices
Of loosening masonry, and there
The mother birds bring grub and flies.
My wall is loosening; honey-bees,
Come build in the empty house of the stare.

We are closed in, and the key is turned
On our uncertainty; somewhere
A man is killed, or a house burned,
Yet no clear fact to be discerned:
Come build in the empty house of the stare.

A barricade of stone or of wood;
Some fourteen days of civil war;
Last night they trundled down the road
That dead young soldier in his blood:
Come build in the empty house of the stare.

We had fed the heart on fantasies,*
The heart's grown brutal from the fare;
More substance in our enmities
Than in our love; O honey-bees,
Come build in the empty house of the stare.

"Meditations in Time of Civil War," *W. B. Yeats*

❧ What characteristics of the honey bee make it an appropriate image by means of which the poet expresses a "sense of the beauty of nature"? What are the images that give substance to the concept of civil war, a time of troubles?

Students, like poets, lawyers, biographers, historians, and popular explainers, can use images to help give form to feelings and ideas. John Wain demonstrates in a passage from his biography of Samuel Johnson how images do that. He has been discussing life in eighteenth century England.

So on we could go, contrasting and comparing, trying to decide which of the two Englands would be preferable to live in, safe in the knowledge that the issue can never be decided. To me personally, to think of the quality of life in the eighteenth century is inevitably, sooner or later, to think of Josiah Wedgwood's leg. Wedgwood, another Midlander who was to trade and commerce in many ways what Johnson was to literature, was troubled in his younger days by some kind of circulatory complaint in one leg. If he happened to knock it against anything, it swelled up and put him in bed for a few days; and, since he was constantly making journeys up and down England in the course of building up his business, he found the waste of time irritating and had the leg amputated.

Most of us, I fancy, would accept the fate of being a mediocrity in business rather than consent to have a leg amputated without anaesthetic. Wedgwood's decision symbolizes many features of eighteenth-century England—the toughness, the realism, the determination to be up and doing, whatever the price that had to be paid. In a thinly populated country such giant individualities stand out clearly. Wedgwood knew that if he did not succeed in the pottery industry, he could not simply subside into comfortable obscurity as the tenth vice-president in some large faceless corporation, with his name on the door and a carpet on the floor. He had to get out there and do what it was in

---

* Yeats here refers to the fact that the Irish uprising against English rule had started with romantic expectations, nourished by dreams of past glory and encouraged by the literary celebration of a Celtic tradition, which included fabulous and heroic exploits. The reality was a bloody defeat.

him to do, or he would be nothing. In such a spirit, also, did Samuel Johnson live his life. . . .

A great photographer, like Cartier-Bresson, creates images which, in capturing "the decisive moment," bespeak more than the actual scene or face they depict. For this reason, a good collection of photographs can provide excellent practice for the student of composition. But even a commonplace photograph can become an image if you bring to it certain questions; you can train yourself to read almost any photograph as an image—and that is precisely what advertisers expect you to do.

If you study the pictures of a public figure chosen by one newspaper with those appearing in another, you can often describe the political viewpoint of either, before reading the editorial pages.

        ❧ Faye had a paper assigned for a political science course with no helpful constraints: "Write 5,000 words on a modern city." She decided to write on Bogotà because she had a huge and very detailed photograph of the city. She "read" the photograph, translating what she saw into images representing the concepts she'd learned in the course. You can try this with almost any assigned paper.

Here are some assisted invitations to exercise a capacity that is natural, innate, linguistically determined: your capacity to construe and construct images.

        ❧ Imagine and describe in single sentences the following:
Landscapes to represent each of these: youth, maturity, old age
Persons to represent each of these: faith, hope, charity
Animals to represent each of these: cleverness, courage, timidity
Places to represent each of these: fear, despair, authority
Weather or other natural phenomena to represent each of these: mercy, justice, equality

        ❧ Develop a context for an object that is valueless in itself but is of great significance to you. Or try to explain someone else's peculiar attraction to (for instance) a greasy, torn jacket, even though there are others hanging in the closet. What concept of self is involved?

∾ A Hippie has sewn the American flag to the seat of his pants: how does The Patriot construe this image?

∾ Look up the word *talisman* in a good dictionary. Describe a talismanic ceremony in another time, far away. Or describe an everyday action (toasting a slice of bread) as if it were talismanic.

∾ Design—or give instructions for designing—a poster to advertise several of the following lectures:
"Disarmament or Arms Control?"
"The Air You Breathe"
"Feminist Fiction"
"Celtic Invaders of the Eastern Mediterranean"
"Behavior Modification Techniques in Correctional Institutions"

∾ Do the same for a poster advertising a speaker whose views you oppose. Make the design express your loathing, fear, distrust, contempt, rage—whatever—but without using any verbal statements of your opinion.
Or consider how you would go about expressing disfavor of a person or a group whose activities you were filming for a television report.

∾ Convert one of the following objects to an image representing a concept. Then compose an editorial denouncing the concept so represented, beginning with a description of the object.

- platform shoes
- station wagons
- paperback novels
- saunas
- a clear, fresh river by a deserted factory

Articulating Relationships

When you understand what's going on in reading or conversing, you are seeing the relationships of one statement to another; you follow what is being said or written. "I don't follow you" means "I don't understand." When you write, the principal question, once you learn to frame it, is: "How do I get from here to there?" The problem of sequence is not—alas—solved by figuring out which words follow which. Getting from here to there is not a matter of lining up words but of articulating meanings.

To be *articulate* means to speak so that every syllable is clear and, by extension, to demonstrate clearly the relationship of one idea to another. *Articulation* derives from the Latin word (*artus*) for *joint:* anatomists speak of the articulation of the skeleton, meaning the relationship of bone, tendon, ligament, and muscle that makes motor activity possible. Without articulation, the skeleton would be merely a clutter of bones; without articulation, there can be statements but no composition. Articulation implies understanding the terms in which the relationships are seen, named, known. You can learn a lot about what articulation involves by considering that little phrase *in terms of*. In describing anything, you identify characteristics in terms of categories * determined by your interest and purpose. *To speak in terms of* is short for *to speak in the terms that the category provides for description and definition.*

The phrase *in terms of* is frequently misused: "What'll we have for supper?" "Oh, I've been thinking in terms of soup and sandwiches." Or: "The Antarctic has a very austere beauty and, of course, on the fringes, it has fantastic wildlife, in terms of penguins and so on." *In terms of* should be used when you mean the descriptive and defining words that are offered by a concept when you are naming the members of the class. (A class, you remember, is the field of a concept's application.) Here are some examples of correct use:

> This problem cannot be understood *in terms of* banking concepts alone; we need to develop a political understanding.

---

* *Category* in the original Greek meant *to speak against the assembly.* To categorize came to mean not just an accusation but any assertion or predication. In logic, *category* refers to any class used in an inquiry or discussion. For our purposes, a philosophical definition is most useful: a category is a class that helps define choices.

In terms of cost accounting, it is a good budget.

If you're considering education *in terms of* its economic benefits, you're in for a surprise.

Consumer education is directed toward changing people's attitudes about purchasing so that they judge various products *in terms of* performance and value rather than *in terms of* appearance and benefits alleged in advertisements.

Any discipline requires the capacity to define *in terms of* certain categories—to be able to classify by differentiating according to criteria derived from those categories. Take the professions, for instance. The lawyer makes a case by arguing along certain lines, *in terms of* such categories as jurisdiction, legality, culpability, etc. Learning the law means learning how the categories work to guide you in arguing a case. The physician diagnoses diseases and malfunctions by reading symptoms *in terms of* normal expectations about the functioning of the human organism. The preacher proclaims the truth as it can be defined *in terms of* dogma, revelation, ecclesiastical law and history, the sacred texts, the lives of the saints and martyrs, etc.

You can think of "in terms of" as a kind of signal that announces that such and such an instance or example or case is to be discussed as a member of a certain class: writing "in terms of" is a way of explicitly classifying. The "terms" are the names provided by the class, the concept, or the category; a *terminology* is the collection of such terms.

          ∾ List the terms in which the duties of the following professionals can be described (HDWDWW?). Write a sentence concerning each, naming the duties and the terms.

- teachers
- soldiers
- engineers
- epidemiologists
- accountants

Articulating relationships as we form and develop concepts depends on a capacity to see the form of one thing in another and to use the form of one to explain and define the other. Such a description is called an *analogy* and it re-presents the way we see relationships. The continuum of the composing process depends on the fact that we can see one thing—shape, event, concept—*in terms of* another. Describing a malfunctioning kid-

ney and describing a bankruptcy case require different terminologies, but to emphasize a point the lawyer can use medical
terminology just as the physician can use legal terminology. The
analogy can clarify certain relationships and help to form the
concept.

There are many varieties of analogy, many different names
for analogous relationships, some of which may be familiar to
you if you have studied poetry: *metaphor, simile, allegory,* for
instance. It won't surprise you to be told that in all its varieties,
analogy is a form that finds form: a form of comparison that
helps discover likenesses; a form of argument that helps you to
discover implications; a form of statement that helps find the
form of feeling and thought you intend to express and represent. Analogy is the principal means of articulating relationships and thus of forming concepts.

One way to sharpen your sense of what "in terms of" means
and to learn how to use analogies is to practice transformations,
deliberately seeing one thing in the terms that are generally
used in describing another class of things. Transforming goes
on all the time as you make sense of the world. Transforming
is a way of seeing what-would-happen-if; it shakes up the categories of understanding and makes you more aware of context.
Here are some assisted invitations to practice transformations.

                              ✎ At the time we were send-
ing a man to the moon, an article appeared entitled
"Landing a Man Downtown." What was it about?

                              ✎ Thorstein Veblen invented
a phrase that exemplifies the inventive uses of analogy:
he called industrialists *"captains* of industry," thus
suggesting the military-like character of capitalist
structures. Using that phrase as a pattern, rename the
following:

students: the _____ of _____
teachers: the _____ of _____
patriots: the _____ of _____

                              ✎ Try another pattern with
these:

_____ are the mice of _____.
_____ are the moths of _____.
_____ are the dinosaurs of the _____.

❧ Analogies can, like every other rhetorical and logical form, be used fraudulently. One way to discover the usefulness of the limits a good analogy provides is to see how easy it is to draw an analogy between *any* two things! Try it with whatever comes to mind: e.g., sunset and pipe tobacco; watermelon and embroidery; Scotland and the bark of a maple tree.

When Wordsworth explained what he and Coleridge intended in their revolutionary new kind of poetry, he said that his aim was to make the familiar *strange* and that Coleridge was attempting to make the strange *familiar*. This Romantic poetics is alive and well in science fiction writing. It is also common practice with inventors and other problem-solvers who deliberately try to see the familiar in fresh ways and to assimilate the strange by pretending that it's familiar by inventing a perspective from which it would be familiar.

❧ See if you can transform some of the objects in the list below, making the strange familiar and the familiar strange. You can transform most easily if you consider the object or idea from an unusual perspective. The technique of horror movies is to distort scale: picnic ants become monsters from the deep lagoon.

Make the familiar strange	Make the strange familiar
a tin can	a Vietnamese grandmother
a patriot	the moon
a traffic jam	the Finnish language
a helicopter gunship	a viola da gamba
a rabbit	the Himalayas
the moon	a sampan
a mosquito	a cow's digestive system
madness	madness

Thinking is seeing relationships; rhetoric is the art of representing that "seeing." Rhetoric is the art of naming, opposing, and defining in order to articulate relationships. Transformations are one of the chief means by which the rhetorician/composer can put things in a new light and thus clarify relationships and form concepts. A whole range of techniques is available for effecting such transformations. Satire, for instance, often employs a distortion of scale to force us to see reality more clearly. In *Gulliver's Travels*—to take the most famous example—Jonathan Swift tells how his hero is shipwrecked among the Lilliputians, in comparison to whom he is a giant, and how, then, on a subsequent voyage, he finds himself among giants. Gulliver is placed in the care of Glumdalclitch, a 40-foot tall nurse who carries him in a padded box at her waist.

> I remember one morning when Glumdalclitch had set me in my box upon a window, as she usually did in fair days to give me air (for I durst not venture to let the box be hung on a nail out of the window, as we do with cages in England) after I had lifted up one of my sashes [windows], and sat down at my table to eat a piece of sweet cake for my breakfast, above twenty wasps allured by the smell, came flying into the room, humming louder than the drones of as many bagpipes. Some of them seized my cake, and carried it piecemeal away, others flew about my head and face, confounding me with the noise, and putting me in the utmost terror of their stings. However I had the courage to rise and draw my hanger [sword] and attack them in the air. I dispatched four of them, but the rest got away, and I presently shut my window. These insects were as large as partridges: I took out their stings, found them an inch and a half long, and as sharp as needles. I carefully preserved them all, and having shown them with some other curiosities in several parts of Europe, upon my return to England I gave three of them to Gresham College, and kept the fourth myself.

Continual reference to the insects and small animals as gigantic monsters prepares us for the scene in which the King of Brobdingnag tells Gulliver, whom he holds in the palm of his hand, that from what Gulliver has told him of the customs and habits of his countrymen, he "cannot but conclude the bulk of your natives to be the most pernicious race of little odious vermin that nature ever suffered to crawl upon the surface of the earth."

Satire offers what Kenneth Burke, a learned and witty rhetorician, calls "perspective by incongruity." Things that don't belong together can, in juxtaposition, give us new insights, help us form concepts. Transforming is at the heart of Burke's theory of rhetoric, which he summarizes as follows: "Instead of viewing words as *names* for *things*, we should view them as abbreviated *titles* for *situations*." * HDWDWW? is a transformer that allows us to do just that—to convert names and things to titles and situations. Other transformers are slogans and stories which Burke calls "entitlements."

Slogans are used to rally and to sell. An advertising slogan presents a product as an answer to a question, the solution to a problem, the fulfillment of a dream, the satisfaction of a need. The answers, solutions, fulfillments, and satisfactions may be entirely spurious—and so may the questions, problems, dreams, and needs.

                    ☙ Consider any of these slogans that may be familiar to you as answers to questions; compose the question (or the statement to which each is a counterstatement).

- Power to the people!
- No taxation without representation!
- Send 'em a message!
- Peace with honor!
- Strength through joy!
- We shall overcome!
- Küche, Kindern, Kirche
- Let us do the driving.
- Guns don't kill people; people kill people.
- Support your local police.
- Better Red than dead.
- The pause that refreshes.

                    ☙ Compose three slogans for the concept of maturity, each expressing a different attitude.

A *story* told to illustrate a concept is one of the oldest literary forms. (*Story* is cognate with *history;* they derive from the Greek *histor*, knowing.) Parables and fables, for instance, spell out the implications of statements about the way of the world, the nature of evil, pride, envy, love, etc., by telling stories that dramatize these concepts. Here are three examples.

A Farmer being on the point of death, and wishing to show his sons the way to success in farming, called them to him and said, "My children, I am departing from this life, but all

---

* *Language as Symbolic Action* (Berkeley: University of California Press, 1966), p. 294.

that I have to leave you will be found in the vineyard." The sons, supposing that he referred to some hidden treasure, as soon as the old man was dead, set to work with their spades and ploughs and every implement that was at hand and turned the soil over and over again. They found indeed no treasure; but the vines strengthened and improved by this thorough tillage, yielded a finer vintage than they had ever yielded before, and more than repaid the young husbandmen for all their trouble.

So truly is industry in itself a virtue.

Aesop, "The Farmer and His Sons"

"The Gardener and the Lord of the Manor"

A devotee of gardening there was,
Between the peasant and the yeoman class,
Who on the outskirts of the village
Owned a neat garden with a bit of tillage.
He made a quickset hedge to fence it in,
And there grew lettuce, pink and jessamine,
Such as win prizes at the local show,
Or make a birthday bouquet for Margot.

One day he called upon the neighboring Squire
To ask his help with a maruading hare.
"The brute," says he, "comes guzzling everywhere,
And simply laughs at all my traps and wire.
No stick or stone will hit him—I declare
He's a magician." "Rubbish! I don't care
If he's the Deuce himself," replied the other,
"I warrant he shan't give you much more bother.
Miraut, in spite of all his cunning,
Won't take much time to get him running."
"But when?" "To-morrow, sure as here I stand."
Next morning he rides up with all his band.
"Now then, we'll lunch! Those chickens don't look bad."

The luncheon over, all was preparation,
Bustle and buzz and animation,
Horns blowing, hounds barking, such a hullabaloo,
The good man feared the worst. His fear came true!
The kitchen-garden was a total wreck
Under the trampling, not a speck
Of pot or frame survived. Good-bye
To onion, leek, and chicory,

Good-bye to marrows and their bravery,
Goodbye to all that makes soup savory!

The wretched owner saw no sense
In this grand style of doing things;
But no one marked his mutterings.
The hounds and riders in a single trice
Had wrought more havoc in his paradise
Than all the hares in the vicinity
Could have achieved throughout infinity.
So far the story—now the moral:
Each petty Prince should settle his own quarrel.
If once he gets a King for an ally,
He's certain to regret it by and by.

LaFontaine

"If sharks were people," the landlady's little daughter asked Mr. K, "would they be nicer to the little fishes?"

"Certainly," he said. "If sharks were people they would have enormous boxes built in the sea for the little fishes with all sorts of things to eat in them, plants as well as animal matter. They would see to it that the boxes always had fresh water and, in general, take hygienic measures of all kinds. For instance, if a little fish injured one of its fins, it would be bandaged at once, so that the sharks would not be deprived of it by an untimely death. To prevent the little fishes from growing depressed there would be big water festivals from time to time, for happy little fishes taste better than miserable ones. Of course there would also be schools in the big boxes. In these schools the little fishes would learn how to swim into the sharks' jaws. They would need geography, for example, so that when the big sharks were lazing about somewhere they could find them. The main thing, of course, would be the moral education of the little fishes. They would be taught that the greatest and finest thing is for a little fish to sacrifice its life gladly, and that they must all believe in the sharks, particularly when they promise a splendid future. They would impress upon the little fishes that this future could only be assured if they learnt obedience. The little fishes would have to guard against all base, materialistic, egotistic and Marxist tendencies, reporting at once to the sharks if any of their number manifested such tendencies. If sharks were people they would also, naturally, wage wars amongst themselves, to conquer foreign fish boxes and little foreign fishes. They would let their own little fishes fight these wars. They would teach the little fishes that there was a vast difference between themselves and the little fishes of other sharks. Little fishes, they would proclaim, are well known to be dumb, but they are silent in quite different languages and therefore cannot possibly understand each other. Each little fish which killed a few other little fishes in war—little enemy fishes, dumb in a different language—would have a little seaweed medal pinned on it and be awarded the title of Hero. If sharks were people they would also have art, naturally. There would be lovely pictures representing sharks' teeth in glorious colours, their jaws as positive pleasure grounds in which it would be a joy to gambol. The sea-bed theatres would show heroic little fishes swimming rapturously into sharks' jaws, lulled in the most delightful thoughts. There would also be a religion if sharks were people. It would teach that little fishes only really start to live inside the bellies of sharks. Moreover, if sharks were people, not all little fishes would be equal any more as they are now. Some of them would be given positions and be set over the others. The slightly bigger ones would even be allowed to gobble up the smaller ones. That would give nothing but pleasure to the sharks, since they would more often get larger morsels for themselves. And the bigger little fishes, those holding positions, would be responsible for keeping order among the little fishes, become teachers, officers, box-building engineers and so on. In short, the sea would only start being civilized if sharks were people."

Bertolt Brecht, "If Sharks Were People," from *Tales from the Calendar*.

          ❧ Compose a fable illustrating some judgment you think can be made of a concept. You can first think up a slogan and then transform it into a fable. Try it with *work* or *play* or both.

          ❧ Just as you can transform objects into events, you can transform statements into stories. Try it with these adages: write a brief story demonstrating the principle or dramatizing the saying and use the adage either as the title or the final line. You will need to develop a context by composing a question to which the adage could be considered an answer. Determine presuppositions by asking HDWDWW? Once you've worked out the logic of the analogy, the story will virtually write itself, but you must be sure to transform the terms of the saying: don't write a story about a stone that rolls continually down a stream bed to illustrate the first adage.

- A rolling stone gathers no moss.
- Make hay while the sun shines.
- Grub first; then morals.
- A bird in the hand is worth two in the bush.
- If you can't stand the heat, get out of the kitchen.

In composing almost any kind of assigned paper, you will need to understand the terminology of the subject. You can't any more write about Third World countries by talking about how "they" face "problems" than you can properly describe the repair of a bicycle over the phone with such terms as "what's-it" and "thingamagig." The organization of a terminology according to what it names is a *taxonomy,* a schematization of class and subclass names. *Taxonomics* is especially important in the natural sciences where a tremendous amount of information must be classified; indeed, until the middle of the last century with the development of different methods and fundamentally different questions, taxonomics constituted science. Studying biology or botany meant learning how to categorize various specimens—examples of the membership of a certain subclass. Here's what the taxonomy of the horse looks like:

Kingdom:	Animalia
Phylum:	Chordata
Class:	Mammalia
Order:	Ungulata
Family:	Equidae
Genus:	*Equus*
Species:	*Equus caballus*
Breed:	Percheron

                    Work out a "taxonomy" for a canoe or a Mustang (car).

Taxonomics by itself wouldn't be of much use; you also need to know how to use the terms, both to discover and to remember, to invent and develop. Taxonomics without field work—getting the facts—is unreliable; field work without taxonomics would be meaningless, since there would be no way of establishing or defining relationships, even if you could see them. Creativity in any art or science, craft or trade, is best defined as a capacity to respond to the ordinary in such a way as to be alert to the extraordinary: To identify the unusual means knowing very well what to expect rather than being anxious to categorize dogmatically. Being tentative about taxonomy is the same thing as being sensible about any kind of limits—neither fearing nor rejecting them, but learning their uses.

It's instructive to consider the way a novice birdwatcher uses the limits provided by ornithological taxonomy, in contrast to the procedure of an experienced birder. The double page in a field guide showing "Warblers in Their Winter Plumage" is very depressing to the novice: 27 little heads in profile, all apparently alike but each with a different label. But this fact of seeming identity is exactly what delights the experienced birder with a life list of 400 birds. The novice may stare hypnotically at the warblers, memorizing the differentiating marks that can be discerned upon close inspection. But once the birder is in the field, how are such details to be remembered? The novice, believing that she has just sighted an extremely rare bird because memorization of length of tail, colors of wing linings, presence of eye stripe, etc., has proceeded without regard for song and flight characteristics and with no attention paid to habitat. The experienced birder knows not to expect a Manx Shearwater on the Mississippi River or a Mallard on the open sea. On the other hand, she has the taxonomy in mind so that if a bird appears bearing certain very precise markings and behaving in a very distinctive manner, it can be identified, regardless of the fact that it has no business being where it apparently is. The novice sees the commonplace as the marvelous, but the experienced birder sees the marvelous among the commonplace.

∾ Birdwatching, I've been implying, is a composing process: it involves the active mind at work naming and defining. The same is true for playing or watching a sport or game. Write a couple of paragraphs about the relationship of knowing the rules to enjoying the game, either as spectator or as player.

∾ Disregarding the fact that you would probably get a dirty look if you said *tax-*

onomy to a ballplayer, can you describe an umpire's job as a matter of taxonomics (the categories and terminology) and observation?

Articulating relationships is a matter of getting together the meanings you are making as you write. This involves you in making choices and, as we have seen, you must have limits to be able to choose. The role of a taxonomy in the natural sciences is precisely that: it offers a set of limits that guide choices as you follow a procedure that will lead to identification and definition; it provides a schema that makes it possible to organize data; it is an organizational form that helps you find particular forms. Two examples of taxonomic form are the botanical key and the flow chart used in a chemistry lab. Both are organized on the principle of *binary opposition*. The choices are made between two and only two alternatives: the stem is *either* round *or* triangular; the filtrate is treated with *either* a sodium chloride solution *or* a silver nitrate solution.

Here are some assisted invitations to practice binary sorting and gathering.

         ❧ Generate a chaos of 20 animal names. Then form two sets into which *all* animals in your chaos can be fitted. You may have to resort to empty sets (e.g., *Tails/No Tails;* Ginny decided on *Salads/Not-Salads:* tuna and turkey in *Salads;* lions and tigers in *Not-Salads.*) A good way to get started is to ask who needs to know.

A botanical key guides classification by offering alternative descriptions of aspects of the form of the specimen. As you choose, you continually narrow the field of possibility, just as in a game of Twenty Questions. A key to the Commoner British Grasses begins as follows; the number in parentheses directs you to the next appropriate set of alternatives, numbered at the left.

1. Basal leaves bristle-like, not easily flattened: (2).
   Basal leaves flat, or if bristle-like when dry can be flattened easily with the thumbnail: (3).
2. Scales of florets with silvery translucent margins: (4).
   Scales of florets opaque, greenish purple or brown: (5).
4. Plants annual, small and slender: (6).
   Plants perennial, robustly tufted: *Deschampsia flexuosa.*

6. Leaf-sheaths rough, panicle open: *Aira caryophyllea.*
   Leaf-sheaths smooth, panicle close: *Aira praecox.*
5. Leaves bent back at right-angles to whitish sheaths; panicle narrow, one-sided, with purple narrow pointed lemmas: *Nardus stricta.*
   Leaves not at right-angles to sheath: (7).
7. Ligules to 4 mm, acute; awn from within floret: *Agrostis setacea.*
   Ligules very short or wanting: (8).
8. Stem leaves flat when fresh, spikelets 8–14 mm long: *Festuca rubra.*
   Stem leaves always tightly rolled, spikelets 5–10 mm long: *Festuca ovina.*
3. Ligule a fringe of hairs: (9).
   Ligule membranous: (10).

         ❧ Develop a key for sorting the contents of your desk drawer; your pockets or purse; your car glove compartment; your dishwasher. Note that the first choice should be between two categories into which *all* items will fit: organic, inorganic; hollow, solid; etc.

Learning something about taxonomics does not mean that you should try to compose according to some prescribed key. A taxonomy provides a model of the process of comparing and differentiating, sorting and gathering; its value to the student of composition is that it shows something about how generalization works. A model can be something you follow, like a pattern, but it can also be a structure that demonstrates a principle of operation. It is in this sense that a taxonomy is a model: it lets you watch generalization as it's happening.

It should be noted—it's an extremely important point—that the binary choices that are defined by a taxonomic scheme represent a judgment of the "real world," not a replica of something "out there." Each set of binary choices is established by the taxonomist on the basis of criteria that are determined by the needs of the observer/definer. You will often hear attacks on "two-valued" orientations: "It's not a matter of black or white; there are many shades of gray in between." The point here is that black/white is an opposition that could help you sort things that are indeed either black or white, but it is also a means of differentiating the shades of gray.

Using taxonomic schemes can help you make compositional choices, but, more importantly, such schema can help you establish the criteria by which to define those choices. They can help you identify your presuppositions and that is one of the important operations in forming concepts. If you keep in mind their function as forms to find forms, you can avoid the danger of mistaking taxonomic schemes for "reality." To sort and gather according to a taxonomic scheme (*either/or*) doesn't mean that you consider that any one thing *must* belong in one category or the other, but only that, given such and such a polarity, you can rank the in-betweens in this way. A taxonomy can't tell you anything about the individual characteristics of any one particular horse or bird; only performance and appearance—the facts as they can be established by observation and experience—can do that. But without a taxonomy, there would be no way of relating one kind to another, of developing classes, of organizing knowledge. By taxonomies we represent the generalizations made possible by language, which gives us the power to name the particular and the general simultaneously.

All terminologies, no matter how abstruse, derive ultimately from the categories of understanding: space, time, causality. Describing the horse, for instance, involves classifying it with other animals having a spinal cord (Chordata) which is a structural element, a part of any vertebrate—a spatial form. The horse is classified in a group (Equidae) that includes animals that flourished millions of years ago and are now extinct—a temporally defined classification. And everything about the horse's appearance—its build and character—is the effect both of evolutionary development and of breeding; in that sense, the horse is a result or an effect.

To see a horse—or a fact, a structure, an event, a situation, a behavior, a phenomenon, an attitude, etc.—as an effect characterizes the modern temper. Determining cause/effect relationships is, of course, the aim of all scientific inquiry, but it is probably a fair description of all rational thought. This comment by C. S. Peirce, the founder of modern logic, is enlightening:

> Whether we ought to say that a force *is* an acceleration, or that it *causes* an acceleration, is a mere question of propriety of language, which has no more to do with our real meaning than the difference between the French idiom "Il fait froid" [it makes cold] and its English equivalent "It is cold." Yet it is surprising how this simple affair has mud-

dled men's minds. In how many profound treatises is not force spoken of as a "mysterious entity," which seems to be only a way of confessing that the author despairs of ever getting a clear notion of what the word means! In a recent admired work on analytic mechanics it is stated that we understand precisely the effect of force, but what force itself is we do not understand! This is simply a self-contradiction. The idea which the word *force* excites in our minds has no other function than to affect our actions, and these actions can have no reference to force otherwise than through its effects. Consequently, if we know what the effects of force are, we are acquainted with every fact which is implied in saying that a force exists, and there is nothing more to know.

Peirce wrote that a hundred years ago in a charming (and difficult) essay called "How to Make Our Ideas Clear." Forming the concept of mechanical force is no longer a scientific or philosophical issue, but the principle he announces is generally applicable to forming concepts. Along with seeing one thing in terms of another, the primary way we have of seeing and articulating relationships is in terms of cause and effect. When we ask, "How did it come about? What's happening? What does this mean?" we seek answers that will explain the *how* and the *why* by relating cause and effect. The rules by which we do that rationally, logically, sanely, correctly, productively, etc., can take a lifetime of study. Meanwhile, here are four ways of thinking about causality which are of use to the writer.

1. *Causal chains.* These can, of course, be fraudulent; reasoning can be merely rationalization. Depending on how "paranoid" we are at any given time, we are more or less liable to fall for spurious reasoning, believing that a collection of "facts" makes a case. The most common logical error is to assume that because one thing is followed by another that the second is caused by the first. (*Post hoc, ergo propter hoc:* After that; therefore, because of that.)

> For want of a nail, the shoe was lost;
> For want of a shoe, the horse was lost;
> For want of the horse, the message was lost;
> For want of the message, the battle was lost.

          ❧ Develop a causal chain in which the first link is a piece of burned toast. Then develop another in which a piece of burned toast is the final link.

Here is a useful account of the nature of inference written by a historian who is interested in detective fiction.

Because historians deal with the inexact, they have developed certain common-sense rules for evaluating evidence in terms of its reliability, its relevance, its significance, and its singularity. Inference is notoriously unreliable, as are eyewitnesses, memories of old men, judgments of mothers about first children, letters written for publication, and garbage collectors. At the moment, I drive a much battered 1954 Cadillac, full of wayward lurchings, unidentifiable rattles, and unpredictable ways upon the road. Recently I shifted a shovel, which I carry in the trunk as proof against New England snows, to a new position. No sooner had I closed the lid than a new and penetrating noise arose from the back of the car which clearly was a metal shovel bouncing about within a trunk. My inference was that this was so, and for a week I drove without investigating the noise. Then the gas tank fell off, proving my inference wrong. . . .

[Notions of relevancy are applied outside the library and] the historian needs to be the most practical of men as well. One of my acquaintances worked with Marine intelligence during World War II. He was asked to help judge how many Japanese had dug in on one of the strategically crucial South Pacific islands, an island which the Marine Corps planned to make their own, whatever the losses, within a few days. No Japanese could be seen from aerial reconnaissance, since their camouflage was nearly perfect. The historian provided an accurate figure, however, for he noted from aerial photographs that particularly dark patches could be identified as latrines, and upon consulting a captured Japanese manual, he learned how many latrines were to be dug per unit of men. The rest was so simple a matter of calculation that even the historian could provide an answer without the aid of a computer.

Robin W. Winks, *The Historian as Detective*, Introduction

✑ What were the presuppositions of the Marine Corps historian?

2. *Cause/effect* : *question/answer* : *form/function*

Scientific discoveries, inventions, new theories all come about because someone has asked a new question that allows relationships to be articulated in a new way. To deduce that your eyes are smarting because a nearby smokestack is belching forth "smoke" takes no great insight; developing a political context for watering eyes may be harder. Here's an example of how relationships are articulated in a new and provocative way by looking for distant causes:

> Perhaps the wisest words on the complexity of the traffic problem [in Manhattan] were uttered long ago by Benton MacKaye, who fathered the Appalachian Trail. To relieve the congestion of traffic in Times Square, he remarked, it might be necessary to reroute the flow of wheat through the Atlantic ports.
>
> Lewis Mumford, *From the Ground Up*

3. *Establish motive and purpose in order to account for results.* Detectives speculate about motive as a way of generating hypotheses that could order a mass of "clues" that may turn out to be evidence for causal relationships. A clue is a fact looking for a context. Historians also form hypotheses to account for what "really" happened. Winks includes in his list of unreliable sources the accounts of old men, but here's one who sounds convincing:

> What made the farmers fight in 1775? Judge Mellen Chamberlain in 1842, when he was 21, interviewed Captain Preston, a 91-year-old veteran of the Concord fight: "Did you take up arms against intolerable oppressions?" he asked.
>
> "Oppressions?" replied the old man. "I didn't feel them."
>
> "What, were you not oppressed by the Stamp Act?"
>
> "I never saw one of those stamps. I certainly never paid a penny for one of them."
>
> "Well, what then about the tea tax?"
>
> "I never drank a drop of that stuff; the boys threw it all overboard."
>
> "Then I suppose you had been reading Harrington or Sidney or Locke about the eternal principles of liberty?"
>
> "Never heard of 'em. We read only the Bible, the catechism, Watts' Psalms and hymns, and the almanac."
>
> "Well, then, what was the matter? And what did you mean in going to the fight?"
>
> "Young man, what we meant in going for those Redcoats was this: *We always had governed ourselves, and we always meant to. They didn't mean we should.*"
>
> S. E. Morison, *The Oxford History of the American People*

❧ Translate each of the *meants* and *means* in the old man's reply.

❧ Imagine a conversation with a veteran of the student protests, 1968–1974. Record it in the form of the Chamberlain-Preston dialogue.

4. *Aristotelian analysis.* The traditional categories can be schematized as follows in the case of a house:

Material cause	Stuff	The stones that compose it
Efficient cause	Agency	The mason who laid them
Formal cause	Structure	The blueprint he followed
Final cause	Purpose	The purpose for which the house was built

❧ Work out an Aristotelian analysis of the causes for a broken window of a commuter train. Which cause would be most likely to be disputed in a court of law?

5. *Systems analysis.* This method can be enormously complex, especially when computers are employed, but what is involved essentially is a dialectical determination of cause and effect so that it can be seen that an effect can itself be a cause; that causes have "side effects" that become causes and start new chains; that our means of interpreting causal relations affect what we see and know. This concept, which is more complex than the concept of defining by effect, is especially important in modern physics where it is known as the Uncertainty Principle. I. A. Richards sees the mutual dependence of what we study and how we study as being central to all language study—and that, as you will see, is everything.

The very instruments we use if we try to say anything which is not trivial about language embody in themselves the very problems we hope to use them to explore. The doubt comes up, therefore; how far can we hope to be understood—or even to understand ourselves—as we use such words? And in the lucidity of this doubt the literature of this subject can take on a queer appearance. Must confidence be in inverse ratio to the security of its grounds? This situation is not, of course, peculiar to the study of language. All studies suffer from and thrive through this. The properties of the instruments or apparatus employed enter into, contribute to, belong with and confine the scope of the investigation. . . . There is no study which is not a language study, concerned with the speculative instruments it employs.

I. A. Richards, Speculative Instruments

Recapitulation

You can name a concept easily enough, but until you can demonstrate how it "applies," how it works to define a field, to gather certain particulars to form a class, it can't be something you can think with; it will simply be a word with a dictionary definition. Forming and developing concepts entails the articulation of relationships. The composer proceeds dialectically with naming the class and describing its members in terms provided by the concept; with seeing relationships between members of a class and between classes; with substantiating those relationships by particularizing (details, examples, instances, cases, the facts); with relating the relationships.

Articulating relationships is important in all exposition, the kind of writing you do when you explain; but the operations of mind involved are the same as those by whose means we make sense of the world. Central to all is the analogizing capacity: it is a fundamental law of mind that we see one thing in terms of another. Analogy as a rhetorical form is based on the fact that all terminologies, no matter how special, derive ultimately from universal categories of understanding: space, time, and causality. We can describe one thing in terms of another because that is the way we have seen the relationships in the first place. Composing is a process of forming concepts and articulating the relationships that they help us to think about.

       ❧ Appearance, as a category, provides such terms as *shape, size, contour, texture,* etc. For each of the categories in the scheme opposite, write out the terms it provides. Nothing is more useful in composing than having such words in your head or on hand. Work on your list and keep it handy when you're writing.

A Pocket Guide to the Logic of Terminologies

Adaptation of HDWDWW?	*Categories*	*Terms*
How does it look? (smell, taste, feel, sound)	Appearance	
Where did it come from? Who made it?	Origin	
What's it made out of?	Material	
How is it put together? Of what is it a part?	Organization, construction, composition	
What does it do? How does it behave?	Activity, Action, Behavior	
How does it work? What effect does it have? What's it for?	Mode of operation Causality Function, purpose	
Who uses it?	Use	
To whose advantage is it that it be invented, made, grown, developed, sold, controlled, etc?	Motive	

---

4. Gathering, Sorting, Gathering

Composing, Revising, Correcting

Composing is like an organic process, not an assembly line on which some prefabricated parts are fitted together. However, plants and animals don't just "grow" mystically, developing from seed to flower and fully framed creatures, without plan or guidance or system. All organic processes are forms in action: the task of the composer is to find the forms that find forms; the structures that guide and encourage growth; the limits by means of which development can be shaped. The method of composing that we've been discussing and practicing is a way of making meanings by using the forms provided by language to re-present the relationships we see.

In that process of forming and developing concepts, writing gets written because you can't articulate relationships without stating and restating. The naming, opposing, and defining that constitute the composing process generate sentences and clusters of sentences that will become paragraphs. Composing by a dialectical method means that you write from the first; the final phase of composing is thus a matter not of going over an outline and "filling in the words" but of rewriting, which means taking another look at what you've written. Revision means a reseeing. That review is a continuation of what has been going on from the start—looking and taking another look. From chaos to oppositions; from statement to paraphrase; from definition to entitlement and building the opposite case: at every stage you interpret what you are composing and those interpretations provide the ground, then, for further composing, further interpreting. Revision is a matter of interpreting your interpretations; it means hearing what you've had to say and deciding if you now know what you mean.

Revision is not the same thing as *correcting:* revising is an integral phase of composing; correcting is not. When you revise, you compose paragraphs. You write sentences; you rewrite paragraphs. It's only when you have several sentences—a paragraph in formation—that it makes sense to try to rewrite any one sentence. When you are getting started and don't really know where you're going, one of the chief purposes of writing is to discover "what you want to say." Stopping to rewrite then is likely to curtail the exploration and to break the train of thought, once that is in progress. Even later, when you are developing concepts and definitions, too much fussiness over sentence structure or paragraphing can confuse the issue. Concentrating on correctness while you're composing sentences would be like polishing the handle before the door is hung.

Andre Gide, in a moment of reflecting on his habits of composing, put it this way: "Too often I wait for the sentence to take shape in my mind before setting it down. It is better to seize it by the end that first offers itself, head or foot, though not knowing the rest, then pull: the rest will follow along."

You compose sentences as forms that represent the way you see relationships; you revise sentences as elements of a larger form that is coming into being. In composing sentences, the dialectic is between saying and intending. In revising sentences, the dialectic is still between saying and intending—that never is finished—but it is now also between this saying and that saying, between this sentence and that one. *The sentences you compose by listening in on the inner dialogue form a sequence that becomes a paragraph when you revise those individual sentences as parts of a bundle.* Since fussing about correctness can interrupt this methodical circle, correcting will have to wait for a later phase. I believe that grammatical analysis is properly the very last stage and that it should not be undertaken until your revision is complete.

The Logic and Rhetoric of Paragraphs

Writers are concerned with statements, arguments, generalizations, classifications, etc.—all matters of logic. In a rhetorical perspective, they appear as sentences and paragraphs. Thought and language are inseparable as philosophical and psychological concepts, but they can be discussed in different terms. Here is one explanation of how logic and rhetoric supply those terms:

> The writer attends to the logical connections between his statements—whether they make sense and hang together without contradicting each other—and he attends to their effect on others, those who hear and read him. In logic, he asks whether it is reasonable that one certain step follows another; in rhetoric, he asks whether it is effective for his purposes. In both, his grammar is a system which underlies and limits his choices; that is, he chooses constructions in words and syntax that will work together to take him where he wants to go.*

Rhetoricians are concerned about unity, coherence, emphasis; introductions, developments, conclusions; transitions, recapitulations, repetitions, and balance. Rhetoric is concerned fundamentally and continually with the dialectical relationship of language and thought: How does this way of putting it differ from that way? How does it change what is said? What changes in language affect my intention? And those questions in turn generate many others about the composition as a bundle of parts. In this section, we will concentrate on the rhetorical aspects of those acts of mind by which we form and develop concepts. As a

---

* Josephine Miles, "English: A Colloquy; or, How What's What in the Language," *California English Journal*, 2 (1966), 3–14.

reminder that rhetorical decisions are contingent on logical choices, here is an account of how the dialectician proceeds.

> This seeing together, this process of getting definitions distinguished and disentangled is two-fold. The Dialectician has to *combine*, that is, he has to discover forms . . . which collect the things he is to talk about, though they may seem very diverse. It is as having these forms that he is talking of them. Their form is their BEING as he is concerned with it. It is what they are. Secondly, he has to divide—he has to separate within the things that share one form, those that share different forms. He has to make the right divisions and see which divisions, for his purpose, are subordinate to which. And in all this he has to avoid mistaking one form or division for another in spite of all the opportunities and invitations language offers him to do just this. It will be seen that every careful reader [and writer] is willy-nilly a Dialectician in some measure.
>
> I. A. Richards, *How to Read a Page*

A composition is a bundle of parts in which each element is both a part and a bundle; a sentence is both a bundle of grammatical parts and a part of the rhetorical bundle called a paragraph; a paragraph is both this bundle of sentences and a part of the whole composition. This dialectic of parts and bundles can be clarified by studying the structure of the paragraph.

The paragraph is a rhetorical form intermediary between the sentence and the whole composition, but it is not adequately described either as a super-sentence or as a mini-composition. There is no grammar of the paragraph and, though it is composed of syntactical units, it is itself not a syntactical unit. In some periods in the history of English prose there is a complete absence of what we would call paragraphs, but that doesn't mean that the compositions are disorderly; it only means that the chief rhetorical unit was the sentence. Sentences could be short or very long indeed, as in this example from the early seventeenth century:

> . . . It is an excellent observation which hath been made upon the answers of our Saviour Christ to many of the questions which were propounded to him, how that they are impertinent to the state of the question demanded; the reason whereof is, because not being like man, which knows man's thoughts by his words, but knowing man's thoughts immediately, he never answered their words, but their

of a shorthand sentence that identifies the *who* or *what* and tᴸ
does. This will give you what journalists call a "lead" and thᴸ
substance for what English teachers and rhetoricians call a
"topic sentence."

Here are some paragraphs with glosses that show what I
mean.

animals /
adaptation
man /
transforming

If, for animals, orientation in the world means adaptation
to the world, for man it means humanizing the world by
transforming it. For animals there is no historical sense, no
options or values in their orientation in the world; for man
there is both a historical and a value dimension. Men have
the sense of "project," in contrast to the instinctive routines
of animals.

Paulo Freire, *The Pedagogy of the Oppressed*

experience
is not
fundamental

I disagree utterly with that modern philosophy which re-
gards experience as fundamental. Experience is a mere whiff
or rumble, produced by enormously complex or ill-deciphered
causes of experience; and in the other direction, experience
is a mere peephole through which glimpses come down to
us of eternal things. These are the only things that, in so
far as we are spiritual beings, we can find or love at all.

George Santayana, *Letters*

logical and
psychological
functions
of names

Nominal definition is an important part of logic, and Carroll
was particularly interested in classification and the use of
names. Alice discusses the matter at some length with the
Gnat, who clearly believes that all names are for the social
purpose of identifying individuals, and that without a name
to be addressed by, an individual is quite cut off from the
rest of society and unable to function within it. Alice, who
sees names chiefly as labels used to classify distinct phenomena, is aware that this is not so, yet she is nonetheless
somewhat concerned about losing her name in the wood
where things have no names. It is interesting to note, however, that it is not her generic name of human child that
concerns her; it is her personal name, Alice, the name that
is part of her identity. Her meeting with the fawn, its
trust and friendliness in the wood, and its immediate fear
and distaste on emerging into the field and remembering
what she is, is, it seems, a comment on the readiness with
which people accept names and words and classifications at
face value, failing to investigate the reality behind them.

Yet another kind of significance is attached to names by
Humpty Dumpty, to whom the purpose of a name is to
describe some important distinguishing feature of the object it signifies. His name means the shape he is; Alice is a
new name to him so he does not know what it means, and
he is horrified and outraged to discover that it violates his
rules by meaning nothing at all.

Kathryn Exon, "Definition"

Try glossing these paragraphs.

Avoid fried foods which anger the blood. If your stomach
disputes you, lie down and pacify it with cooling thoughts.
Keep the juice flowing by jangling around gently as you
move. Go very light on the vices such as carrying on in
society—the social ramble ain't restful. Avoid running at
all times. Don't look back. Something may be gaining on you.

Leroy (Satchel) Paige

A work of (whatever) art can be either "received" or
"used." When we "receive" it we exert our senses and imagination and various other powers according to a pattern
invented by the artist. When we "use" it we treat it as assistance for our own activities. The one, to use an old-
fashioned image, is like being taken for a bicycle ride by a
man who may know roads we have never yet explored. The
other is like adding one of those little motor attachments to
our own bicycle and then going for one of our familiar rides.
These rides may in themselves be good, bad, or indifferent.
The "uses," which the many make of the arts may or may
not be intrinsically vulgar, depraved, or morbid. That's as
may be. "Using" is inferior to "reception" because art, if
used rather than received, merely facilitates, brightens or
palliates our life, and does not add to it.

C. S. Lewis, *An Experiment in Criticism*

I'd forgotten what an exciting place a neighborhood can be.
Somehow I think the only way a definition of "neighborhood" can be rendered is by the sight of six or eight kids
playing kick the can. It's a symbol of activity, interaction,
sight and sound. The children have awakened to this place.
They are spontaneous and joyful here. Matt barely had time
to eat yesterday, he was so busy helping build a soapbox car
from resurrected wheels and parts. Today he's off planning
a carnival. When I see him on the bike, his nimble body
fluid and free and leaning into the speed of the mechanism,

his hair flying, shirt flying, I feel pain at the juxtaposed mental image of his stiff little back, so controlled, at the piano, or at his solitary task of model building. Then I ask myself why we ever chose a home without neighbors, save the strutting pheasants on the field. As I imagine A————, it seems a stiff, unnatural community. There were no sand lot baseball games got up this summer. The children engaged in no spontaneous play; rather, most children we know were sent to camp or summer recreation programs. There was play, but it was organized play—gymnastics, hockey leagues, tennis lessons. "Organized play": there's some vague contradiction in those terms. Like "houselion" or "tame wildcat." "Play" should be free and ingenuous, not planned.

Marlene Ostrowski, "Returning to a Place"

There really is, then, a system to our perception of the world, a certain method to our everyday knowledge of what is around us. One way to actually see this system at work is to consider the plight of the very near-sighted person who must go the day without his glasses. Such a person would be unable to distinguish words from even a slight distance, but if he had to turn down Elderberry Street, and had to pass several streets before doing so, he would have the means still of "reading" street signs, though the names on the sign would appear only a blur. For he would not turn down Oak Street or Fir Street simply because the words *Oak* and *Fir* do not take up the same amount of space on the sign as the word *Elderberry*. Though the words themselves would appear as blurs, the near-sighted person would be able to judge by the length of the blur on the sign which street he was at. A short blur, then, would indicate a *not-Elderberry* street. The distinction becomes one of length, of size, but not of letters. By using such a method of "seeing," this near-sighted person could probably function the entire day without his glasses. If he were in a supermarket, for instance, to buy a bottle of soda, he would be able to distinguish the beverage section by looking for glassy, bulbous shapes. If he was in a drugstore to buy a notebook, he would direct himself to horizontal arrangements opposed to bulky, irregular ones. Unable to identify actual facial features, he may know that John is approaching because of that width of shoulders, that size of head, that shape of physique, manner of moving all belong to the person he knows as "John." It is important to keep in mind here that a very near-sighted person, without glasses, really sees only a world of blurs—details simply do not come into view, except at very close range. For the near-sighted individual, recognition of persons, things, is often based on dimension, basic shapes, and simple outlines rather than particular details. In a way, everyone uses a system like that of the near-sighted person when he confronts the world each day; certain shapes and sizes represent certain types of objects and in this way we are able to make sense of all that is around us.

Judy Waters, "Images and Concepts"

Composing a gloss is a way of stabilizing a cluster of sentences so that you can consider them collectively as well as individually. A gloss gives you a handle to pick up the bundle with; it's a way of seeing if the parts will really hold together. Glossing is a way of seeing if you have the makings of a paragraph. Sometimes, the gloss will give you the bundle tie that your would-be paragraph has been missing; you can build the gloss back into the paragraph as the opening sentence or wherever else you think it fits. If you can't compose a gloss, it's a good indication that what seemed a cluster actually has no potential unity: The sentences may be too disparate or there may be too wide a range of detail to allow for generalization or there may be too many generalizations that remain undeveloped. Glossing lets you test the paragraph's grip. In short, composing a gloss is a critical means of reviewing the paragraph as a bundle of parts.

Another way of developing that critical skill is to read good paragraphs analytically, attending to how the parts are bundled. It is a misconception of the relationship of reading and writing in the study of composition to think that study of the patterns of sentences written by somebody else can teach you how to match your own sentence patterns to the shape of your thinking. But it is also a misconception to believe that you can learn to write complexly articulated sentences without studying such sentences. Critical reading is no panacea, but there's no substitute for its benefits.

The most important thing that the student of composition can learn from slowed-down reading is to appreciate the complexity of the relationship of topic and grammatical subject. *Topic* derives from the Greek word for place * and refers both to

---

* Our word "commonplace" is a survival from rhetorical terminology: the "places" were carefully ordered and memorized, "common" to all students of rhetoric.

the beginning and to the end: The topic is your point of departure and what you aim to develop. What, for instance, is the subject of the following sentence? What is the topic?

> There was no reachable post-office as yet; not even the rude little receptive box with lid and leather hinges, set up at convenient intervals on a stout stake along some solitary green way, affording a perch for birds, and which later in the unintermitting advance of the frontier, would perhaps decay into a mossy monument, attesting yet another successive overleaped limit of civilized life; a life which in America can today hardly be said to have any western bound but the ocean that washes Asia.

Now, grammatically, the subject is *post-office* and the verb is *was* and yet the sentence is not "about" post-offices or even "about" the little box that wasn't there. The negative statement serves as the skeletal structure or framework for the topic. The paragraph opposes what was to happen with a time when these events had not yet occurred; note the phrases that establish this temporal structure: (*no*) *as yet . . . later . . . would decay . . . today.* The sentence is not "about" the nonexistent "reachable post-office" but the western movement that brought civilization to the shores of the Pacific.

As soon as we use language for purposes other than simple, direct reference—*The cat is on the mat*—or simple, direct expression—*Get that cat outta here!*—we have the problem of how to match thinking and language, of how to take advantage of the fact that linguistic forms discover ideas, as ideas find the forms of language. In conversation, we do not usually stop and figure out exactly what words we will utter before we speak; everything happens at once. In reading, too, we let what's been said (read) help us read what's coming next. All reading skills are based on the dialectic of expectation and response; an efficient reader does not read word by word, but thought by word and word by thought. An efficient writer works the same way, letting form find form: letting syntactical structures—sentence patterns—help discover what's to be said; letting intention and purpose find the form by which it can be re-presented. The more critical reading you do, the more practice you have in writing by a dialectical method, the more continuous this mutual support of saying—writing—and thinking will be.

Nevertheless, you can listen in on the inner dialogue and come very close to re-presenting the process of forming a concept and still write incorrect, ungrammatical sentences. Why?

Because the semantics of a sentence—the relationships it articulates, the oppositions it develops, the meanings it makes—are
not necessarily identical with the base clause, the grammatical
foundation provided by the subject and predicate. Because the
linguistic structures you are using are subject not only to your
intentions but to *conventions* that have the force of law. If you
disobey them, you will distract a reader who is aware of the
correct form; if you disregard too many, you won't be making
yourself clear. Word forms and syntax provide limits that you
can learn to use to help you form statements, but they are not
entirely flexible, any more than words are in their lexical definitions. You can learn to use the conventions of language to
your advantage, conceiving of them as forms to find forms rather
than as hurdles or roadblocks. Studying the structure of paragraphs is one way.

We have considered the Melville sentence as a bundle of
parts. Now here it is as a part of a bundle:

> But a scene quite at variance with one's antecedents may
> yet prove suggestive of them. Hooped round by a level rim,
> the prairie was to John Marr a reminder of the ocean.
>
> With some of his former shipmates, chums on certain
> cruises, he had contrived, prior to this last and more remote
> removal, to keep up a little correspondence at odd intervals.
> But from tidings of anybody or any sort he, in common with
> the other settlers, was now cut off: quite cut off, except from
> such news as might be conveyed over the grassy billows by
> the last-arrived prairie-schooner—the vernacular term, in
> those parts and times, for the emigrant-wagon arched high
> over with sail-cloth, and voyaging across the vast cham-
> paign. There was no reachable post-office as yet; not even
> the rude little receptive box with lid and leather hinges, set
> up at convenient intervals along some solitary green way,
> affording a perch for birds, and which, later in the uninter-
> mitting advance of the frontier, would perhaps decay into a
> mossy monument, attesting yet another successive over-
> leaped limit of civilized life; a life which in America can
> hardly be said to have any western bound but the ocean that
> washes Asia. Throughout these plains, now in places over-
> populous with towns overopulent; sweeping plains, else-
> where fenced off in every direction into flourishing farms
> —pale townsmen and hale farmers alike, in part, the de-
> scendants of the first sallow settlers; a region that half a

century ago produced little for the sustenance of man, but today launching its superabundant wheat-harvest on the world;—of this prairie, now everywhere intersected with wire and rail, hardly can it be said that at the period here written of there was so much as a traceable road. To the long-distance traveller the oak-groves, wide apart, and varying in compass and form; these, with recent settlements, yet more widely separate, offered some landmarks; but otherwise he steered by the sun. In the early midsummer, even going but from one log-encampment to the next, a journey it might be of hours or a good part of a day, travel was much like navigation. In some more enriched depressions between the long, green, graduated swells, smooth as those of ocean becalmed receiving and subduing to its own tranquillity the voluminous surge raised by some far-off hurricane of days previous, here one would catch the first indication of advancing strangers either in the distance, as a far sail at sea, by the glistening white canvas of the wagon, the wagon itself wading through the rank vegetation and hidden by it, or, failing that, when near to, in the ears of the team, peeking, if not above the tiger-lilies, yet above the yet taller green.

Luxuriant, this wilderness; but, to its denizen, a friend left behind anywhere in the world seemed not alone absent from sight, but an absentee from existence.

Though John Marr's shipmates could not all have departed life, yet as subjects of meditation, they were like phantoms of the dead. As the growing. . . .

Herman Melville, *John Marr*

Thus, Melville, who in *Moby Dick* describes the whales as "mowing" through the ocean, in this sketch depicts the prairie in terms of the sea. That metaphor is the rhetorical binding agent for these intricately fashioned sentences, which, with their multitudinous details and melodramatic generalizations, would otherwise be very hard to follow. And you can see that the sentence we have studied takes its place in a passage whose purpose is to describe, define, compare, contrast; to assert, argue, and narrate—any rhetorical function you could name is performed by this passage.

If you can compose a paragraph, you can compose a series of paragraphs and once you have the series, you will see better how to revise each of them. Here is a lively description of the writing and rewriting of paragraphs, of their role as sorters and gatherers, by the Schoolboys of Barbiana, a group of dropouts in Northern Italy who, with the help of a friendly and thoughtful priest, formed their own school where they learned to teach one another.

school of art The craft of writing is to be taught like any other craft.

a humble This is the way we do it:
technique   To start with, each of us keeps a notebook in his pocket. Every time an idea comes up, we make a note of it. Each idea on a separate sheet, on one side of the page.

Then one day we gather together all the sheets of paper and spread them on a big table. We look through them, one by one, to get rid of duplications. Next, we make separate piles of the sheets that are related, and these will make up the chapters. Every chapter is subdivided into small piles, and they will become paragraphs.

At this point we try to give a title to each paragraph. If we can't it means either that the paragraph has no content or that too many things are squeezed into it. Some paragraphs disappear. Some are broken up.

While we name the paragraphs we discuss their logical order, until an outline is born. With the outline set, we reorganize all the piles to follow its pattern.

We take the first pile, spread the sheets on the table, and we find the sequence for them. And so we begin to put down a first draft of the text.

We mimeograph that part so that we each can have a copy in front of us. Then, scissors, paste and colored pencils. We shuffle it all again. New sheets are added. We mimeograph again.

A race begins now for all of us to find any word that can be crossed out, any excess adjectives, repetitions, lies, difficult words, overly long sentences and any two concepts that are forced into one sentence.

We call in one outsider after another. We prefer that they not have had too much school. We ask them to read aloud. And we watch to see if they have understood what we meant to say.

We accept their suggestions if they clarify the text. We reject any suggestions made in the name of caution.

Having done all this hard work and having followed these rules that anyone can use, we often come across an intellectual idiot who announces, "This letter has a remarkably *personal* style."

laziness Why don't you admit that you don't know what the art of writing is? It is an art that is the very opposite of laziness.

The Schoolboys of Barbiana, Letter to a Teacher

❴ Here is a news release which was clearly not written by the method the Schoolboys propose. See if you can revise it in two paragraphs.

The Sol LeWitt exhibition of fifty drawings by the seminal figure in concept art will open to the public on March 4 through April 13 at the Museum of Art.

Born in Hartford, Connecticut in 1928, LeWitt received his B.F.A. at Syracuse University in 1949 and now lives in New York City.

LeWitt's work has been cited as the beginning of the movement called "Conceptual Art."

This is highly cerebral art, but in the graphic art of Sol LeWitt the ideas do produce work that while intellectual, is generally quite beautiful and serene. In LeWitt's work, the concepts or ideas are not of great interest; they are actually quite simple. They do contain an element of games and humor which makes them all the more appealing.

In this exhibition there are working drawings for structures LeWitt has made, drawings that involve mathematical systems to explain the pieces. Also included are what LeWitt terms "mistake drawings" that is drawings in which the logic was apparent but not real and so abandoned.

LeWitt has had a total of 36 selected one-man exhibitions since 1965 among which are Kunsthalle, Berne; The Dayton Art Institute, Dayton; Massachusetts Institute of Technology, Cambridge; The John Wiber Gallery, New York; Lisson Gallery, London; Pasadena Art Museum, Pasadena.

He has been in a total of 91 selected group exhibitions since 1964. Much has been written about the artist in "Art Forum," "Arts Magazine," "Arts International," and "Art News."

A paragraph is analogous to any unit in other kinds of composition that is midway between the smaller parts and the whole. For instance, the *modular units* with which you can construct a house play a role like that of paragraphs, since each unit is made up of individual parts (wood and metal framing) and also constitutes, along with other units, a larger whole (a wall, for instance). If you consider a measure of music as analogous to a sentence, then the *section*—the series of measures set off by a double bar—would be analogous to the paragraph. Jerry learned to paragraph when he began thinking about the form of a *mathematical proof;* I don't know how he managed to draw a parallel, but I believe that it is instructive to try to identify a stage or a phase that is analogous to the paragraph in a process with which you are familiar. In that way, you form the concept of the paragraph as both a part and a whole.

     ❧ You can learn a lot about composing a series of paragraphs by studying the way a good writer gets from one to the next. Note how the metaphor in the composition below helps sustain the continuity.

The young people who are rebelling all around the world, rebelling against whatever form the governmental and educational systems take, are like the first generation born in a new country listening to their parents' tales of the old country and watching their parents grapple, often clumsily, often unsuccessfully, with the new conditions. They have no firsthand knowledge of the way their parents lived far across the seas, of how differently wood responded to tools, or land to the hoe. They see the tasks which their unaccustomed elders are performing as poorly done; they feel that there must be a better way, and that they must find it.

For now, nowhere in the whole world are there any elders who know what the children know, no matter how remote and simple the societies in which the children live. In the past there were always some elders who knew more— in terms of experience, of having grown up within a system —than any children. Today there are none. It is not only that parents are no longer a guide, but that there are no guides, in the older sense of the term, whether one seeks them in one's own country, or in China, or in India. There are no elders who know what those who have been reared in the last 20 years know about what the next 20 years will be.

All of us who grew up before the war are immigrants in time, immigrants from an earlier world, living in an age essentially different from anything we knew before. We still hold the seats of power and command the resources and the skills which have been used in the past to keep order and organize large societies. We control the educational systems, the apprenticeship systems, the career ladders up which the young are required to climb, step by step.

The elders are separated from the young by the fact that they too are a strangely isolated generation. No generation has ever known, experienced, and incorporated such rapid changes, watched the sources of power, the means of communication, the definition of humanity, the limits of their explorable universe, the certainties of a known and limited world, the fundamental imperatives of life and death—all change before their eyes. They know more about change than any generation has ever known and so stand over against and vastly alienated from the young, who, by the very nature of their position, have had to reject their elders' past. Just as the early Americans had to teach themselves not to daydream of the past but to concentrate on the present and so in turn taught their children not to daydream but to act, so today's elders have treated their own pasts as incommunicable, and teach their children, even in the midst of lamenting that it is so, not to ask, because they can never understand. We have to realize that no other generation will ever experience what we have experienced. In this sense we have no descendants. At this breaking point between two radically different and closely related groups, both are inevitably very lonely as we face each other knowing that they will never experience what we have experienced and that we can never experience what they have experienced.

As long as any adult thinks that he, like the parents and teachers of old, can become introspective, invoke his own youth to understand the youth before him, he is lost. But once the fact of a deep, new, unprecedented, worldwide generation gap is firmly established in the minds of both the young and the old, communication can be established again.

Margaret Mead, "The Generation Gap"

The following assisted invitations can be responded to most usefully in small groups; you need an audience to help you test your sense of paragraphing as a form.

∾ Write a press release about some activity of public interest. Suppose that you have a maximum of 250 words and proceed with the knowledge that the newspaper may cut the last 50 words.

∾ Gloss the paragraphs on pp. 243 and 244, if you have not already done so. Compose your own paragraphs on the same topic of each of these, developing the gloss as your topic sentence.

∾ Here are 12 jumbled sentences in search of the paragraph they once were. Compose a paragraph with/for them.

1. Freedom is, I think, a mixed concept.
2. The true half of it is simply a name of an aspect of virtue concerned especially with the clarification of vision and the domination of selfish impulse.
3. It is in the context of such limitations that we should picture our freedom.
4. We behave well in the areas where this can be done fairly easily and let other areas of possible virtue remain undeveloped.
5. And can we, without improving ourselves, really see things clearly?
6. We are largely mechanical creatures, the slaves of relentlessly strong selfish forces, the nature of which we scarcely comprehend.
7. At best, as decent persons, we are usually very specialized.
8. There are few places where virtue plainly shines: great art, humble people who serve others.
9. There are perhaps in the case of every human being insuperable psychological barriers to goodness.
10. The false and more popular half is a name for the self-assertive movements of deluded selfish will, which because of our ignorance we take to be something.
11. The self is a divided thing and the whole of it cannot be redeemed any more than it can be known.
12. And if we look outside the self what we see are scattered intimations of *Good*.

Deciding when to start a new paragraph is an interesting task for the composer because the choices made (and remade) can illuminate obscurities and show up weaknesses. Paragraphing is partly a matter of logic and rhetoric, but it's also a matter of temperament: Mark Twain said he began a new paragraph when he felt like having a drink. A paragraph can consist of a single sentence, if you think the need for emphasis or a change of pace requires it. If you will review the Melville passage (pp. 164–165), you will see that one very long paragraph is followed by a paragraph of one sentence.

ᜰ In reading the following paragraphs, decide where you think they could have been divided or trisected. What changes, if any, would you make in the course of reparagraphing? What advantages are there to having the passage as a single paragraph?

The dominant note which Navajo life strikes is joy, and buoyant confidence in the powers within the breast and in the world. And active happiness, positive health, are social duties among the Navajos. But equally, the Navajos do not entertain, and would scornfully reject, that view of life which is called "pangloss," or willful, fact-denying, sentimental optimism. Famine, war, drought, cold, and the dark storms that are within the human soul, they have always known, and have never tried to be oblivious towards them. Darkness and evil, not only light and love and joy, are indwelling deep within the nature of things, and their attempts to invade the soul are never-ending. Once, for a long cosmic interval, gigantism and darkness and evil predominated in the whole earth; then through a mighty effort the forces of beauty, love and joy subdued them, and scattered them afar, but never annihilated or sought to annihilate them; and to man then recreated or newly born, the Blessing Way was given, and many other symbols, precepts, rites and disciplines, and norms of conduct and feeling; and these, as lived by man, are the City of God, but Darkness and active evil assail the City and invade it forevermore. Thus the cosmic and human drama is sustained by the Navajos, and the insecurity of things is wrought into a structure of beautiful security, a "dance over fire and water" whose rhythms are sometimes wildly impassioned but more often stately and gradual. And in these terms, Navajo religious art builds for eternity through building into the human and social tissue and soul, none the less for the fact that its material constructions * are demolished on the very day that they are completed.

John Collier, On the Gleaming Way

Kleist uses visual description to impress upon the reader the highly emotional state of a character or the psychological tone and effect of a situation. He twice informs us of Kohlhaas's sorrow by placing a tear on his cheek (95, 118) and expresses the Junker's dismay with a reference to his "white and quivering lips" (131). Rather than telling the reader that Kohlhaas is sad and that the Junker is dismayed, the reader is invited to observe the signs of this emotion; she is called upon to witness them as if she herself were living through the events, and to respond emotionally, herself, before translating that emotional state into an abstract concept of sadness or dismay. And Kleist also requires the reader to witness incidents without the help of interpretation. He merely uses his position as writer to direct our attention to various details, such as the pile of dung in the square (133), which relates with full significance the repulsive state of the horses, and the people in the crowd with "their handkerchiefs crammed into their mouths" (133), which demonstrates the subsequent humor to be found in the situation. Yet, in his descriptions of situations or the environment, he achieves the most outstanding effects not by these single references alone, but by their repetition. In the final scene, with the reference to the blue and white feathers, he repeatedly draws our attention to that embellishment and then back to Kohlhaas, firmly creating the line of vision and tension between the incendiary [Kohlhaas] and the Elector. And he uses this technique of repetition to draw the mind's eye of the reader to the pile of dung. So, the reader comes to know the characters through visual description of their emotional states, and the scenes through visual description of a significant object

---

* Sand paintings "which are created as an element of the healing ceremonies and the ceremonies which renew the occult nature-man relationship."

within the situation, but it is through repetition of these elements that the reader becomes deeply acquainted with the characters and scenes.

Kristin Bomegen, "Imagery in Kleist's *Michael Kohlhaas*"

You can learn to use paragraphing as a way of expressing your own way of seeing relationships—the way you think. How your temperament leads you to employ logic and rhetoric determines style, but a sense of audience is essential if your style is to develop grace and power. A paragraph is a treat for the eye and an encouragement to the reader; it is like a pause in a formal speech. (Cicero warned students of oratory that interest would flag after the beginning of the oration but that it would pick up as soon as the audience felt that the end was in sight. The trick, then, was to keep beginning and to warn far ahead of time of the ending and thus virtually eliminate the middle of the discourse!) You can learn to use paragraphing in the interest of keeping your reader's attention: We all like to know where we are, what's happening, and when it will end. Studying paragraphs and paragraphing is the best way, I believe, to learn to strike a balance between the needs of your reader-audience and your own expressive needs.

          ❧ Using any of these definitions, compose a paragraph that defines a paragraph.

- A paragraph is a rhetorical form that gathers and sorts statements.
- A paragraph is both an effect and a cause, a gathering and a gatherer.
- A paragraph is a form of punctuation.
- A paragraph mediates between the sentence and the whole composition; it is an intermediary structural unit.
- A paragraph is a means of making meaning.
- A paragraph is half a page of elite type on an 8½ by 11 sheet with 1¼-inch margins.

Revising

The great thing about writing is its two stages: first trying to make yourself understand; then putting it to other people.

Anthony Powell

> Writing and rewriting are a constant search for what it is one is saying.
>
> John Updike

The review procedures in the following section should be put to the test. Use any assigned paper that you have composed through the point of forming and developing concepts, ready for paragraph and sentence review. If you don't have a paper on hand from another course, prepare a draft. Aim for a paper of at least five or six paragraphs.

As a refresher, here is a checklist for the phases of concept formation. You should also reread pp. 79–80, 112–113, and 153–155.

A Procedural Guide to Concept Formation

1. Generate chaos by responding to conceptual terms. Deliberately see relationships in terms of space, time, and causality; deliberately consider various perspectives and contexts.
2. Substantiate the terms of HDWDWW? that will give you names for agent, action, manner, and purpose, if they are not already in your chaos.
3. Draw a line down the middle of the page to generate oppositions between and among the names of your chaos and the terms of HDWDWW?
4. Develop oppositions as sentences; let sentences cluster.
5. State the opposite case.
6. Formulate definitions: work out classifications by interpreting and generalizing.
7. Articulate relationships by means of entitlements (images, slogans, stories); analogies; identifying causal relations.

Considering the relationship of any one sentence to the paragraph it helps to bring into existence is a bootstrap operation. In order to avoid the priority dilemma—which comes "first," the sentences or the paragraph?—you have to revise sentences and review/compose the paragraph simultaneously. The trick is to learn to use the paragraph as a form that guides the re-forming of sentences; composing a gloss is the best way to do that. We have already discussed glossing as a way of developing a topic sentence or "lead" (pp. 158–162), and if you have done that, you can then use the gloss as an instrument of revision. It can help you see if you're making yourself clear because it lets you hear what you're saying. The gloss is like a garage door or a brick wall against which you can throw or hit a ball: the way the ball bounces tells you how you threw or hit it.

Along with glossing you can also use paraphrasing in revision. Paraphrasing serves the same function as chaos does earlier: it encourages choice, a sense of the alternatives. When you paraphrase, you beat around the bush until you drive out the rabbit of intention. Restating is essential to concept formation; when it comes to sentence review, paraphrase is equally important, since it allows you a means of checking what you've written against what you think you mean. The paraphrase gives you a vantage point from which to assess the strengths and weaknesses of your sentences. It can help you to decide whether to cut, to mend, or to adjust; to amalgamate the sentence with others or to substitute the paraphrase, if it seems superior to the sentence under review.

And the third way to revise/compose a paragraph is to consider it the answer to a question. If you can't formulate the question to which your paragraph could be considered a response, then you probably don't have a paragraph.

The conventional criteria for judging a paragraph are *unity*, *coherence*, and *emphasis*, but you can't expect to discover if your paragraph is well-formed by asking, "Is it unified? coherent? emphatic?" You have to develop critical questions and it's in order to do so that you gloss or paraphrase or formulate the question the paragraph answers.

The *unity* of a paragraph can be easily tested by using the gloss: any sentence that does not state or support or illustrate the opposition you've developed in the gloss can be eliminated. (Don't cross it out too thoroughly, since this sentence might come in handy in another place.) In the following discussion, therefore, we will concentrate on paragraph revision as a matter of assuring *coherence* and *emphasis*.

Coherence means "hanging together": you couldn't have coherence without unity, but unity without coherence is very common—the most common rhetorical fault, I would say. It is inconceivable that you could have emphasis without coherence, but unified and coherent paragraphs frequently are written without any emphasis. You will recognize this as characteristic of the style of many textbooks where the only means of emphasis used is to print topics in boldface type. In an incoherent paragraph, the sentences may all concern the same topic, but there will be no rationale for the order. One sentence will seem to call for further explanation or to promise examples, but then the next sentence will go on to something else. Many handbooks suggest that the way to make a paragraph cohere is to use road signs such as "for example . . ." or "on the other hand. . . ." These little phrases can be valuable clues for your reader, but only if the relationships they signal are the ones that are indeed being set forth. If two sentences do not in fact present a contrast, then "on the other hand" will not help; if you aren't in fact expressing a second thought or a reservation, then "however" won't make sense. I think it's a better policy to work out the relationships between sentences and *then* add the road signs, if you think they're needed.

A root cause of incoherence is frequently that you are working with sentences that all present details and examples, but *of what* remains unclear. Composing the gloss can reveal the fact that you haven't developed a generalization that can unite the particulars; in other words, it will be difficult to gloss the would-be paragraph. But if you can do so, the next step is simply to develop a sentence from the gloss and build it back into the paragraph, probably at the beginning.

Another root cause of incoherence is generalizations so vague that there isn't any clear way to decide what should come next; you have the feeling that you could as well read backwards as forwards. Vague generalizations are also likely to lead you into syntactical snarls; without substance to give them structure, articulations get fouled, like lines on a boat blowing loose. Checking your verbs can help test the substantiality of generalizations. The relationships in a sentence are articulated by means of the verb; if you check the verbs in successive sentences, you can more easily determine the relationships *between* the sentences. If most of them read *is* and *are*, you can do something about that right away by naming the relationships more precisely. And be warned: *contains* is generally an inadequate substitution. Use the Pocket Guide to the Logic of Terminologies (p. 153) to help identify the kind of relationship you are articulating, a step that can help you find verbs of a more precise and substantial character. Letting *is* and *are* and *has been* etc. do all the work puts too great a strain on them; *is* is a very good cord for tying some bundles, but don't wear it out.

In reviewing the paragraph to see if it is coherent, you will simultaneously be concerned with *emphasis:* Getting sentences to cohere, getting a paragraph into shape, entails deciding what needs to be soft-pedaled or given second place. Subordination and emphasis are best considered together, since a choice concerning one will also concern the other. You subordinate in order to emphasize the main point, much as you build the opposite case in order to form a concept. Without subordinating, what you get is *parataxis*—and if that sounds like a disease, it is. Each element is given the same weight and assumes the same shape. The resulting paragraph is like a train of boxcars:

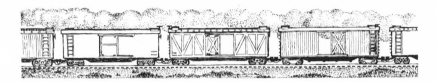

Paratactic order yields a paragraph like this one:

> The Yam Festivals are held each year before the harvest in Umofia. The purpose of the Festivals is to honor Ani, the goddess of the earth and the source of all fertility. The land is very important to the farmers in the villages and this is why the festivals are the largest and most celebrated in Africa.
>
> A great deal of preparation is made for this holiday and one is expected to have a big meal and many guests. . . .

Note that the author here begins another paragraph when he comes to describing the preparation for the yam festivals. Now if the paper were entirely devoted to the yam festivals, a separate paragraph concerning preparation would be legitimate, since obviously there would be many facts and details to set forth and particulars to be developed; every aspect of the yam festivals would need to be discussed—origin, function, organization, etc. But the paragraph I have quoted appears in a short paper on tribal customs in Africa and the topic of yam festivals is only one of many items. There is no reason for devoting to it more than one paragraph, which could include a description of preparation as well as comment on purpose, etc. Without subordination, there is no way to make the main point about the yam festival in the larger context of a paper about social and religious institutions and celebrations.

In finishing your paper, when you come across a series of boxcar sentences, it is a sign that your paragraph lacks emphasis. Unless you have subordinated, how will your reader be guided in identifying the main point?

An alternative to judicious subordinating is to subordinate everything. James Thurber explains the dangers of that procedure in the following passage: *

What most people don't realize is that one "which" leads to another. Trying to cross a paragraph by leaping from "which" to "which" is like Eliza crossing the ice. The danger is in missing a "which" and falling in. A case in point is this: "He went up to a pew which was in the gallery, which brought him under a colored window which he loved and always quieted his spirit." The writer, worn out, missed the last "which"—the one that should come just before "always" in that sentence. But supposing he had got it in! We would have: "He went up to a pew which was in the gallery, which brought him under a colored window which he loved and which always quieted his spirit." Your inveterate whicher in this way gives the effect of tweeting like a bird or walking with a crutch, and is not welcome in the best company.

It is well to remember that one "which" leads to two and that two "whiches" multiply like rabbits. You should never start out with the idea that you can get by with one "which." Suddenly they are all around you. Take a sentence like this: "It imposes a problem which we either solve, or perish." On a hot night, or after a hard day's work, a man often lets himself get by with a monstrosity like that, but suppose he dictates that sentence bright and early in the morning. It comes to him typed out by his stenographer and he instantly senses that something is the matter with it. He tries to reconstruct the sentence, still clinging to the "which," and gets something like this: "It imposes a problem which we either solve, or which, failing to solve, we must perish on account of." He goes to the water-cooler, gets a drink, sharpens his pencil, and grimly tries again. "It imposes a problem which we either solve or which we don't solve and. . . ." He begins once more: "It imposes a problem which we either solve, or which we do not solve, and from which . . ." The more times he does it the more "whiches" he gets. The way out is simple: "We must either solve this problem, or perish." Never monkey with "which." Nothing except getting tangled up in a typewriter ribbon is worse.

---

* From "Ladies and Gentlemen's Guide to Modern English," *The Owl in the Attic and Other Perplexities* (New York, 1931), pp. 106ff.

The chief subverters of emphasis are jargon and cliché. Jargon is terminology that is (or may be) appropriate and indeed essential in a particular field of study or activity, but that can be tiresome and misleading when it is used in other contexts. A biologist needs the word "viable" in describing experiments; when a politician uses it to mean "workable, in my opinion," he is attempting to sound "scientific." You can easily train yourself to spot jargon in your own writing and in what you read by paraphrasing and interpreting any statement that seems wordy:

> The Institute is engaged in the design of experiments to identify parameters of creativity and to correlate those parameters of creativity with the characteristics and behavioral patterns of the creators.

> *Translation:* The Institute will provide occasions for observing how creative people work—but if we don't make it sound complicated, we won't get our grant.

Clichés—and jargon terms quickly become clichés—are moribund metaphors, literary expressions, old proverbs, specialized expressions that have been used so frequently that they are no longer sharp or provocative. (Cliché is a French word, a printing term that refers to a kind of plate used in the nineteenth century to print photographs. After a few printing runs, such plates became worn and flattened so that the impressions they made were fuzzy or blurred.) A gifted public speaker can bring clichés to life. Dr. Martin Luther King, Jr. could preach a sermon that was fabricated mostly from clichés, but by the rhetorical arrangement and the cadences he composed, by the way he played them off against anecdotes from his own experience, he made them his own. Oratory in this style is like the art of quilting: it's not the scraps but the design and stitching that count.

That said, it's better to avoid clichés. The most important point is to tune your ear so that you can recognize a cliché in your writing; then you can decide if you want to keep it. Seeing that you've written, say, "stark contrast" may remind you to review your statements to find if you've set things forth so that the contrast is indeed "stark." If it is, you may want to cut out the cliché; if not, you'll know that some further forming/finishing is called for.

You write sentences; you rewrite paragraphs. The paragraph in rhetoric is analogous to the concept in logic: by its means you sort and gather. Composing paragraphs is a matter of articulating the gathered relationships.

Reviewing the paragraphs in the section that follows will allow you to familiarize yourself with the procedure for a critical revision of any composition. It's a lot easier, of course, to review somebody else's writing—these are from students and professional writers—but it is nonetheless good practice. The paragraphs are arranged according to the seriousness of their sickness: the earlier ones suffer from a simple lack of substance or unity; the later ones show symptoms of more complex maladies. This metaphor of medical diagnosis is useful, I think, because it underlines a fact about medical science that is analogous to any critical method. Once tests have been run and a diagnosis is completed, the treatment is simple, if not automatic. The doctor's skill is in recognizing symptoms and interpreting them in the context of the patient's history; then, once the diagnosis is made, the lowliest intern can look up the treatment plan and prescribe medication. The analogy with composing, revising, and correcting is that recognizing rhetorical and logical faults is more fundamental than knowing how to correct them; on the other hand, knowing what constitutes a healthy state of affairs provides important limits for interpreting the signs of disease. I have outlined a critical review procedure on the basis of this analogy.

A Procedural Guide to Paragraph Composition and Review

A. *Clinical techniques*
  1. Gloss each paragraph
  2. Paraphrase any suspicious sentences
  3. Formulate the question to which the paragraph could be considered an answer

B. *Diagnosis: a checklist of critical questions* *
  1. How is this sentence related to others? Does it define or qualify? generalize or interpret? assert or exemplify?
  2. Should it be revised in order to clarify assumptions? to subordinate? to emphasize?
  3. Would its role in the paragraph be strengthened if its position in the sentence sequence were changed? if it were

---

* I have derived these questions from the following comment by Josephine Miles: "The major grammatical and rhetorical choice is the degree of predication, of assertion to be stressed or subordinated, or assumed."

amalgamated with other sentences? if it were rebundled? if it were eliminated—or moved to another paragraph? (Clinical procedure: Cover all but first sentence with a note card; formulate what you expect to be the substance of the next sentence; check sentence as written against your supposition; then proceed with the questions concerning positions, etc.)

C. *Treatment plan: optional grammatical and rhetorical adjustments*
1. Develop generalization to gather particulars (Develop gloss into a statement and incorporate)
2. Substantiate generalizations
3. Develop particular examples to support generalizations
4. Name relationships more precisely than by writing "is"
5. Repeat yourself for emphasis (a phrase in apposition; grammatical transformations of key terms)
6. Add road signs where necessary to avoid confusion and to add emphasis.
7. Subordinate, amalgamate, eliminate; rearrange

∾ Here are some poorly composed paragraphs for you to practice on. It's always easier to revise someone else's writing, but if you work methodically, you can more easily transfer what you learn to help you in revising your own compositions.

1. Silone's humor tends to vary in many different ways. It can range from severely sarcastic to extremely anatomical. At times it can be very dry and then again it can be very comical. In the book it seems that he did not flood the chapters with constant humor but instead evenly placed it in key positions throughout the entire story.

2. When a person realizes that this dignity is something to be respected in all persons, then they discover values in that duty which God wills mankind to follow. Those values are truth, justice, charity, and freedom. These values are part of mankind's responsibility to God to uphold human dignity.

3. The arrangement of the interior of the transit vehicle should allow for free movement of passengers throughout the entire vehicle. If this is not the case, the passengers will bunch up in the immediate vicinities of the doors. The behavior of the passengers, usually referred to as "exit ori-

entation," can be seen very often in building elevators during off-peak hours. The passengers already in the vehicle insist on remaining just inside the doors in preparation for leaving. As a result, other passengers cannot readily enter or leave the vehicle.

4. The United States public housing program was first developed in the late 1930s as a method of stabilizing the American economy by creating jobs and providing low-rent homes for families struggling out of depression poverty. After World War II and the Korean War, public housing was used to house veterans until they were financially able to find homes on the private market. Public housing was seen then as a method for housing the "temporarily poor." Since then, public housing has come to be, both in law and in the public view, a way of housing the "permanently poor," those who will probably not work their way out of poverty in a space of a few years. Almost simultaneously with this new rationale for public housing, public housing has been subject to great criticism, and surely public housing has failed in many ways. Many projects, especially large projects in large cities, suffer from intense vandalism, lack of proper maintenance, and are crime-ridden, dismal places to live.

5. The function of the church is much simpler than that of the house and consequently the plan is simpler. The church is more of a unified whole dedicated to one main goal, adoration of god. In contrast, the various individuated units of a house are each used for a different purpose. A general characteristic of all churches is size. Largeness, like the shape, is a result of both practical and spiritual considerations. The large size of the church signifies its spiritual domination through physical domination of the surrounding city or town. Size is also a necessity to contain the congregation attending masses. Finally, size is made possible through greater financial resources than those available for building a house. A house is financed by one family; a church is paid for by the wealthy prelates and by the donations from the town, city, or if it is to be a particularly large church, the country in which it will be built.

6. When we are hungry, the only thoughts occupying our minds deal with satisfying this hunger in any way possible and only when we are no longer hungry can our minds com-

fortably concentrate on other things, but this biological need must be satisfied first. Someone who is hungry feels as if they could be assured that they would have an abundance of food at their disposal now and forever, they would never want for anything else, and if desperately hungry where the food came from and what it consisted of would be of little importance. Once this need has been satisfied and their stomachs and minds no longer occupied with the urgency of hunger, their world no longer revolves around food and they can begin work on satisfying the next in the hierarchy of their needs.

7. Claude Monet in his painting "Village Street" and Pablo Picasso in his painting "Circus Family" picture people outdoors on a warm summer afternoon. Though we don't see the sun, we feel its warmth on the burnt yellow ground. Both Monet and Picasso have an old woman sitting on the left side of the picture, watching the activity. A certain mood of peace and contentment is reflected from the pictures. One gets the feeling of timelessness; as though nothing before or after that moment is important. The people are placed in the center of the paintings, against the blue sky and the yellow of the sun.

❧ Evaluate these three paragraphs on the same topic, the idea of "community" as it emerges in a reading of the short stories of Sarah Orne Jewett.

8. The characters of *The Country of the Pointed Firs* lives seem to be very isolated from the rest of the world outside of their stomping grounds. The way in which they talked about another state seems as though it were another country. Their lives are built on mostly simple events. Their lives are so simple that they would appear boring out of context. Miss Jewett made beauty out of her characters with what little material made available to her. The characters didn't seem to reveal any real startling situations. But in context the excitement that arises from the coming of a yearly reunion is comparable to that of the excitement generated by that of the yearly Stanley Cup playoffs. The characters enjoy sitting around having a cup of tea and chatting as much as some people enjoy sitting around drinking a six-pack of beer and watching a Sunday football game.

9. The community of Dunnet Landing was that of father and son. It was said that everyone loved each other in that community. People would sing, dance, and play with each other until late at night. Some houses gave more beauty to the island because of their presence overlooking the sea. Sailors that arrived on the island would remark how close a relationship between the people of the island is. It gave the island a more attractive setting than other islands in eastern Maine.

10. Through lifetimes of self-sufficiency, Jewett's women of the Maine coast have become strong, indomitable characters. Their husbands die young fighting for an existence in a hostile world or spend their lives on distant seas. Women like Almiry Todd must learn to fend for themselves and meet life's crises with strength and courage. At best, life along the coast of Maine is difficult: Winters are harsh and long, desolate and lonely; spring is indeed welcome after the long winters and a time of reunion for families and friends. These women find happiness in the true and simple pleasures of life—each other and the beauties of nature. A yearly family reunion or a sail in the harbor are big events in their simple country lives. When life moves slowly and is regulated by nature, anything outside of the ordinary is exciting and topic for speculation among the village residents. The lives of these delightful women of the Maine coast reflect the beauty and the hardship of the landscape itself.

Finishing

Archimedes, a Greek mathematician given to considering the problems of method, asserted that he could move the world —if he had a stick long enough and a place to stand. This is a principle that is centrally important to more than just mechanics: In revising a composition you have to establish some place "outside" the composition from which to regard it. That place can't be established by simply asking, "Am I being clear?" or, "Is this paragraph coherent?" Rather, you will need critical questions that can establish a place from which to gain perspective; they will be dialectical in character: "If these sentences are to be a paragraph, what phrase would adequately name the topic they develop?" "If these three glosses in sequence come before that next sequence, what is the relationship between them?" "If the composition ends with a paragraph that can be glossed in such and such a way, does this gloss make sense when juxtaposed with the gloss of the opening paragraph?"

In the final stage of revision, when you have the whole composition before you, in order to take it all in, you need to see it from a distance, to get a perspective that lets you see everything at once. The more territory you have to survey, the higher up or the farther off you will have to be. You can consider the following suggestions as ways of providing Archimedean places.

First of all, copy out your paragraph glosses in sequence and number them. Read them through without checking the paragraphs and see if you can account for the order. Some rearrangement might be called for. After you've experimented, perhaps, with new arrangements, give the sequence a title. This will be called the *supergloss* and it should include at least two terms from HDWDWW? At another time—preferably another day— read through the entire composition and, without checking it again, write an *abstract*, a summary or condensed statement that presents the topic, the argument, and the chief support for the conclusions reached. Don't waste words by saying, "In this paper I have tried to show some of the more important influences on the development of one or two factors." Get directly to the topic and the points you make about it; explain yourself in as precise * a manner as you can. For a paper under 600 words, the abstract could be a single sentence; if the composition is 5,000 words (20 pages), the abstract should be not more than 250 words. Use these limits to give you a sense of how long an abstract should be.†

Preparing the abstract without having the composition in front of you means that you are working from what you think you've said. The abstract thus can represent your intentions, a checkpoint from which to review the individual paragraph glosses, what you've actually said. The abstract acts like a sieve: it should catch *all* the paragraph glosses, filtering out those that are trivial or irrelevant. Of course, if several paragraph glosses are not caught—that is, if some paragraphs are completely un-

---

* In France, *précis* writing forms the basis for the study of composition, as well as for critical reading and interpretation.

† You can get the hang of how to write an abstract by reading a dozen or so. The library will have various collections of abstracts appearing in scholarly journals.

related to the abstract—then you have trouble: either the paragraphs are indeed beside the point—or there is something the matter with the sieve. You can revise the paragraphs by reordering, amalgamating, or eliminating; the abstract can be repaired by checking it against the supergloss, the title of the paragraph sequence. If the abstract is too general, it won't function: you can't catch minnows in a crab net.

Another means of judging the integrity of the composition is to check the introduction against the conclusion, at which point you may discover that one or the other is missing! Some compositions can reach the final stage without a proper introduction, but that is easily supplied by composing a version of the supergloss. If the conclusion is missing, you can rewrite the introduction or adapt the abstract.

If you think of them as the limits within which you are working, the introduction and conclusion can help you with one of the most difficult tasks of composition, namely, the review of transitions: How did you get from beginning to end? by which routes? over what terrain? using what kind of map? stopping over where? how many detours? how many excursions off the beaten path? Paragraphs are, in a certain sense, arbitrary; nevertheless, once you have indented, indicating thereby that you want your reader to consider a group of sentences as a whole, that paragraph should be clearly related to what has gone before and what follows. As you read one paragraph, can you say, without looking, what comes next? Can you name the relationship of paragraph A to paragraph B? C to D? and so on. Checking your paragraphs against the introductory and concluding paragraphs will help you to clarify the role of each in the sequence of paragraphs that makes up the whole composition. Number, or renumber, the paragraphs in the order you think best serves your argument or best preserves balance in the composition. (Don't waste time recopying. Writing out a single passage over and over is a habit some writers develop as a strategy to put off the hard task of articulating paragraphs.) Suppose you find that you have three paragraphs in succession that are devoted to particular cases; you might want to steal a short paragraph from earlier in the paper that deals with points more generally. You could indicate this change simply by numbering the paragraphs on whatever page they appear, in the sequence you think best. Now, once you've worked on another section of the paper, it might then appear that three particularizing paragraphs are exactly what is needed. Renumbering is a lot simpler than copying out once again, according to the new order. The trick is to work out ways of keeping your options open.

Once you have a sound sequence established, you will then be in a position to check or compose the recapitulations that keep your readers informed of where they are in your discourse: recapitulations—the word means going back to the head (*cap*) or beginning—inform readers of the degree of generality that's been reached; the relationship of the opposite case to your explanation; the way the particular details specify and build context; etc. In reviewing recaps, watch for empty statements like this one:

> Examples of how these philosophies can produce two completely different reactions to the action are easily found.

Ask HDWDWW? to remind you which terms need substantiating.

You can then check transitions against the paragraph glosses. If you work on transitions without first gaining an overall view of your composition, the temptation will be to shift paragraphs around aimlessly. Just as you should avoid rewriting sentences when you're getting started, so you should save the reordering of paragraphs until you have a clear view of the whole, an Archimedean point. Then you can decide what transition is called for by the gloss sequence and check to see what in fact you've written. This is the only way I know to alert yourself to overdependence on road signs, some of which may indicate transitions unrelated to what has been written.

A review of transitions will be unnecessary in a short paper, since the paragraph glosses will have revealed the gaps and holes in the structure, and it will be perfunctory for most paragraphs in a six- to ten-page paper. But it can be extremely useful in deciding the fate of a paragraph that could go anywhere or nowhere. Sometimes, adding a single sentence (the idea for which you might steal from the conclusion) can salvage a paragraph, putting it to work in a useful role in the composition. Finishing a paper in such instances is like finishing a jigsaw puzzle: getting the last pieces to fit is a lot easier than getting started and what generally happens is that resolving one dilemma or solving one problem gives you the means of taking care of other troubles. Everything begins happening at once and that is a sign that the dialectic is in operation.

With transitions reviewed and paragraphs adjusted, you can revise the supergloss and then read through the whole composition in the light of that summary. At this point, you might well decide to compose a new title, since the composing process may have yielded a paper that has grown beyond its earlier limits. And with that, you're finished with the sorting and gathering that constitutes the concluding phase of the composing process.

Recapitulation

A dialectical method of composing can help you do the following:

1. To cultivate a habit of "careful disorderliness."
2. To listen in on the inner dialogue and to make it sensible to others.
3. To make your own map of any territory you need to explore.
4. To generate chaos; to tolerate chaos; to learn the uses of chaos.
5. To develop contexts by naming from different perspectives.
6. To develop criteria for judging degree and kind of specification and to substantiate accordingly.
7. To define the presuppositions of a list; to develop the context of situation by interpreting a list.
8. To form oppositions and thus identify relationships.
9. To specify and substantiate the terms of relationships.
10. To articulate relationships and thus to make meanings.
11. To use the paragraph form to gather sentences.
12. To review paragraphs by glossing and paraphrasing them as answers to implied questions.
13. To revise in order to assure unity, coherence, and emphasis by considering beginnings and ends, generalizations and interpretations, definitions and articulations as dialectically related, thereby carrying out "a continuing audit of meanings."
14. To use the forms of language to find the forms of thought, the forms of thinking to find linguistic forms.

5. Correcting

The Role of Editing

When you are correcting sentences, you need to remind yourself that even if your readers can understand you, that doesn't mean that ungrammatical sentences can be left as they are. You correct in order to meet the expectations of your readers; unless you follow certain conventions, they will be distracted from what you're saying. Correcting is a courtesy to them, but you're doing yourself a favor too, since otherwise you can't be sure that you're making yourself understood or that you won't shift attention from your argument to superficial matters.

The idea of correcting goes against the grain in some people, because so much of it is a matter of following conventions. If you are an unconventional person, if temperamentally or politically you distrust conventions as symptoms of authoritarian practices, you will have to come to terms with this problem, just as those who are all too willing to do what is expected have their own problem to cope with. One solution is to decide that, since most conventions are troublesome and useless anyway, the fewer the better. This solution produces writing that consists of sentences in the form *The-cat-is-on-the-mat*, helped out by the jargon of sincerity: "you know" . . . "it's like" . . . "I mean" . . . etc.

Another solution to the problem of deciding whether or not to conform is to write in modes in which it doesn't matter; you can become a superb letter-writer or rabble-rouser or sociologist and pay very little attention to the rules of grammar and syntax; indeed, you can turn them to account (Ring Lardner, Richard Daley, Dwight Eisenhower). And, most common of all, the solution can be to write for a limited audience. The advantage is enormous, since a "peer group" can be encouraging, gentle in expressing negative feelings about your syntax, and personally supportive, even when being picky.

The disadvantages, as I see them, are equally great: You can become used to the idea that people only want to know what you mean, not what you, in fact, have said. This is not the way it is in The Real World where there can be very little concern about meanings and an obsession with "what-has-been-said." In The Real World, it is a familiar experience that a report that was received sympathetically by your co-workers can be torn to shreds by a reviewing committee; that a statement of protest that you and your co-workers have researched carefully and which you are certain will change hearts and minds will be read by others with consternation, contempt, disbelief, *if it is read at all.* A newspaper reporter does not submit her copy (the text of what she has written) to an encounter group, to sympathetic editors who want her to say whatever makes her feel comfortable; a supervisor does not persuade management by writing a personal narrative of how he came to be so upset about evaluation procedures; a political science major won't usually be able to satisfy the course requirement for a term paper by submitting a notebook of observations; and it is likely that a seminar paper will be heard not by loving and friendly people who at the worst might be confused by your syntax and ask for another version, but by mean-minded, intemperate, self-serving competitors who might try to seize on a mixed metaphor and try to claim that it is a symptom of intellectual dishonesty, moral turpitude, and professional incompetence.

In The Real World, a lot of people are convinced that "by their grammar, ye shall know them." It is unfortunately true in The Real World of college courses that an instructor who finds your judgments unacceptable will concentrate not on what he finds untrue or badly argued (or, indeed, factual and well-argued and all the more distasteful) but instead will criticize the grammatical errors. A paper that may have important insights and plenty of original thinking can be downgraded easily if it is presented in a careless manner, or in a manner that seems careless because of grammatical and mechanical mistakes.

It is my view that if you commit yourself to a few principles of correcting, you can then make a clearing in the thicket of rhetorical, logical, and syntactical constraints and thus more easily see what it is that you have to set about learning. It is cheering, I think, to realize that the conventions of your language have evolved over the centuries. You are part of that history: every sentence you compose in some way determines that history, modifying the language, strengthening or weakening it. It is your language because you were born knowing how to speak it. (If you are not a native English speaker, you will have many more linguistic conventions to learn than the rest of us, but you will have the same means of learning them as we do those of your language.) In learning the conventions that help assure the "effective communication" that handbooks pay tribute to, you are learning to become your own authority by knowing what's best for your sentences. That, in my view, is the happiest solution to the problem of conformity.

Revising and correcting are both important, but they require different procedures. Every efficient writer is her own editor, but editing is not part of the composing process. That's why it can be and should be handled separately from the process of revision.

As you may have had occasion to discover, you can make sense of the explanation in a grammar workbook and complete the exercises there and still not be able to correct your own sentences. The reason is that when you're undistracted by its role in making meanings, you can more easily see/hear that there is something wrong with the way the sentence is constructed. Real sentences, however, occur not in isolation but in the context of passages and paragraphs, books and papers, courses and lives. Since a faulty sentence can be recognized and corrected more readily when it is considered as a bundle of parts, you need some way of focusing on that "bundle" rather than on what you think you mean or what you wanted to say or what you think the sentence says.

Such a concentration can be encouraged, I think, by the simple technique of reading your paper backwards, a sentence at a time. This procedure creates an isolation that focuses attention on sound patterns, idioms, agreement, reference, and so forth. It can make your sentences sound alien, like those in a workbook, and for the purposes of correction, that is all to the good.

Some Common Errors

In the following pages you will find examples of the kinds of errors that you can train yourself to locate by this technique of reading backwards. Remember that when you locate an error, you can sometimes correct it by rather simple adjustments, but that at other times you will need to revise it; and that calls for returning it to the context provided by the paragraph.

I have included here only a handful of the possible errors that we all can get trapped by, but these seem to me to be among the most common and the most annoying to both reader and writer.

(*Note:* Corrected versions of faulty sentences are in boldface type.)

WORD TROUBLE

Of course, all faulty sentences suffer "word trouble," but some errors can be fixed by simply cutting or adding a word or two, without getting into any heavy analysis. As a starter, here are some errors that can be corrected with minimal effort: they result from having (1) too many words, (2) too few words, or (3) the wrong words.

• *Simple redundancy: more words than you need in one sentence.*

Example: The woman in front of the roulette wheel stares at the wheel with an apparent disgusted look.

You ought to be able to get rid of one *wheel*, and if she has a *disgusted* look, you don't need to say it's *apparent*, which means "the way it looks."

The woman sits staring with disgust at the roulette wheel in front of her.
The woman at the roulette table sits staring in disgust at the wheel.

What a sentence "needs" is problematic: you have to decide whether each word pulls its weight. When Macbeth says that he's "cabin'd, cribb'd, confin'd," he's repeating himself on purpose and that purpose is to express his growing anxiety that he is not secure in his power. It's not repetition that is the problem in redundancy, but *purposeless* repetition.

• *Short circuit: too few words to accommodate the needs of the grammatical elements.*

Example: He is concerned with how society has, is, and may change.

Has, is, and *may* do not in themselves carry the meaning; it's only when they are used with *change* that they can do that. The catch is that by grammatical convention, the form of *change* is different in each instance: *has changed, is changing, may change.*

He is concerned with how society has changed, is changing [or being changed] and may change.
He is concerned with change in society, past, present, and future.

If you force a construction to carry more than it's designed to handle, you overload the circuit, the sentence structure. When you feel that adding the words needed to correct the grammatical error make the sentence seem long-winded, you may be right. In that case, paraphrase and reconstruct.

• *Faulty diction: wrong words.*

Example: Let me first *extend* the symbolism of the potato.

Explore? develop? extend it *to* other vegetables?

Let me first explain the symbolism of the potato more fully.

You use the wrong word when you've confused two words or because you don't in fact know the dictionary definition of the word you've used. There is no way to catch these errors, except when they are due to simple carelessness rather than to ignorance. The more you read critically, the more reliable your ear will become. In most cases, faulty diction occurs when the writer is putting on a manner that is not his own.

SNARLS: VERBAL CONFUSIONS

What I am calling "snarls" are syntactical errors that result from joining constructions that are at odds with one another linguistically, or failing to observe the conventions that govern the use of those grammatical elements that articulate the parts of the sentence. What the writer intends may be clear, but reading the sentence can make you dizzy.

Snarls result when you (1) mix metaphors, (2) mix constructions, or (3) confuse the terms of comparison and differentiation.

• *Mixed metaphor.*

Example: Miss Welty has dived into the realm of the balance between external forces in the world and the emotions of the individual.

You can *dive* into all kinds of things, not just water; a *realm* is a kind of place, but it can refer figuratively to anything that can be said to be an "area" of thought or action; *balance* is both the name of a state of being and the name for a device used to measure an unknown thing against something of known weight: Each of these words can be used metaphorically to describe an action or concept, but when they are all used together, each undercuts the other.

Miss Welty has explored the realms of emotion.
Miss Welty has examined the balance between personal emotion and . . .

Whole books are written about the structure of metaphor. Why? Because metaphor is central to the making of meaning. Metaphor, myth, and language itself all come from a single source, which is the human capacity to see the form of one thing in another. Bad teaching of poetry has led some students to believe that all images should be visualized, that the point of an image is to make you think in visual terms of what's being described. That is sometimes true of an image and sometimes not. Some metaphors present an image that brilliantly illuminates the visual character of what is being described; the prime function of other metaphors is to name indirectly a quality that is shared by two things or an idea and a thing, or two ideas. When Marvell wants to describe the meadows by a river just after they've been drained, he sketches this picture:

> For now the waves are fall'n and dried,
> And now the meadows fresher dyed;
> Whose grass, with moister color dashed,
> Seems as green silks but newly washed.

On the other hand, when Gerard Manley Hopkins writes,

> Self yeast a dull dough sours

we are not meant to see the inside of a poorly run bakery.

Learning to read poetry is in part learning how metaphors work. That's why many teachers believe that composition students who study carefully the rhetorical forms of poems can learn something about creating rhetorical forms in prose, even in the unexciting, workaday prose of course papers.

It's very difficult to formulate rules about using metaphor but here are two my students have found tolerable:

> Don't use a metaphor unless you can use it to think with; don't use it as icing.
> If you do use a metaphor, trust it with the work you assign it. Don't explain it, don't draw it out at great length, and don't tack one metaphor onto another.

For an excellent—and very amusing—discussion of the rhetoric of metaphor, see H. W. Fowler, *Modern English Usage.*

Mixed constructions: fractured idioms and incongruously matched syntactic elements.

Example: It's asking too great a drain on the writer.

Asking too much or *it is too great a drain,* but not parts of each spliced together.

It's asking too much of the writer to require that . . .
The demand you make is too great a drain on the writer.

Mixing constructions, like mixing metaphors, loses the point of both. It is an error that comes from writing one phrase at a time without regard for the structure of the sentence: it results from assembling the parts without bundling them. As you sort things out and decide which construction you want to complete, you will see that meanings shift; different ways of unsnarling will formulate different intentions. That's why it's a good idea to develop at least two different versions so that you can see which comes closest to what you intend to say.

Mangled comparisons and differentiations. Many errors result not from getting lost in your argument but from losing your way in the structure of a sentence. Although the confusion in saying then becomes a confusion in meaning, in some cases the very elements that have caused the confusion can be used to straighten things out. The best way out of the mazes created by mismatched correlatives or incomplete idioms is patient paraphrasing and a sorting out of what goes on one "side" and what on the other.

Example: Their work is not much alike.

alike   *Alike* is a shorthand way of saying that two things are similar. It therefore can be used only when the subject is in the plural; a plural verb is thus required. Translating *alike* to mean *X is in the state of being like Y* can help you be sure that you have named both X and Y. That initial *a*, which in some other words is a sign of the negative (*a*moral, *a*pathetic, *a*symmetrical), here signals a state of being (cf. *a*maze, *a*but, *a*lign, *a*wake, *a*kin, and the beautiful archaic form, *a*borning). Note that when *a* signals a state instead of the negative it is never stressed in pronouncing the word.

Their paintings are not very much alike.

Example: In pre-revolutionary China, the status of women was much like those in other non-Westernized countries.

(much)   *Like* signals a comparison of two subjects or objects
like   —two things or concepts: X is like Y. But the X and the Y have to share the same degree of generality. (They have to both be vegetables or both be parsnips.) In its uncorrected form, this sentence states that the *status* is like *women.* Like can be qualified with *quite, much,* and *a lot.* "*Very like*" is archaic, but *very likely* is a common qualifier used about acts or events.

In pre-revolutionary China, the status of women was much like that [of women] in other non-Western countries.

Example: It is this unity of perception that makes a reading of the two paragraphs together a more rewarding task than either of them separately.

more
(or less)
than

More and *less* are used with *than* to state comparisons formulated as measurements. *More* and *less* are quantitative terms, which by extension can be used of qualities as well. *Than* functions like the pivot or fulcrum of a balance.

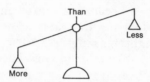

When you're reviewing a sentence with *than,* in order to be sure that you are weighing comparable items/concepts/terms in the balance, you should check to see if you can restate exactly what is *more* (or *less*) *than* what.

It is this unity of perception that makes a reading of the two paragraphs together a more rewarding task than reading either of them separately.

It's not the paragraphs that are being weighed but the task of reading them, singly or together.

Example: He reasons that man created God rather than God being the creator of man.

rather
than

Rather is the comparative form of an adjective (*rath*), which has not survived in Modern English. It meant *first* or *early; rather,* therefore, originally meant "firster" or *earlier.* Like *than,* it is a temporal term, which by extension came to mean "first" in the sense of "preferable." To say "I would *rather* have this one than that one" is like saying "I would take this one *first, then* that." As is the case with *more than, rather than* can be separated, as in the example just given. But this usage should be avoided until you know what you're doing. The rule to follow is that whatever choices are being articulated, you should present them in parallel form: a certain grammatical element on one side of the balance must be matched on the other side.

He reasons that man created God rather than that God created man.

It's also a good idea to have on hand *instead of* and *whereas.* Here they are in revisions of faulty sentences using *rather than:*

Example: There is too much emphasis placed on discipline *rather than* education.
There is too much emphasis placed on discipline instead of education.

Example: The difference is that in a novel rather than a discourse we deal with the personal effort.
The difference is that in a novel we deal with the personal effort, whereas in a discourse, we do not.

Example: "The City and the Hive" deals with man's differences to the animal kingdom; the Gardners' study deals with our similarities.

different from

similar to

Stating differences and similarities causes less trouble if you refer to them as characteristics *"of X,"* rather than as *"X's";* don't make possessions out of similarities and differences. It is also useful to let the job of comparing and differentiating be done by the verbs *differ* and *resemble* (or *corresponds to, reminds us of, calls to mind, duplicates,* etc., according to context). If you do speak of differences, remember that they are *between* X and Y, not *to.* And don't undo the effect of your articulator by adding another: "The observer of American life and its accompanying values can see a marked difference between the appearance of a high-priced so-called luxury sedan *as opposed to* that of a more economically priced one." If you've written *difference between X and Y,* you don't also need *as opposed to.*

"The City and the Hive" deals primarily with the differences between man and the rest of the animal kingdom; the Gardners' study stresses the similarities.

Example: Simple acts like donning woolen sweaters instead of raising the thermostat and organizing car pools instead of one car wasting the fuel that four could use would enable us to postpone a long-term commitment to the plutonium economy.

instead   *Instead of* means *in the place of:* X is where Y used
of to be or should be. It's a fulcrum that must weigh elements of the same grammatical kind. You can avoid
many cases of "faulty parallelism" if you check out
what is being placed where *what* was. Use your ears:
in the case above, you'll know there has to be another
ing.

**Simple acts like donning sweaters instead of raising the
thermostat and organizing car pools instead of wasting fuel
in individual cars would enable us to postpone a long-term
commitment to the plutonium economy.**

Examples: Each is a means of communication and work on
the principle of using waves.
Perhaps the illusion common to both Jake and Gatsby is their
respective concepts of themselves.

In all phases of composition, you need to know how to
single out and to form groups. When you use *one, each,
self, other, everyone, anybody,* etc., to particularize, you
"My brother can avoid difficulties by remembering that they are all
and my singular and all take singular verbs; likewise, when you
selves . . ." group by means of terms like *both* and *others,* there is
Tommy Smothers no problem, so long as you keep to the plural. So far, so
good; confusions arise when you want to do two things
at once—to group, but also to stress the single thing
held in common; to differentiate, but not at the cost of
disregarding commonality. The trouble comes in the
course of ascribing X to both Y and Z or in asserting
that A and B are both related to C. It is very easy
to get syntactically derailed. In the first sentence,
means, which sounds plural because of the *s,* may have
created static so that the writer didn't remember that
each is her subject and that it requires a singular verb,
works. Or she may have thought that after the *and*
she could return to the pair she's discussing—radio
and television—and refer to them in the plural. But
once the sentence is started in a certain way, syntactical requirements can't be ignored: *is . . . and . . . works.*
In the second sentence, the subject is singular—*the
illusion*—and it is given the proper verb form, *is.*
What's confusing is the shift to the plural in *their concepts* (even though it is not grammatically incorrect to
have a singular subject and a plural subject comple-

ment); and "respective" doesn't really help. What is needed is a syntactic element that can allow a shift of emphasis from singularity (*the illusion*) to the matter of the two *concepts*. *Each* can clear things up:

Perhaps the illusion common to both Jake and Gatsby is that each believes he understands himself.
Perhaps the illusion common to both Jake and Gatsby is the concept each has of himself.

Another way to eliminate interference from a plural when you want to be singling out, or from a singular when you want to be grouping, is to interrupt the syntax by means of punctuation.

Society plays a very large role when it comes to how each of us see our self.
Society plays a very large role when it comes to how we— each of us—see ourselves.

(Using the pair of dashes allows you to interrupt the syntax momentarily for emphasis, but you return to the plural *we* and thus to a plural verb, *see,* and the plural *selves.* It's important to note that an interruption has to be carefully controlled.)

LOGICAL CONFUSIONS

These errors can be described in grammatical terms and they can be corrected by following "the rules," but they are difficult to recognize and to analyze in any but logical terms.

· *Pleonasm: logical redundancy.*

Example: This growth has been paid for at the expense of the environment.

To say that something *has been paid for by* somebody else and that it has been *at the expense of* somebody else are two ways of saying the same thing: you can use either expression, but you can't use parts of each to make a third.

This growth has been paid for by our willingness to destroy the environment.
This growth has been at the expense of environmental quality.

This error is, I would say, the most common rhetorical/ logical fault in all sorts of composition. I invented the term "logical redundancy" in an attempt to differentiate it from the kind that is simply a matter of too many words. In rhetoric texts this error goes by the name of *pleonasm,* which is Greek for "too much of a muchness." The reason that pleonasm is harder to recognize than instances of simple redundancy is that the duplication can't be spotted just by seeing that there are more words than you need. But, fortunately, pleonasm is easier to correct than it is to explain. What is required is that by paraphrasing you draw out the implications of each idiom or expression in order to see how to go about unsnarling. This is a case when it is especially useful to isolate a sentence by reading your paper backwards; you can suddenly hear the absurdity when you aren't attending to its role in the paragraph.

Example: In pursuit of this quest he encountered many dangers.

The term *quest* includes the idea of a *pursuit* of a goal or trophy.

In his pursuit of X he encountered many dangers.
In this quest he encountered many dangers.

• *Classification errors.* This is the most common source of trouble in faulty sentences that do not suffer from grammatical weaknesses but that are, nevertheless, obscure or confusing because terms have been used inappropriately and concepts have been named with a degree of generality that is illogical for the context.

Example: The Reynolds portrait of Dr. Johnson couldn't have been painted in the 1500s.

Since neither the painter nor his subject lived in the sixteenth century, this statement is a truism, but of course the words do not accurately represent the writer's intention. Mistaking the particular for the specific—confusing an actual person/place/thing with a kind/sort/class is especially common in writing about historical events and personages.

Options: a. Use *such . . . as* in order to create a class to which you can then refer.

Such a portrait as that of Dr. Johnson could not have been painted in the sixteenth century.

b. Convert matter to manner by using *"so————a way"* (or *manner* or *mode*). Convert noun to verb: *portrait* becomes *portrayed.*

A scholar of the sixteenth century would not have been portrayed in so direct and personal a way.

c. Rename the subject in specific terms by deciding which aspect you intend to discuss and then define by using the terms *class, type, kind, sort,* etc.
The style of Reynolds's portrait of Dr. Johnson is not typical of sixteenth century portraiture.

Example: The imagery Kleist uses is one of the most fundamental differences between himself and others.

Imagery here is limited and is defined as "the imagery Kleist uses"; it therefore can't refer to imagery other writers use, which is what this construction implies. Once a word is given a syntactical setting, it must function in that setting; if you need it in another sense or with another reference, you must create a new setting, develop another syn-·tactical structure. In this case there are several options, each developing a meaning slightly different from the others.

Options: a. You can name two specific kinds, both members of a class.
The imagery Kleist uses is fundamentally different from that found in the other writers we have studied.

b. You can change the focus to another concept.
It is his use of imagery that is the fundamental difference between Kleist and the others.

c. You can specify and make the specification the point of reference.
It is the dream-like quality of his imagery that distinguishes Kleist's style.

Here is a schema showing the relationship of concepts and specifications (see page 103):

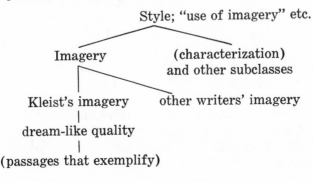

Style; "use of imagery" etc.

Imagery   (characterization) and other subclasses

Kleist's imagery   other writers' imagery

dream-like quality

(passages that exemplify)

MULTIPLE INJURIES

Although it is always easier to correct the errors in somebody else's prose, it nevertheless is good practice. If you slow down the procedure, you can more easily develop certain principles of grammatical analysis so that the tasks of editing can be simplified. It can be intensely frustrating to spend half an hour on one sentence, but you probably will learn more from the experience than you would in doing 20 workbook sheets. Here are 27 execrable sentences for practice. They are from student papers and the published productions of professional writers, including English teachers.

1. The building has a phenomenal ability to blend with the landscape as well as the season.
2. The artist's view of society's responsibility is one of financial support.
3. The future of wildlife may be entering a more hopeful era in Massachusetts.
4. In our eye, we have larger eyes and many more cells.
5. The police are permitted to break open a door or window to execute the warrant if refused admittance or loss of life may be involved.
6. The fears surrounding the Communist scare have been reborn somewhat due to the numerous extremist political factions present in the U.S. today.
7. Counseling is always available for use in developing more mature relationships with adults rather than utilizing passive rebellion, an important reason for failure in a high ability student.
8. There were no other manuscripts other than those given to those people who had to work on the book.
9. Is the Widow of Ephesus any less virtuous at the end of the story as compared to the beginning?
10. It was an event viewed in Iran as a harbinger of future changes to come.
11. He undercuts himself with overstated events and our emotions are lost with the plantation falling into the river.
12. The face of the land is being murdered, but much of the visible history lives on, if not in our eyes, then in our minds and hearts.
13. He provides a summation that ties things together.
14. Plant form provides a comparison to physical form, showing the formal similarities and differences between organic and inorganic matter.

15. After examining these paragraphs, certain distinctions and a broader generalization about a common denominator can be made.
16. Paul eventually had built up such an imaginative world of his own that it is smashed and with it, Paul, who dies.
17. Businessmen think of overpopulation in terms of another baby, another customer.
18. The late President's concern, he went on, was not with whether he had ever been under surveillance while in the White House, but rather one of, "Did you have a wiretap on me when I was in the Senate?"
19. It is more than ordinarily essential to consider Leonardo's Last Supper "as a whole," for it is at once a depiction of an essay in, and part of a deliberate quest for, wholeness, its success is the result of bringing each of these modalities to bear on the others, and the common denominator by which this is done is the key, not simply to its meaning, but to an understanding of how it functions as art, and why.
20. The remainder of the sentence gives the reader moment to pause.
21. We can trace an incremental degree of finer perception, greater awareness, and deeper understanding as the sense of the meaning becomes more abstract.
22. Rather than the psyche or the unrealized sexual self or the strange deed of a man that changes every one else's life domestically, etc., Kleist deals in *Michael Kohlhaas* with feelings and events which form causes and effects.
23. It is my opinion that a balance between the Vincent, Frankfurter, Jackson opinions on the one hand and the views of Black and Douglas on the other should be joined together to somehow find a common ground that satisfies the needs of national security as well as individual freedoms such as free speech.
24. A new auto is one of the worst investments one can make in terms of depreciation and marginal utility per additional dollars invested.
25. Human beings, like all living things, multiply in number— some by procreation, the rest through pollination.
26. Her writing has the tough precision of poetry and the closely observed naturalness of everyday life.
27. Her poetry provides a unique exploration of a woman's emotions toward Christ in a way that no man, however devout, could explore.

part iii

CONSTRUING AND CONSTRUCTING

1. Getting to Work

The Psychology of Composing:
Writer's Block and Writer's Compulsion

Writing involves your feelings, no matter what the topic or circumstances; writing a term paper can involve you "emotionally" just as deeply as composing a sonnet could. Whatever else it is, writing is not a mechanical operation.

Writing certainly involves temperament. Some people can, for instance, carry on an inner dialogue without taking notes. They simply sit down, when the time comes to write, and pour it out, but the "it" has been invented and shaped and formed by means of language over a long period of time. The pouring out is not as mysterious as it seems; nevertheless, it is baffling to those whose temperament would not allow for that kind of intensity. Some writers compose at the typewriter because they can type faster than they can write and because they can't think consecutively until they see what they are saying in type. Others write by hand because they need to doodle; that kinetic activity acts as a kind of starter motor. Many writers can't start until they have the right pen, the right paper, the right chair, the right writing surface. This Goldilocks Complex, it's fair to say, is frequently a way of putting off the job of writing. All of us are capable of using one or another obsession to forestall coming face to face with the blank piece of paper. On the other hand, a little compulsiveness never hurt any writer. If the search for the perfect pen can help you defuse some of the anxiety you may feel about writing, go right ahead with your collection; if you can write with greater ease on green-tinted legal paper without holes, go find a pack. Schiller, the great poet of German Romanticism, kept rotten apples in his desk: they provided an irritant for his restlessness to focus on so that the main channel of creative energy could be kept free. Tobacco serves the same function, but inhaling the aroma of rotten apples is better for your health.

Writer's Compulsion can help remove Writer's Block, insofar as that is a matter of rationalization about not getting to work. "Writer's Block" is a catch-all term used by nonwriters to keep themselves from examining their difficulties; occasionally, though, it names something very real, a resistance beyond the reach of games and harmless compulsions, beyond what a method of composing could cure. For every student who is unable to write because not-writing serves some psychological need, there are six who can learn the uses of chaos and how to search for limits. Not being able to write is a very real and upsetting experience, but it is not a supernatural affliction. You can learn to separate the hangups from genuine anxiety and thus decide if you need to talk to somebody about further remedies.

Working Rules

Many of the psychologically troubling aspects of composing can be dealt with by developing working habits, which can include giving into harmless compulsions if they make you feel more comfortable. The way to develop such habits is to have the experience of seeing how they can save time and energy. The following "rules" can be useful in forming good working habits. They concern limits, schedules, and note-taking.

Working Rule No. 1: Work within the specifications of the assignment. The method of composing set forth in Part II can help you find your own limits for any topic and to use them to make sound decisions about composition, but no method is reliable if it doesn't also keep you mindful of the limits set by the assignment itself. (Larry had a paper to write on the James-Lange theory of emotion. He wrote about how he disagreed with this theory and how very much superior he considered his own to be. He was astonished when his paper was returned marked "This doesn't follow the assignment. Unacceptable.") An efficient writer keeps in mind what is expected by the instructor. You should have on hand from the start a description of the assignment you've been given or the one you've worked out for yourself on the basis of an assigned topic. This descriptive statement should include a reminder of the relationship this paper bears to others in the course; specifications concerning the use of sources and the degree to which "your own ideas" are encouraged or welcomed; the date the paper is due; a definite indication of the minimum or maximum number of pages or words. If length has not been specified in the assignment, you must decide, since length of paper establishes an essential limit. (Count 250 words to the typed page. If you must write by hand, be sure to leave an adequate margin. If your handwriting is not very good, write on every other line.)

Understanding the limits is part of the composing process. A method of composing should help you make good use of them. I once saw the instruction sheet that a student had inadvertently turned in along with a bought paper. The student had prepared an explanation of how this paper fitted into the course; a description of what other papers he had written and what grades he'd received; how he wanted this paper focused, the texts he wanted cited, the quotations he wanted used: In short, the assignment was carefully interpreted, the ground carefully prepared. The next step should have been to set his own limits, and by that time the paper would have been half done! But the student wrongly thought that the writing would be the only work, and on the basis of that faulty notion, he rightly concluded that it could just as well be done by someone else. If you have, say, 6 weeks for writing a paper and your instructor does not ask for a progress report (or a first or second draft) at an earlier stage, then you should require it of yourself: one of the functions of this book is to teach you how to teach yourself how to write in circumstances in which no instruction is offered.

Working Rule No. 2: Establish a schedule that takes into account the amount of time needed for typing or writing out a clean copy. The way you use your time when you compose is determined by your temperament, your other papers, your life. Some of these constraints are "necessary": they are not subject to your will or choosing. But you can learn to be honest about that and not confuse conditions that you can't really change and those to which you can adapt, to say nothing of those that you can radically change. In my present teaching position, I have students whose schedules are as complicated as my own. Most of them have jobs; some of them work 15 or 20 hours a week. They do not have a lot of time to throw away; if they are to get their course reading done, their lab work done, their writing assignments done, they have to learn to plan their time. I try to persuade my students that they should compose even a short (five to six pages) paper over a period of 2 weeks, say, and not save it for a weekend or two successive weekends. Some aspects of composing require long stretches of time—revision, for instance. But there are various aspects of forming concepts and working out interpretations and generalizations that can be done in bits of time.

You can help yourself make hard decisions if you establish a target time and date and then work out a schedule from that point backwards. All writers benefit from one last overview of the whole composition. I am a great believer, therefore, in false deadlines: if the paper is due Monday at 10 A.M., plan to have it ready for typing by noon Saturday. This will give you time for the final review, which can make the difference between a "good" paper and a "thoughtful, well-written" paper. (After Chuck had experimented with this way of working out a backwards time frame, he remarked that he now understood what a former teacher had meant when he said that he "wrote" in the shower. Chuck learned very quickly how to use odd bits of time for thinking about his paper, learning how to compose it over a longer period of time than the weekend before it was due.)

If you have a hard time starting (despite rotten apples in every drawer) or stopping, you can try giving yourself only 15 minutes at a time for writing. Even if you're in high gear or even if you've written not a single word, don't let yourself go over the time allotted. I ask my students to equip themselves with a kitchen timer or a parking meter buzzer that can be set for 5 or 10 minutes or any other fraction of an hour. This is a more humane and a more productive method than one devised by an Italian philosopher of the Renaissance who had his servant tie his hair to the back of his chair, giving him strict orders not to yield to the philosopher's pleas to be untied short of the 3 hours he allotted himself. Once you've sharpened your sense of how long a time 15 minutes (or 5) is, you can know better how long a time you need for working at various phases of composing. It's a good idea to decide rather carefully what your next stint will be devoted to, before you close shop. Hemingway remarked that he never left his desk without taking one step toward the next job of writing, whether it was the next paragraph or the next chapter or the next novel.

Options should be kept open, but not wide open, and not for more than a third of your total working time. The novice writer spends 2 weeks of research on a topic, which she then decides is boring or too difficult. She pushes everything aside and starts over; the 2 weeks are simply lost, written off. The only way to avoid this waste of time is to define the options more carefully. Between the rigidity of the Formal Outline and a mindless looking around waiting for something to turn up is a method that can help you generate critical questions and thus establish a field in which your explorations can be carried out.

Working Rule No. 3: Work out a system of taking notes, but don't be a slave to it. A distinguished historian made the point in a lecture on research methods. "I use pink and blue cards, 3 x 5," she said. "The pink ones are for primary sources; the blue, for secondary sources. When I run out of blue cards, I take a pink card and write 'blue' at the top." Keep your method flexible and efficient so that note-taking can be a phase of the composing process.

Here are some suggestions: If you just fill out note cards and let it go at that, you are making a monumentally difficult job for yourself (unless you plan to fit the note cards, each with its own little "fact," into a prefabricated grid, in which case nothing in this book will be of interest to you). To keep from piling up the note cards without any notion of what kind of structure they could help to build, you can keep formulating what your paper is about, what you think you are doing. You can take notes on your notes; write questions and responses: don't save up the task of critical review. For every page of notes—or for every half dozen cards—you should write two or three sentences in which you note to yourself how those parts could be bundled with others. In my view, the best way to take notes is in a spiral notebook like the one you've been using, with the right-hand side reserved for direct quotations from your reading and the left-hand side for queries, statements of purpose, summaries, tentative amalgamations, bundle-ties of all sorts. Don't write on the back of the paper or note card except for a brief continuation of a quotation and even then the important terms that appear in the continuation should be noted on the top side. Why? Because you may want to use the actual sheets of paper torn out or the note cards to represent a sequence. A pile of sheets or a little group of cards can be a proto-paragraph (*proto-* Greek, first of a series; earliest form). Dogs and cats and roommates are hazards, to say nothing of strong gusts of wind and 2 year olds, but a large flat surface in a still room provides one of the best devices for getting a composition together.

The principal reason that I warn students against the conventional prescriptions for note-taking and research—filling out note cards, developing a formal outline—is that these activities can mask the fact that the mind is not engaged and that the composing process has not even started.

Working Rule No. 4: Don't throw anything away until your paper is finally copied. Keep all the scribbles and notes and drafts of statements of purpose, lists of oppositions, etc. Since naming and defining continue right through to the very end, you should keep what you have on hand; it can afford the materials to help in all sorts of problems in the later stages of composing. (And, indeed, you could write another paper from the leftovers! Like making another film out of all the stuff on the cutting room floor.)

Complaints, Queries, and Suggestions

The following questions and answers might be a source of comfort, since they help define just what kinds of problems in composing are "universal"; they are typical of students of composition everywhere. The responses are not formulated as "rules," nor are they meant to be definitive; they are representative of the responses I make in conference.

1. *How can I write about something I'm not interested in?* Whenever a topic seems dull or difficult or vague, one way to approach it is to consider who might care, even if you don't. Or put it this way: to whose advantage is it that this subject remain dull? A little self-analysis won't hurt either: "Why am I uninterested in beet sugar manufacture? Why should I care about the Hundred Years War or the Putney Debates? the settlement of the Great Plains or the First Amendment? In what circumstances is it conceivable that I might care about the topography of the Iberian peninsula?" This suggestion is not meant to encourage that strategy that is rediscovered annually by a million students, writing the theme about writing the theme, but only to remind you that if you think of composing for an audience that does have an interest, such a notion can provide useful limits to help in defining the topic.

"Writing from experience" is a favorite concept of many English teachers, but they don't always make clear just how learning to write an interesting account of a personal experience can have anything to do with writing a formal paper on, say, the development of modern Japan (to take the single most popular topic in introductory courses in economics, modern history, political science, etc.). If you write about what Emily Dickinson means to you, the reception your paper gets might be warm and enthusiastic; it might be contemptuous. A method of composing ought to free you from a dependence on your personal enthusiasms; otherwise, you will be condemned to taking courses given by people who look kindly on whatever mode of writing you feel comfortable with. A method of composing ought to help you discover what bearing your experience has on what you are writing about, whether it's a narrowly defined topic ("The Use of Busing in Charlestown, pursuant to the orders of the Federal Court of Boston, September-October, 1975") or one very widely conceived ("Rituals"). First of all, "experience" must be interpreted to mean not just "what has happened to me," but what you have thought about in your reading and in other areas of your life. I would claim that the exercise of imagination in forming concepts can bring us as close to the realm of experience as the study of statistics can.

The point here is to keep "experience" from being narrowed to the merely personal. Experience is the ground from which we depart, not the sole subject of our intellectual and moral concerns. Making your experience available as a resource in writing means learning to generalize so that you can discover what there is in common between what you know from experience and the topic. That doesn't mean that you write about how the space program reminds you of the summer your uncle decided to build a submarine in the garage; it means that in thinking about the personal experience, you discover some of the limits that will help you form the concepts necessary for a discussion of the public/scientific/political enterprise that is called "the space program."

2. *"My professor, when you ask him to explain, just puts it in other words; he doesn't explain."* Sometimes instructors are, in fact, confused about what they are asking for in an assignment. In such cases, your questions could help. On the other hand, if you haven't mastered the principal concepts of the course, you won't be able to understand the explanations. If an instructor offers study questions, use them; translate them; compose your own. At any stage of the composing process, you can develop your own study questions; they not only can guide critical inquiry, but they can also help you decide where you are in

your paper, what you think you are saying; they can help you to identify road blocks. (Finally, they can help you decide whether it is you or the instructor who is obtuse.)

Whatever the topic, you will need a terminology. It may be simple or it may be highly technical. If it is ordinary, everyday language, you may need analogies to help freshen your sense of what the terms mean; if it is specialized language, you will need either analogy or careful exemplifications in order to explain references. In most cases, it will be unnecessary to incorporate such explanations in your paper; the point is, rather, that *you* need to understand the range of reference and the uses of special terms. Here's a question from an exam in *Psychology 19: Human Sexual Behavior:*

> Give an example in which social class predicts differently for males and females in terms of premarital sex behavior, according to the Kinsey studies.

The jargon has to be understood: "predicts" is used in a way peculiar to statisticians; "in terms of" is used illogically and should be translated to read "with respect to." A student cannot usefully complain about barbaric language; the causes are much deeper than anything an individual instructor could control easily. It's up to the student to understand the use of terms peculiar to a subject. In this instance, the answer one student gave earned no credit and this comment from the instructor: "You should read the question more carefully."

3. *"You keep talking about how we should start writing right away, about chaos and all that. But I was always told not to start writing until I knew what I wanted to say. I thought you were supposed to have an outline before you could write."*

The composing process starts and stops and starts again; it goes in circles; it spirals; it can involve being "in the dark," though at other times, composing is like going over a well-worn path. In any case, you can't see where you've been until you get to where you're going. A method of composing that requires that you work out an outline before you start writing cannot possibly help you find the parts or guide you in bundling them: an outline is like a blueprint and, in the design of a building, drawing the blueprint is the final stage of the architect's work. You can't use an outline as a method to compose your paper unless you already know your topics, the line of argument or plan of presentation, the principal examples or supporting evidence—in which case, you won't need an outline!

One reason that students hold on to the formal outline as a kind of security blanket is the familiar fear that if they actually do start writing, there won't be more than a paragraph. The matching fear is that there is simply no way under heaven to bring any kind of order to what is on hand without writing at least 345 pages. The fear that you have too little to say leads to tinkering with sentences, fussing over tiny details. The fear that you have too much leads, paradoxically, to further reading and writing, to heaping more on the pile in the hope that somehow it will sift down into manageable shape.

Cultivating a "careful disorderliness," learning the uses of chaos, can help you escape from this dilemma. Without a method, the chance is that you will simply go to the other extreme of the formal outline, writing one sentence and then another. And another. The trouble with that non-method is that there's no way to get started again, once you get stalled. Here is a familiar sight: A student sits staring into space with a blank tablet of paper and a pen at the ready. A sentence gets written and then another. A long wait. Another sentence. A long wait followed by careful, loving rereading of The Three Sentences. More staring into space. A rereading of The Composition suddenly is brought to an end as the sheet of paper is ripped off the tablet, crumpled into a throwable ball. There is a long silence. Quickly, a sentence gets written, then another . . . and so on.

What's happening here is that the would-be composer has nothing to guide him but the sentence he's written down. There is no place to go where materials might be afforded and no other direction than the one indicated by the opener, vague as it might be. The result is generally about like this:

> One of the most important things about Chekhov's stories is his skillful characterization. For example, in "A Trifling Occurrence," he tells us that Bielyaiev is "a well-fed, pink young man." He also says that he is fond of the racetrack. We really feel that we know this character.

And with that remark, the composition comes to a full halt. There is no place to go except to another "example"—but of what? To speak of Chekhov's "skillful characterization" is like saying that water is wet. It leads nowhere except to the high school book report, the main purpose of which is to persuade the teacher that you've read the book.

One of the chief benefits of learning to look kindly on chaos is that it gives you some place to go when you're lost or provides new purposes to get you started again when your composition has come to a full halt.

4. *"I start out with what I want to say, but then I get a new idea and I can't fit it in, so I scratch out what I've written and start over again. I keep doing that."* A sheep dog doesn't run in a straight line. Keep starting and keep beginning; just don't throw anything away. Starting sentence composition too soon can stop the composing process. "In the realm of mind, to begin is to know one has the right to begin again" (Gaston Bachelard).

5. *"I didn't mark my book or take notes when I did the reading because I didn't know what to look for."* Learning to pose questions without answering them immediately is the essential critical skill and the essential power, too, of creativity. Underlining, even taking notes, is useless unless you are in a dialogue with what you're reading, and dialogue means posing questions. That felt pen that provides a yellow or pink background for important passages, which you carefully indicate by running the marker over the lines of print, is probably the most subversive of all the reading skills equipment on the market. Pages with rectangular pastel islands suggest anything but a careful reading, which depends on questions, paraphrases, transformations, glosses, abstracts, oppositions of all kinds. Remember that the process of construing—making sense of a text—involves the same acts of mind as constructing—creating a composition. Glossing paragraphs and writing a one-sentence abstract for each chapter—whether of a novel or a textbook—will yield greater dividends than highlighting the Important Passages.

6. *"In this paper, do you want us to be objective or can we say what we think?"* *Subjective* and *objective* are too problematic to be useful terms. By the time you explain what you mean by each, according to which context, you'd probably be better off with other terms altogether. It may be that within the context of a certain course "objective" has been defined so that it can be critically useful, but I think that it's important for all writers to understand the premise that there is no such thing as context-free evaluation; that you cannot name without presuppositions; that the "objective" facts and figures you employ have been collected and arranged by a "subject"; that facts substantiate, not The Truth, but one's judgment of the truth. Language is not a veil between us and reality but our means of knowing reality. A means is always subject to objective evaluation, but those limits have, in turn, been established by a subject. What we know, we know in terms of some form or other. The

question properly should be about the kind of form required, not whether you are supposed to be "objective."

7. *"I don't like to read critical introductions; I'm afraid I'll plagiarize without knowing it."* Learning how to cite sources of facts and ideas and wording involves more than just learning correct footnote form, and there's no point in trying to get around it. Critical introductions to novels or standard works of any kind provide information that is in the public domain, simply gathered and packaged in a convenient way. Particular insights and formulations should be cited—who said it where?—and credited or directly quoted. You will need practice in deciding just what is a particular formulation. You should ask the teacher in any course requiring a formal paper for instructions about crediting sources if they have not been provided. Studying carefully the kind of information cited in scholarly articles and critical studies in any one field can help you develop a sense of what is to be credited. I once knew an anthropologist who required her students to credit the sources for the information that the Eskimos are a circumpolar people. Learning how to determine what needs crediting can be a useful exercise in differentiating fact and opinion, which is, of course, an important aspect of forming concepts.

8. *"I don't know how to say what the author says without just quoting him."* One of the chief problems in critical writing is presenting the argument of a writer without misleading paraphrase or without depending on lengthy quotation. You can't solve this problem by varying the phrase "The author says," which is what John does in this discussion of George Orwell's views of socialism in the second half of *The Road to Wigan Pier*.

> Orwell paints an interesting picture of the English working class's lack of acceptance of the supposed virtues of socialism. He states that socialists, as a group, are their own worst advertisements. He goes on to explain that it is not only the Englishman's fear for what will happen to his Sunday trousers in a revolution that holds him back,* but his revulsion at the "fruit juice drinkers, nudists, sandal

---

* This is an allusion to Brecht's "Buddha's Parable of the Burning House" in which an analogy is drawn between those people in a burning house who ask if it's raining outside and if there's somewhere else they can go and those who are concerned not with the necessity of radical social and political change but only with their own welfare, symbolized by their Sunday trousers.

wearers, vegetarians" who seem to swell the ranks of socialists. This class consciousness was not seen in any other
societies we read about and would seem to cast an unfavor-
able light on the relative importance of social mores and
political ideology for the English working class. Orwell then
seems to side with the workers in claiming that there are
no artists or men of great imagination who are active socialists. He deplores this but does not find fault in socialism,
only in the stereotypical socialist. But he does lament the
fact that socialists have not given us a song worth singing.

Orwell goes on to talk about the relative merits of mech-
anization, condemning it while admitting that we can't live
without it. He also strongly condemns those who fear for
their trousers but who in reality possess Sunday best
clothes only in their heads. He sees this false association
with the upper class as a big stumbling block to the socialist
cause, and one that has to be gotten over.

Once you firmly establish that you are paraphrasing, you
can write without announcing the fact continually. When you
come to a memorable phrase, quote it, as John does in his third
sentence. When the subject changes, you can remind your readers that they are reading a *redaction,* an old-fashioned term
meaning "reduction," a "boiled-down" version of the original.
Of course, there will be times when you want to stress the fact
that a writer is changing his mind or contradicting himself.
In the last three sentences of the first paragraph, John is as
interested in Orwell's ambivalence as in the attitudes themselves: *Orwell seems to side . . . deplores . . . also laments* are
all ways of focusing on Orwell. But in the next paragraph, *Orwell goes on to talk . . . he also strongly condemns . . . he sees this*
are phrases that could easily have been cut.

When you've reached the point at which you are ready to
develop your own counter-argument, you'll have the same sort
of problem with *"In my opinion . . ."* as you faced with *"He
also says. . . ."* Learning to set up a framework in which it is
clear that what is being declared represents your ideas and is
indeed the way you see things can save you from the use of
such phrases as "Frankly, . . ." and "I definitely believe . . . ,"
which are distracting. It takes a good deal of practice before you
can differentiate pomposity from authority and judge when you
have earned the right to declare your own opinion without more
than one announcement.

9. *"I just tossed that off, but you liked it; what I really worked on—that was the one you didn't like."* "Really working" unfortunately bears no necessary relation to quality. What is "tossed off" is often better writing because it gives expression to concepts and feelings whose forms you have been familiar with and probably have a deep understanding of.

10. *"But that's what I meant! How can you say I didn't say it when you've just been able to explain what I meant?"* Learning to recognize the difference between what you think you've said and the meanings your language has made possible is one of your primary tasks in composing.

11. *"It's all very well to talk about 'method' and I grant you that it can be very useful in getting started, but I have to get this paper written and what I need for that is not a 'method' but a plan. I can't risk ending up completely disbelieving what I started out with."* One reason for having a method is to know when and how to plan. Ending up somewhere other than the place you thought you were going when you started out may be to your advantage: if you don't proceed in such a way that that can happen, if you don't allow for the possibility of changing your mind, then it is a certainty that you will learn nothing from writing the paper. A method of composing should help you understand what kind of process composition is. Any process can be broken down into three phases: beginning, middle, end. These phases or stages can be differentiated for the purpose of analysis, but that doesn't mean that you can say, "Right there is where the beginning ends; right here is the point at which the ending begins." In some processes, the stages follow one another very precisely, one step after another. When you bake a cake, you reach the point when the batter is at the right consistency and the oven is at the right temperature and you know it's time to put the cake in to bake. But composing is not that kind of process. All you can do to differentiate the three phases of composing is to say something like, "Right about here I can begin drawing things together. . . . Somewhere about now I could go back to the beginning and see how I can get it to match the conclusion." But there's nothing to say that you can't start off by working with the middle and figure out the beginning as the very last step. (Novelists I have talked with say that the first chapter is often written last.)

The most common problem in writing longish papers (15 or 20 pages) is how to balance the analysis of a set of themes, issues, events, or texts with a chronological account. I don't think you can decide on a strategy until you have reached the stage of gathering and sorting paragraphs, but once you are there and are ready to rewrite, then you should decide—and stick with the decision. Composing alternate titles can help you determine which kind of format is best suited to the material you have on hand. You can write several introductions and conclusions, which can help you identify the conceptual issues that might have been disguised by the chronological account. Sometimes you will find that working out the chronology has served its purpose in helping you form and develop concepts and that it needn't be a structural element in the paper. You have to learn to differentiate the topic and the history of your attempt to deal with it: the discovery you make a week before the paper is due does not have to be part of the conclusion. Options can't really be identified and established until you have defined your purpose, though it is true that experimenting with options can help establish purposes. Deciding which options best serve which purposes is the composer's continuing task. Deciding them marks the beginning of the final phase of composing.

The relationship between organization and purpose can be seen if you consider this example. Suppose you are going to organize a series of programs featuring the cantatas of J. S. Bach. Here's how defining purposes would define the options for arrangement.

- To show the development of Bach's style in this form:
    Cantatas presented in order in which they were written with some skipping around to point up contrasts.
- To show Bach's mastery of the form and his influence:
    Cantatas representative of this mastery, juxtaposed with excerpts from works of other composers.
- To demonstrate range of style, kinds of treatment of texts:
    Cantatas presented according to the occasion for which they were written.
- To demonstrate the performing styles of contemporary choral directors and singers:
    Cantatas presented which best show off the performing styles of certain musicians.

There is a dialectic at work, of course: if you discovered that there is no "development" in Bach's cantata style, that he began complexly and kept it up, then that fact would limit the number of purposes and, hence, the number of rational arrangements.

2. Critical Reading and Critical Writing

Naming, Opposing, Defining

When you read critically, you analyze how the parts are bundled to make the whole: the fundamental question for the reader, as for the writer, is, "What goes with what?" Critical reading is simply the reverse of composing and we could call it "decomposing," except for the fact that that word suggests organic deterioration. *Critic* derives from a Greek word that meant *to judge, to discern, to be able to discuss*—all capacities necessary to forming concepts and making meanings in both reading and writing. As we've frequently noted in this book, how you construe is how you construct. For that reason, the method of composing we've developed in Part II is adaptable to reading. Here are some suggestions, then, for using naming, opposing, defining in the process of critical reading.

1. *Naming the names.* Recognizing and listing conceptual terms—naming the names—is not difficult when the writer is deliberately developing concepts. In almost all the paragraphs in this book, that is the case. Nevertheless, explicitly identifying a writer's conceptual terms is good practice for reading documents and other texts in which concepts don't jump off the page. For instance, if you are giving the Bill of Rights a careful, critical reading, there is no signal to tell you which terms are conceptually complex, calling for something more than a lexical definition. Take the Second Amendment:

> A well-regulated militia being necessary to the security of a free state, the right of the people to keep and bear arms shall not be infringed.

Practice in identifying conceptual terms can alert you to the fact that any central name or word or fact should be carefully examined and interpreted; thus *militia* sounds like a down-to-earth name for *local citizens with guns*, but once you have developed a historical context, you can see that it does not belong in the same class with *Americans protecting private property with firearms*. The meaning of "the right of the people to keep and bear arms" has nothing to do with the claims of the National Rifle Association.

In reading essays, articles, or any text in which technical language is necessary in forming the concept, it's a good idea to prepare a *lexicon*, which is a list of words serving a special purpose. A gardener's *lexicon* would include names of equipment and processes as well as the names of plants. Preparing a lexicon is essential in keeping track of a complicated terminology, but it also has its uses in helping you keep familiar terms carefully differentiated. If you're reading about the energy crisis, for instance, it would be useful to include in your lexicon the terms *fuel, energy, power, resources,* along with examples of their use. They are all familiar, of course, but each is used to indicate a different function or state. Coal in the ground has one name; coal in the furnace or in a statistical table has other names. Developing a lexicon prepares you for naming the classes accurately and appropriately, an act that is essential to forming concepts.

Naming conceptual terms—underlining or copying them in the margin—is preliminary to recognizing them in grammatical transformations (if *variation* is a key term, it is likely that *vary, invariant,* or *varying* will occur somewhere in the passage); and it is also essential for an understanding of the ground of analogies, images, or other entitlements. It can be disconcerting to be reading along and suddenly find yourself in the midst of something that seems to have nothing to do with what you thought you were reading about. ("What in the world does plum pudding have to do with epic diction?" See paragraph by C. S. Lewis, p. 87.)

2. *Opposing: Developing contexts, identifying the relationships of various conceptual terms.* Glossing is as useful in critical reading as it is in composing; it provides an excellent instrument for determining the structure of a paragraph—your own or someone else's. If you develop the opposition of the gloss, you will have a summarizing statement; composing it can help you understand the logical and rhetorical structure of a paragraph in a way that passive underlining cannot. You can then label as *A* or *B* each sentence or part of a sentence that moves toward one or the other term of the opposition. Sometimes a sentence that you have not been able to follow will suddenly make sense when you work out this kind of schema. Why? Because you construe on the basis of what you have already figured out; you develop expectations on the basis of interpretations. Critical reading is a matter of knowing what to expect and being able to identify it when you meet it.

Another way to use opposition as a form to find form is to set the first sentence of a paragraph over against the concluding sentence. Can you account for the last in terms of the first? What has been defined? Has an opposite case been developed? What relationship is articulated in the conclusion that was not implicit in the opening? This kind of analysis will help you understand the structure of a good paragraph—and it will encourage you in seeing the spurious arguments and inadequate substantiation of a poor one.

3. *Defining: articulating the relationships between inter-pretations and generalizations.* A definition, you will remember, names the class and differentiates the members of that class. You should use your dictionary continually in reading difficult passages, but remember that forming concepts takes you beyond lexical definition (see page 94ff). A concept is formed by interpreting examples, cases, instances from which one could generalize and form a class, the field of the concept's application. Unless you are reading pure theory, you will find a balance of general statement and substantiation in almost every paragraph of expository prose. One of the primary tasks of critical reading is identifying the supporting statements and judging their relevance. Asking HDWDWW? will help you determine if the examples are intended to substantiate agent, act, manner, or purpose. With the help of your gloss, you can locate the sentence that has the highest degree of generality, the most general statements. Relating other sentences to it will then help you follow the argument. (You will find a demonstration of this method of critical reading in the introduction to Paragraph Sequence III.)

There are two ancient rhetorical/logical principles you can use to guide all critical acts:

Save the particulars: as you gloss and paraphrase, you should try to account for everything in the paragraph; your gloss should represent the skeletal structure of the argument so that the relationship of all elements to that bony structure is clear.

Nothing too much: the principle known as "Occam's Razor" is a correlate; don't include the inessential when you are trying to re-present the main point.

These principles are not magical charms. They cannot save you from the hard job of analysis and restatement, but they can remind you of the uses of limits: a skeleton doesn't have to be the whole body; its purpose is to articulate the parts that make the whole. A gloss or paraphrase or abstract is a skeletal structure by which you can represent those relationships that are meanings.

Heuristics

Any device, principle, or structure that can help you construe and/or construct is a *heuristic*. (Deriving from the Greek word for *find*, *heuristic* is both an adjective and a noun.) Heuristics are forms that find forms. Here are a few that are adaptable for use in the critical reading of the Paragraph Sequences to follow.

1. What you learn from a thoroughgoing analysis of one passage can help you construe a comparable passage. Look for the verbs that articulate the central opposition. Once you locate the word or phrase that *juxtaposes, equates, polarizes, ranks,* or otherwise *bridges* the two terms of the opposition, this articulator can be a powerful instrument for analyzing the definitions in another passage. One writer's terms can be entirely different from another's, and yet they can both be developing the same concept. (It's more disconcerting to discover that, although two writers can be using the same terms, they are actually forming quite different concepts.) Once you see what's being defined by the way certain examples are interpreted and how a generalization is developed from certain particulars, you can learn to recognize that concept, even though it bears another name. Identifying the context in which the concept is developed requires that same "continuing audit of meaning" that is essential to the composing process. Most of the techniques explained in our discussion of a method of composing are adaptable to critical reading. You can, for instance, determine if the argument of one paragraph is analogous to that of another by making "ratios" to guide your alignment of terms, to help you interpret the logic of the analogy.

2. Thinking in three's is another way of carrying out the audit of meaning. Threeness is a form having a physiognomic and perceptual basis; it is a structure that typifies spatial and temporal forms and it characterizes virtually all cultural and biological activities. Indeed, one philosopher sees "the act concept" as the form of forms, as essential to all human thought and activity, to all the arts, to all experience.* Here are some trios and triads.

left, middle, right
top, in between, bottom

---

* Susanne K. Langer, in *Mind: An Essay on Human Feeling*, Volume I, Chaps. 8–11.

beginning, middle, end
space, time, causality
head, torso, limbs
animal, vegetable, mineral
thesis, antithesis, synthesis
statement, development, recapitulation
theme, conflict, resolution
nature, history, spirit
text, explication, exhortation
id, ego, superego

If you list the three principal conceptual terms of one thinker and enclose it, you will have a sort of tower; Professor Perry Miller of Harvard used to call such category arrangements "grain elevators."

3. One of the best ways to practice critical writing is tracking down, smoothing out, following up arguments, agreements, and confusions which take shape in the course of discussing difficult passages with other readers. If you discuss these paragraphs in small groups in which various inner dialogues are brought out in the open, then interrupting the discussion to write for 10 minutes can give everybody good practice in using context and in catching the rhythm of dialogue. My students are frequently amazed to discover how substantially and succinctly they write when they are working in the context of small group discussion and under the pressure of time. The starting point can be arbitrary or it can be decreed by a discussion leader who decides when there's enough chaos.

4. You can also carry on a conversation with the writer by composing a follow-up paragraph in which you develop what you think needs to be said in order to clinch the argument or to bring out implications that might support or undercut what has been said. This is an excellent way to see if you have understood what you've read; it's useful for times when you are your own critical audience but, of course, members of a small group reading one another's follow-up paragraphs can make it more valuable.

5. While you're still struggling to learn a method of composing, it may be hard to believe that you might some day want to concern yourself with balance and cadence, subtleties of emphasis, and complexities of repetition; nevertheless, it can happen and it's a good sign. When and if you tire of your writing "voice," there is an old remedy that is amusing as well as in-

structive: imitation. The traditional way of teaching composition was to set a certain theme or topic and require students to compose in the manner of a master stylist whose essay on the same topic had been painstakingly analyzed. Such practice has a lot in common with translation and it serves very well to slow down the process of composing sentences so that the interaction of syntax and meaning can be observed. The trouble was that the topics were generally banal or "irrelevant" and the distance between the student writer and Francis Bacon or Thomas Carlyle was often felt as a shameful fact. The exercise I am proposing is closer to parody than old-fashioned imitation; it is, in any case, a lot more fun than other kinds of "model" composition.

It's called "persona paraphrase" * and the procedure is as follows: you use a passage of prose as a model to guide you in constructing a sequence of sentences, each of which is as close syntactically to the model as you can make it, but the subject matter of your sentences is entirely different. The model acts to shape your sentences, somewhat the way an armature provides a framework when you are modeling a clay figure. There are two important requirements: (a) The logical relationships you are trying to articulate should be analogous to those the model articulates. You couldn't model the figure of a horse on an armature made for a bird in flight—or could you? Maybe a winged horse would result. The point is that you must observe the dialectic, letting the syntax of the model help determine what you are saying, up to a point. Any one model can't be appropriate to just any assertion. (b) You need to be deeply immersed in a problem, to have on hand a full lexicon of terms and well-developed concepts. It's because they are complex and strange that these models can be critically useful: they are like rest and recreation points from which you can return to your own sentences with renewed vigor and restored spirits; you can also bring back some ideas about articulation and emphasis. Here are two examples using single sentences.

1. *Model:* Jules Roy, *The Fall of Dienbienphu.*

Paraphrase: Carol Rainwater, who was working on a short paper on theories of the origin of language.

The world that separated Uncle Ho from the representatives of France

---

* For a full explanation, see Phyllis Brooks, "Mimesis: Grammar and the Echoing Voice," *College English* (35), 1973, 161–168.

The quality that distinguishes man from the members of the
animal kingdom
was not simply a means of expression or comprehension,
is not merely a matter of awareness or mentation,
a language or a civilization;
an utterance or a vocalization:
for if Uncle Ho's civilization was not yet industrial,
since man's vocalization is not only self-expressive,
it had nothing to learn from that of M. Letourneau or M. Dejean.
it has nothing to do with that of the wolf or the lion.
It was the same world which would later separate M. Lacoste
It is the identical quality which should always distinguish the
ape
from Belkacem Krim in Algeria:
from the human on earth,
that of men who fought, not for portfolios, mandates, or
that of creatures who verbalize, not (only) for expression, communication or
constituencies, but for the freedom of their people.
self-protection, but for an understanding of their world.

2. *Model:* Sören Kierkegaard, *Repetition.*

Paraphrase: Rebecca Saunders, who was in the process of
converting her very full journal notes on the creative process to
a short paper on that topic.

This is a world in which each of us,
This act of creation is a process in which each of us,
knowing his limitations, knowing the evils of superficiality
scrutinizing his ideas, knowing the dangers of arrogance
and the terrors of fatigue, will have to cling to what
and the humiliation of nervousness, must choose from what
is close to him, to what he knows, to what he can do,
he has carefully thought out, from what he has "the feel of,"
to his friends and his tradition and his love,
from the familiar, and his culture and his true passions,
lest he be dissolved into a universal confusion
lest he fall into a popular delusion
and know nothing and love nothing.
and create nothing and understand nothing.

Some writers find it easier to work with sentences in the setting of their paragraphs and prefer, therefore, to use entire paragraphs as models. Many of those in Paragraph Sequence III can serve this purpose. For those who prefer single sentence models, here is a repertory:

1. Sprung from the nomads of the Asiatic hinterland and for long dependent upon other nations for transport at sea, the Turks, when they had captured Constantinople, found it to their advantage to revive the commercial arrangements that had existed between Byzantium and the European states.

2. I must study politics and war, that my sons may have liberty to study mathematics and philosophy, geography, natural history and naval architecture, in order to give their children a right to study painting, poetry, music, architecture, tapestry, and porcelain.

3. Romanesque, too, is the conception of the figure with opposed directions of the head and body, a form that resembles a vital type in Greek art of the archaic period, when the painters and sculptors infused movement into the primitive figures by contrasting positions of the limbs, sharply turned from each other. It is an essential factor in the expressive force of the tympana and capitals of Vezelay and Autun.

4. I never saw a more beautiful country, nor more lively prospects, hills so raised here and there over the valleys, the river winding into diverse branches, the plains adjoining without bush or stubble, all fair green grass, the ground of hard sand easy to march on, either for horse or foot, the deer crossing in every path, the birds towards the evening singing on every tree with a thousand several tunes, cranes and herons of white, crimson and carnation perching on the river's side, the air fresh with a gentle easterly wind, and every stone that we stooped to take up, promised either gold or silver by his complexion.

5. Sir James Macdonald, in part of the wastes of his territory, set or sowed trees, to the number, as I have been told, of several millions, expecting, doubtless, that they would grow up into future navies and cities; but for want of enclosure, and of that care which is always necessary, and will hardly ever be taken, all his cost and labour have been lost, and the ground is likely to continue an useless heath.

6. The thatched houses, so warm and safe in winter storms, have been condemned to extinction by an unimaginative authority which prefers two-storey wooden Swedish prefabricated houses planned for a totally different climate, the height of which exposes them to every gale that blows in Uist.

7. Washed up thankfully out of the swirl and buffet of the city, they were happy to lie there, but because they were accustomed to telling the time by their nerves' response to the different tensions of the city—children crying in flats, lorries going heavily, and bicycles jangling for early morning, skid of tyres, sound of frying, and the human insect noise of thousands talking and walking and eating at midday—the tensionless shore keyed only to the tide gave them a sense of timelessness that, however much they rejoiced mentally, troubled their habit-impressed bodies with a lack of pressure.

8. Like the crow and black duck, the green heron is at once a wary and venturesome bird, endowed with sufficient intelligence to discriminate between real and imaginary dangers and often making itself quite at home in noisy, thickly settled neighborhoods where food is abundant and where it is not too much molested.

9. When somebody says "image" or "images," I think primarily and somehow exclusively of those wonderful little round pictures in my mind of persons, places, things, sounds, smells, events, scenes of the recent past which occur to me daily, either triggered by some idea, word, thought, or deliberately called up simply because I have wished to think of something fond, happy, or sad, though one could question how much is deliberate and how much is unconscious calling up.

3. Forming: Paragraph Sequence II

The paragraphs in this sequence are selected from the writings of artists and critics concerned with artistic making. Each one has something to say about how or why or what the artist composes. If you ask HDWDWW? in reading each selection, you will be developing a lexicon, a list of terms, which then can help in rereading each selection in the context that the other paragraphs provide. Critical reading means, for one thing, rereading. You can take a phrase or a statement that you find obscure in one selection and try to translate it into the terms of another selection. What one artist says about the *how* of artistic composition can illuminate what another artist has to say about the *why*. And, of course, you may find profound differences of opinion about purpose as you compare the images that are used to describe it, the entitlements given to the process and function of artistic creation. Pair the paragraphs in different ways. I've arranged them so that between any two in sequence there are interesting echoes and overlaps, but if you read the sequence backwards, you may find other pairings that are equally illuminating. One passage offers a perspective on another; one group of statements provides a context for another.

Remember: there are no right answers nor is there any final truth hidden in these selections. They are intended as points of departure for your own thinking about works of art and about your own experience, if you've ever danced, painted, sculpted, designed a house, written a poem, composed a piece of music, or taken a picture.

Note: These artists and critics have written essays of various kinds, tracts, articles, lectures, letters and so forth, and although they appear as paragraphs, that is not how they were published. These are all passages from larger works. It is inappropriate to say, "In her excerpt, Barbara Hepworth explains . . ." or "Max Black says in his paragraph. . . ." Instead you can name the form in which they are writing or you can refer to the rhetorical form—*argument, analogy, description,* etc. The excerpts are ours; the arguments are theirs. For our present purposes, when you want to allude to these writers, it is best to say simply: "Ackerman explains that . . . ," "Gertrude Stein says that . . . ," "Paul Klee develops a metaphor which . . . ," etc.

1. All the clues for [a theory of dance composition] come from life itself. Every movement made by a human being, and far back of that, in the animal kingdom too, has a design in space; a relationship to other objects in both time and space; and energy flow which we call dynamics; and a rhythm. Movements are made for a complete array of reasons involuntary or voluntary, physical, psychical, emotional or instinctive, which we will lump all together and call motivation. Without a motivation, no movement would be

made at all. So, with a simple analysis of movement, in general, we are provided with the basis for dance, which is movement brought to the point of fine art. The four elements of dance are, therefore, design, dynamics, rhythm, and motivation. These are the raw materials which make a dance, and so fundamental are they that, without a balanced infusion of each, the dance is likely to be weakened, and without any two of them it will be seriously impaired. To be sure, all four parts of movement will be there in some degree no matter what is done, but to use them skillfully so that all the mutations are understood and can be intelligently chosen to support the idea, takes quite a lot of study.

Doris Humphries, The Art of Making Dances

2. I don't feel any difference of intention or of mood when I paint (or carve) realistically and when I make abstract carvings. It all feels the same—the same happiness and pain, the same joy in a line, a form, a color—the same feeling of being lost in the pursuit of something. The same feeling at the end. The two ways of working flow into each other without effort . . . [the two methods of working] enhance each other by giving an absolute freedom—a freedom to complete the circle. . . . Working realistically replenishes one's *love* for life, humanity and the earth. Working abstractly seems to release one's personality and sharpen the perceptions, so that in the observation of life it is the wholeness or inner intention which moves one so profoundly: the components fall into place, the detail is significant of unity.

Barbara Hepworth, "Letter to Herbert Read," quoted in
Herbert Read, The Philosophy of Modern Art

3. If a photograph is to communicate its subject in all its intensity, the relationship of form must be rigorously established. Photography implies the recognition of a rhythm in the world of real things. What the eye does is to find and focus on the particular subject within the mass of reality; what the camera does is simply to register upon film the decision made by the eye. We look at and perceive a photograph, as a painting, in its entirety and all in one glance. In a photograph, composition is the result of a simultaneous coalition, the organic co-ordination of elements seen by the eye. One does not add composition as though it were an afterthought superimposed on the basic subject mate-

rial, since it is impossible to separate content from form. Composition must have its own inevitability about it.

In photography there is a new kind of plasticity, product of the instantaneous lines made by movements of the subject. We work in unison with movement as though it were a presentiment of the way in which life unfolds. But inside movement there is one moment at which the elements in motion are in balance. Photography must seize upon this moment and hold immobile the equilibrium of it.

The photographer's eye is perpetually evaluating. A photographer can bring coincidence of line simply by moving his head a fraction of a millimeter. He can modify perspectives by a slight bending of the knees. By placing the camera closer to or farther from the subject, he draws a detail—and it can be subordinated, or he can be tyrannized by it. But he composes a picture in very nearly the same amount of time it takes to click the shutter, at the speed of a reflex action.

Sometimes it happens that you stall, delay, wait for something to happen. Sometimes you have the feeling that here are all the makings of a picture—except for just one thing that seems to be missing. But what one thing? Perhaps someone suddenly walks into your range of view. You follow his progress through the view-finder. You wait and wait, and then finally press the button—and you depart with the feeling (though you don't know why) that you've really got something. Later, to substantiate this, you can take a print of this picture, trace on it the geometric figures which come up under analysis, and you'll observe that, if the shutter was released at the decisive moment, you have instinctively fixed a geometric pattern without which the photograph would have been both formless and lifeless.

Composition must be one of our constant preoccupations, but at the moment of shooting it can stem only from our intuition, for we are out to capture the fugitive moment, and all the interrelationships involved are on the move. In applying the Golden Rule,* the only pair of compasses at the photographer's disposal is his own pair of eyes. Any

* The Golden Rule is a formula for proportions in designing sculptural, architectural, and other spatial forms. The ratios are 3:5:8. Thus, in the Golden Rectangle, the width is to the length as the length is to the sum of the two.

geometrical analysis, any reducing of the picture to a schema, can be done only (because of its very nature) after the photograph has been taken, developed and printed—and then it can be used only for a post-mortem examination of the picture. I hope we will never see the day when photo shops will sell little schema grills to clamp onto our view-finders; and that the Golden Rule will never be found etched on our ground glass.

If you start cutting or cropping a good photograph, it means death to the geometrically correct interplay of proportions. Besides, it very rarely happens that a photograph which was feebly composed can be saved by the reconstruction of its composition under the darkroom's enlarger; the integrity of vision is no longer there. There is a lot of talk about camera angles; but the only valid angles in existence are the angles of the geometry of composition and not the ones fabricated by the photographer who falls flat on his stomach or performs other antics to procure his effects.

Henri Cartier-Bresson, *The Decisive Moment*

4. The composition is the thing seen by every one living in the living that they are doing, they are the composing of the composition that at the time they are living is the composition of the time in which they are living. It is that that makes living a thing they are doing. Nothing else is different, of that almost any one can be certain. The time when and the time of and the time in that composition is the natural phenomena of that composition and of that perhaps everyone can be certain.

No one thinks these things when they are making when they are creating what is the composition, naturally no one thinks, that is no one formulates until what is to be formulated has been made.

Composition is not there, it is going to be there and we are here. . . .

Gertrude Stein, "Composition as Explanation"

5. It is known that this preoccupation with locale is frequent among the creative who find in their imagination richer sources of inspiration than in copying reality. It was in a Burgundian village that Debussy patiently studied the play of waves for *La Mer* and in his lodging in the Batignolles that he condensed, without having crossed the Pyrenees, the intoxicating perfumes for *Ibéria*. Two well-known anec-

dotes of Fauré and Ravel confirm this observation. To an admirer who begged him to reveal the divine countryside which had dictated the sublime harmonies of the *Nocturne No. 6 in D flat Major, Op. 63* to him, Fauré answered with a secret satisfaction, "the Simplon Tunnel." And Ravel, during a trip to Morocco, confessed, "If I were involved in composing Arab music, it would be much more Arabic than the real thing."

Emile Vuillermoz, Gabriel Fauré

6. A kind of urbanistic thinking prompted Palladio to draw together the discrete functions of the villa into a compact organism; he wrote in the Quattri Libri that a house is nothing other than a small city. Behind this metaphor there was a social theory of architectural history: man, according to Palladio, first lived and built alone, but later, seeing the benefits of commerce, he formed villages by bringing houses together. By analogy, a farm center would become more economical and natural as its functions were drawn together. Mere clustering, however, would not do. Palladio believed in a hierarchy of functions, and compared the dwelling to the human body, the noble and beautiful parts of which the Lord ordained to be exposed, and the ignoble but essential parts to be hidden from sight. The metaphor of the organism reminds us that every Palladian work is designed as if members are joined symmetrically to a central spine. Whether or not the villas were planned consciously to be built outward in symmetrical units from the spine—as against being raised all at once, storey by storey—this process proved to be eminently suitable to the uncertain economy of the time. The master's dwelling had to be habitable, but from there on Palladio's patrons added just what they could afford of the annexed loggias and towers.

James Ackermann, Palladio

7. You can step up to an oil painting and suddenly see the image almost dissolve in the concrete material of which it's made. You can walk up to a painting of Constable's and suddenly the surface of the river and the clouds seems to fly apart and you just see great lumps of oil paint. You can't do this with either a photographic or a television image. You are in the fixed position of viewer. The difference is that the television image or the film image is not an object: it is an imitation of an object. The whole point

about painting is that it is an object in its own right which can be taken to be an image of reality as well as an object in its own right, whereas the television image has only one place of existence—as something on a screen. . . . An oil painting is the residue of a very complicated negotiation between an actual person and a series of actual materials during which the artist walked up to his canvas, blobbed bits of stuff onto it, stepped back to see how it looked, went up to it again. He had a relationship to the canvas—of man as smearer—and then he stepped back from his canvas and had a relationship to it as a replica of reality. And what he leaves behind is a history of this dual relationship. The television image is nothing whatever. It is simply a disturbance on the surface of a piece of luminous glass which has no existence apart from the reality that it represents.

Jonathan Miller, "TV Guide," *New York Review of Books*, Oct. 7, 1971

8. "What," it will be Questioned, "when the Sun rises, do you not see a round disk of fire somewhat like a Guinea?" O no, no, I see an Innumerable company of the Heavenly host crying, "Holy, Holy, Holy is the Lord God Almighty." I question not my Corporeal or Vegetative Eye any more than I would question a Window concerning a Sight. I look thro' it & not with it."

William Blake, *A Vision of the Last Judgment*

9. May I use a simile, a simile of the tree? The artist has studied this world of variety and has, we may suppose, unobtrusively found his way in it. His sense of direction in nature and life, this branching and spreading array, I shall compare with the root of the tree. From the root the sap flows to the artist, flows through him, flows to his eye. Thus he stands as the trunk of the tree. Battered and stirred by the strength of the flow, he moulds his vision into his work. As, in full view of the world, the crown of the tree unfolds and spreads in time and in space, so with his work. Nobody would affirm that the tree grows its crown in the image of its root. Between above and below can be no mirrored reflection. It is obvious that different functions expanding in different elements produce vital divergences. But it is just the artist who at times is denied those departures from nature which his art demands. He has even been charged with incompetence and deliberate distortion. And yet, standing at his appointed place, the trunk of the tree, he does nothing other than gather and pass on what comes to him from its

depths. He neither serves nor rules—he transmits. His position is humble. And the beauty at the crown is not his own. He is merely a channel.

Paul Klee, *On Modern Art*

10. The poet, described in ideal perfection, brings the whole soul of man into activity, with the subordination of its faculties to each other according to their relative worth and dignity. He diffuses a tone and spirit of unity, that blends, and (as it were) *fuses*, each into each by that synthetic and magical power, to which I would exclusively appropriate the name of Imagination. This power, first put in action by the will and understanding, and retained under their irremissive, though gentle and unnoticed, control, *laxis effertur habenis* [swept along, unreined], reveals itself in the balance or reconcilement of opposite or discordant qualities: of sameness with difference; of the general with the concrete; the idea with the image; the individual with the representative; the sense of novelty and freshness with old and familiar objects; a more than usual state of emotion with more than usual order; judgment ever awake and steady self-possession with enthusiasm and feeling profound or vehement; and while it blends and harmonizes the natural and the artificial, still subordinates art to nature; the manner to the matter; and our admiration of the poet to our sympathy with the poetry.

Samuel Taylor Coleridge, *Biographia Literaria*

4. "Do You Know Your Knowledge?": Paragraph Sequence III

Consciousness . . . mind, life, will, body, organ (as compared with machine), nature, spirit, sin, habit, sense, understanding, reason: here are fourteen words. Have you ever reflectively and quietly asked yourself the meaning of any one of these, and tasked yourself to return the answer in *distinct* terms, not applicable to any of the other words? Or have you contented yourself with the vague floating meaning that will just save you from absurdity in the use of the word, just as the clown's botany would do, who knew that potatoes were roots, and cabbages greens? Or, if you have the gift of wit, shelter yourself under Augustine's equivocation, "I know it perfectly well till I am asked." Know? Ay, as an oyster knows its life. *But do you know your knowledge?*

Samuel Taylor Coleridge, *Notebooks*

The paragraphs in this sequence concern topics and employ terms like those in Coleridge's list—conceptual terms. There are many difficult passages, but the experience of reading them carefully can work to give you practice in discovering complex meanings without having them broken down into bits and neatly packaged for ready consumption; to offset the influence of the idea of "speed reading"; to help you learn to talk back without settling for "I don't agree." There is a trade-off: the paragraphs are hard, but they are well-written and they repay careful study. Construing them will, I hope, encourage you to construct paragraphs of your own. The best way to learn something about critical writing—re-presenting analyses of what you read and think—is to keep at it in the process of critical reading. To know your knowledge is to search for meanings, to discover and articulate relationships—and that's what the composing process is.

In developing a critical method of reading, you need to slow down the process so that you can find out what you are doing and thereby how to do it better. If you spend, say, 45 minutes on one paragraph or several hours on a set of four, what you learn in the course of that analysis can be of service in reading the next set, and so on. Furthermore, careful study can help you cut down, eventually, the amount of time wasted in aimless reading, vague worry, and teeth-clenching anxiety. Working on this small scale—with paragraphs rather than with entire essays—can help you develop your own techniques for identifying, ordering, and arranging concepts so that you can learn to think with them and not just about them.

Here is a demonstration of the process of critical reading in slow motion. The paragraph is taken from an essay by I. A. Richards entitled "Functions of and Factors in Language."

(1) Messages are generated by Contexts; they are conveyed by signals. (2) Messages are living. (3) They are animated instances of meaning, determinations from the context field; the signals which convey them are dead. (4) My thinking, doubting, wondering at this moment is living activity; so is the nerve-muscle-joint process guiding my pen as I compose my Message. (5) But the motions of the pen itself are inanimate, as are the configurations its point is tracing on the paper, the signals. (6) The typist, the printer, the library, etc. put the page before you. (7) As you read the inanimate lines of print, a living activity of thinking,

doubting, wondering—despairing perhaps—arises in you. (8) That is the Message coming into being again. (9) It was not in the pen or on the page. (10) So too with a speaker: his gestures, postures, facial expressions, actions and the rest, together with what his voice does in the sound wave channel—anything that videotape can take down: all that is signal, merely. (11) Not until it is interpreted by some living recipient does anything that should be called the Message appear. (12) It is essential to a Message that what forms in the Addressee or other recipient should be of the same order of being with what has formed in the Addresser. (13) He may get it all wrong (and often does) but there is an IT. (14) The two apparitions are both meanings. (15) But a sound track and a system of meanings are not things of a sort, able to agree or disagree.

Lexicon: messages   contexts   signals   meanings

Gloss: contexts → messages → signals → messages

Gloss in form of statement: The message that is addressed/received is not in the same category as the signals by means of which it is sent and received.

Oppositions

Message (A)	Signal (B)
Living, animated	Dead
Cf. thinking, motor activity	Inanimate: motions of pen, marks on page, lines of print
Reading—living activity message comes into being	Cf. speaker's gesture, expressions, etc. "Anything videotape can take down"
Interpreted by living recipient	
What forms in addressee What forms in addressor: both "apparitions"	
System of meanings	Sound track

Oppositions by sentences

1) A,B	6) B	11) A
2) A	7) B,A	12) A
3) A,B	8) A	13) A
4) A,A	9) A	14) A
5) B	10) B	15) B,A

Final sentence

Beginning sentence

$$\frac{\text{a system of meanings}}{\text{generated}} \quad : \quad \frac{\text{a sound track}}{\text{conveys}}$$

Questions that the paragraph answers

"*Is* the medium the message?"

"Do we have a thought that we encode and send as a message to be decoded by the receiver?"

"Is meaning something that can be represented by squiggles or rumbles directly?"

"Are meanings created, made, imagined, formed?"

Working out oppositions by sentences helped me see that I'd misread sentence 10 the first time through: I took the "So too . . ." to refer to the living activity of a speaker's presentation, but, though that is, of course, a "living activity," Richards sets it in opposition *with* "anything that videotape can take down"; it is set *over against* the speaker's message. *So too* is a signal that an analogy or a ratio is forthcoming, but you still must interpret in such a way that the ground of the analogy is clear.

Of course, this is a paragraph, not an essay, and so there are loose ends. We can assume that preceding paragraphs probably have explained how meanings are "generated by contexts" and how they can be said to be "determinations of the context field"; it's a good guess, too, that the paragraph to follow will return to the notion of "apparitions." In the paragraphs you will be studying in this sequence, there will certainly be loose ends, but they needn't distract you. The paragraphs are isolated from their original contexts, but each is given a new setting, which for our present purposes—practicing the techniques of critical reading and experimenting with strategies of critical writing— is adequate. Furthermore, since the paragraphs all concern in one way or another the problems and issues one confronts in studying the composing process, this book itself provides a context. Most of them come from books that are readily available in the library in case you want to read the rest of an essay.

Here is a suggested procedure for using the context provided by Paragraph Sequence III.

1. Gloss all four paragraphs in a set. Use your dictionary, but remember that you can't depend on it to form the concept for you.

2. Give the hardest paragraph the works—a sentence by sentence analysis. (See demonstration above.)

3. Decide whether the other three writers support or contradict the statements in the paragraph you've thoroughly analyzed. Use ratios and grain elevators. (See pp. 221–222.)

4. Give the set of four a title. Compose it in oppositional form and be sure that it's general enough to cover all four paragraphs. Use this tentative title as a guide in writing a paragraph or two in which you form the concepts that emerge from your analysis of the four.

After several weeks of reading, writing, discussing, and carrying through any procedure of critical analysis that you find useful, you would have on hand all the concepts necessary for writing an essay on knowing your knowledge.

Here are some questions and topics that have developed in my classes when we've read and discussed these passages.

1. **a,b,c,d**   Can you support Langer's argument with anything Black or Grene is saying?
How does Swift's parody illuminate the conception of language Black and Grene are developing?
Who comes closest to Swift's academicians in your experience?

2. **a,b,c,d**   Reread p. 118 where you will find Richards's list of "our most important words." Does it help to explain the opposition he is making here in this passage, which follows in the original?
Write a history of naming.
One student of language has remarked that "while primitive man may have perceived many abstract categories, he would not have felt any pressing need to talk about them." Query: what does "talk about" mean? How could he have "perceived abstract categories" without language in which to "talk about" them? Does Walker Percy help you work out an answer?
Could primitive man have danced his "abstract categories"?

3. **a,b,c,d**   Explain Gombrich's notion that "the historian's method is circular." Using the paragraph by Gombrich as a model for a persona paraphrase, write about the topic of Set 1 or 2.

If the scientist and the historian both proceed by the same method, why isn't history a science? or is it? What division is "History" in in your school?

What is "natural history"?

4. **a,b,c,d**   Write a dialogue between Oppenheimer and Camus about pain.

Where would Camus place himself in the scene Allport describes? Does the Kwakiutl Indian seem to have Camus' "need for coherence"?

What is a scientific object?

It isn't necessary to follow slavishly my procedure for critical reading. Here's how Robin got started with a critical reading of the second set of paragraphs (2. a,b,c,d). These notes represent an hour's work.

2a.   technical words=fine tools of discipline
concepts=crude utilitarian tool
rule: the more central, necessary its meaning is in our picture of X, the more deceiving the word will be.

These words are used most in philosophy but it isn't philosophers who are ambiguous—it's the position of their ideas, or the hinges on which their thoughts hang.

Does this paragraph hang together? I don't like the way it makes me feel about myself. Does all this hardware imagery make a substantial case? does it give us something to "handle" when we discuss whether "words like experience" are good, exact explanations?

If scientific words are technical words, what are "words like experience"? Richards doesn't give them a label.

But why *is* an "important" . . . "central" . . . "necessary" word "deceiving"???? Richards needs examples and definitions that are more exacting himself!

2b.   The function of a name: always limited to emphasizing a particular aspect. Value of a name depends on this restriction and limitation. *not* a function of name to refer exhaustively to a concrete situation.

Naming/isolation is a positive act *because* we select & fix our perception . . . but not as scientists do—in comparison common speech seems vague. Our everyday terms and names are *milestones* on way to scientific concepts because we receive our first objective or theoretical view which results from a constructive intellectual effort.

Main point: language seems vague but it's necessary for scientific achievement.

So what? What is he doing?

Cassirer spends more than half the paragraph on a comparison which separates everyday speech and scientific speech. At the end of the paragraph he puts them into relationship again. He doesn't seem so negative, like Richards is.

2c.　imagination linked to passion
　　　　　　　　　to *absence* of knowledge about the physical world

ancient chaos, every man's desire
connects chaos to imaginative ability
"had immortal models about them" Who or what is "them"?
Concept of immortal linked to free expression of chaotic feelings. Is this a "thought of weight and measure"? In other words, is Yeats's explanation of the origins of religious belief in external creative forces, and immortality large enough—?
Yeats uses words like *soul, imagination, immortal:* are they hinges? How does he feel about science, scientific definition? He says you'd better *not* limit your language.
If ambiguity is a good thing, then all these guys may be saying the same thing. Now how does Percy fit in?

2d.　rash of positivist to limit truth to *how* not *what*
copy theory?　　gives acct of *what*
What about the what: it is true we cannot know what it is itself intuitively . . . ?

a semiotist = someone who doesn't explain
　　　　　　 = someone scandalized by metaphor because it confuses two things

how something is w/
／s. else
BUT unless we name, we shall not know＼
　　　　　　　　　　　　　　　　　something at all

agrees c Cassirer

We "know" through comparison
both truth and error are served
if truth is attenuated it means nothing
beyond structural similarity is belief/knowledge that something
"is" and also that "it is something"
What does Percy think about naming? He says he doesn't want
to limit truth through definition but he does say that we must
call a thing *some name* in order to KNOW it. Where does this put
Percy?
What is a third trait "of the thing" that is discussed and affirmed by a "symbol (relation)"?
Note: read Percy next time first
Does metaphor come *before* naming?

Paragraph Sequence III

1a. Language, the most versatile and indispensable of all symbol-
isms, has put its stamp on all our mental functions so that I
think they always differ from even their closest analogues in
animal life. Language has invaded our feeling and dreaming and
action, as well as our reasoning, which is really a product of it.
The greatest change wrought by language is the increased scope
of awareness in speech-gifted beings. An animal's awareness is
always of things in its own place and life. In human awareness,
the present, actual situation is often the least part. We have
not only memories and expectations; we have *a past* in which
we locate our memories, and *a future* that vastly overreaches our
own anticipations. Our past is a story, our future a piece of
imagination. Likewise our ambient is a place in a wider, symbol-
ically conceived place, the universe. We live in a *world.*

Susanne K. Langer, Philosophical Sketches

1b. [One] project was a scheme for entirely abolishing all words
whatsoever; and this was urged as a great advantage in point of
health as well as brevity. For it is plain that every word we
speak is in some degree a diminution of our lungs by corrosion,
and consequently contributes to the shortening of our lives. An
expedient was therefore offered, that since words are only names
for *things*, it would be more convenient for all men to carry
about them such things as were necessary to express the particular business they are to discourse on. And this invention would
certainly have taken place, to the great ease as well as health

of the subject, if the women, in conjunction with the vulgar and illiterate, had not threatened to raise a rebellion, unless they might be allowed the liberty to speak with their tongues, after the manner of their ancestors; such constant irreconcilable enemies to science are the common people. However, many of the most learned and wise adhere to the new scheme of expressing themselves by things, which hath only this inconvenience attending it, that if a man's business be very great, and of various kinds, he must be obliged in proportion to carry a greater bundle of things upon his back unless he can afford one or two strong servants to attend him. I have often beheld two of those sages almost sinking under the weight of their packs, like pedlars among us; who, when they met in the streets, would lay down their loads, open their sacks, and hold conversation for an hour together; then put up their implements, help each other to resume their burthens, and take their leave.

Jonathan Swift, Gulliver's Travels, Part III

1c. . . . The secret [of linguistic innovation, the capacity for generating sentences, inventing new words, etc.] seems to reside in something no less fundamental than the apprehension of relationships in general. If so, that may be a reason why it is hard to come to grips with. To take a simple example: understanding the meaning of the word *on*—as in *The cat is on the mat*—means, among other things, to be prepared to understand combinations of the form *X is on Y* for an indefinite range of values of X and Y. A child or a foreigner would not be held to have learned the meaning of *on* unless, having previously learned the meaning of *the dog* and *the chair*, he knew without specific instruction what was intended by *The dog is on the chair.* Thus the requisite generalization and application to novel cases enters at the ground floor, as it were, with the basic understanding of relational rules. It would be wrong to think of words as independent blocks which have, somehow and mysteriously, to be put together again in possibly novel ways to produce unified structures. We start with the "structures" (sentences) whose meanings are apprehended as wholes. As we begin to analyze these holophrases into elements that can be arranged and recombined, we learn at the same time how to reorganize them. Thus analysis and synthesis are inseparable aspects of the mastery of linguistic structure: to be able to divide is necessarily to know how to connect, and *vice versa.* If there is any residual "mystery," it is the basic one of how we perceive complexity in unity

—how we ever manage to *see* parts related in a whole. But this mystery we must leave for psychologists and philosophers to wrestle with.

Max Black, The Labyrinth of Language

1d. But can any names, such as the general quality words, red, feline, colored, etc., of which I am trying to build my firmly factual language, work uniquely for *this* percept? Both the words themselves and the things designated are *instances of universals*. The *same* word, e.g. "cat," designates the same thing, cat, in the sense that a mark or sound of the same class designates a thing of the same class. But no occasion of "cat" or cat is identical with any other. It is in each case a similar occurrence or object. How do I know that it is similar, and similar enough to be subsumed under the same class? By memory, a Humean empiricist would say. But even granting that, meeting cat 2, I recall cat 1, I must *make* the comparison. I must liken cat 2 to cat 1 and find them similar by a standard, a standard which is the concept cat. I do not mean to suggest that there is an explicit or even an "unconscious" inference involved here, every time I recognize a cat as a cat. But as my world is colored, so too it is cat-inhabited and at the same time *structured through language:* I dwell in a coherent and mutually inter-acting framework of word-classes and thing-classes; only within such a frame do individual sounds and written shapes and individual animals become what they are. The power to generalize which speech demands is the power to sort out according to effective norms both utterances and natural events.

Marjorie Grene, The Knower and the Known

2a. [Richards is discussing "our most important words."] . . . The very usefulness which gives them their importance explains their ambiguity. They are the servants of too many interests to keep to single, clearly defined jobs. Technical words in the sciences are like adzes, planes, gimlets, or razors. A word like "experience," or "feeling," or "true" is like a pocket-knife. In good hands it will do most things—not very well. In general we will find that the more important a word is, and the more central and necessary its meanings are in our pictures of ourselves and the world, the more ambiguous and possibly deceiving the word will be. Naturally these words are also those which have been most used in philosophy. But it is not the philosophers who have made them ambiguous; it is the position of their ideas, as the very hinges of all thought.

I. A. Richards, How to Read a Page

2b. The function of a name is always limited to emphasizing a particular aspect of a thing, and it is precisely this restriction and limitation upon which the value of the name depends. It is not the function of a name to refer exhaustively to a concrete situation but merely to single out and dwell upon a certain aspect. The isolation of this aspect is not a negative but a positive act. For in the act of denomination we select out of the multiplicity and diffusion of our sense data, certain fixed centers of perception. These centers are not the same as in logical or scientific thought. The terms of ordinary speech are not to be measured by the same standards as those in which we express scientific concepts. As compared with scientific terminology the words of common speech always exhibit a certain vagueness; almost without exception they are so indistinct and ill-defined as not to stand the test of logical analysis. But notwithstanding this unavoidable and inherent defect our everyday terms and names are the milestones on the road which leads to scientific concepts; it is in these terms that we receive our first objective or theoretical view of the world. Such a view is not simply "given"; it is the result of a constructive intellectual effort which without the constant assistance of language could not attain its end.

Ernst Cassirer, An Essay on Man

2c. Men who lived in a world where anything might flow and change, and become any other thing; and among great gods whose passions were in the flaming sunset, and in the thunder and the thunder-shower, had not our thoughts of weight and measure. They worshipped nature and the abundance of nature, and had always, as it seems, for a supreme ritual that tumultuous dance among the hills or in the depths of the woods, where unearthly ecstasy fell upon the dancers, until they seemed the gods or the godlike beasts, and felt their soul overtopping the moon; and, as some think, imagined for the first time in the world the blessed country of the gods and of the happy dead. They had imaginative passions because they did not live within our own strait limits, and were nearer to ancient chaos, every man's desire, and had immortal models about them. The hare that ran by among the dew might have sat up on his haunches when the first man was made, and the poor bunch of rushes under their feet might have been a goddess laughing among the stars; and with but a little magic, a little waving of the hands, a little murmuring of the lips, they too could become a hare or a bunch of rushes, and know immortal love and immortal hatred.

W. B. Yeats, "The Celtic Element in Literature"

2d. Without getting over one's head with the larger question of
truth, one might still guess that it is extraordinarily rash of the
positivist to limit truth to the logical approximation—to say that
we cannot know what things are but only how they hang together. The copy theory gives no account of the *what* we are
saying *how* about. As to the what: since we are not angels, it is
true that we cannot know what it is intuitively and as it is in
itself. The modern semiotist is scandalized by the metaphor,
flesh is grass. . . . He is confusing an instrument of knowing
with what is known. The word *flesh* is not this solid flesh,
and this solid flesh is not grass. But unless we name it *flesh*
we shall not know it at all, and unless we call flesh grass we
shall not know how it is with flesh. The semiotist leaves unex-
plained the act of knowing. He imagines naively that I know
what this is and then give it a label, whereas the truth is, as
Cassirer has shown so impressively, that I cannot know anything
at all unless I symbolize it. We can only *con*ceive being, sidle up
to it by laying something else alongside. We approach the thing
not directly but by pairing, by apposing symbol and thing. Is it
not premature to say with the mythist that when the primitive
calls the lightning serpentine, he conceives it as a snake and is
logically wrong? Both truth and error may be served here, error
insofar as the lightning is held to participate magically in
snakeness, truth insofar as the conception of snake may allow
the privately apprehended inscape of the lightning to be formulated. I would have a horror of finding myself allied with those
who in the name of instrumentality or inner warmth or what
not would so attentuate and corrupt truth that it meant nothing.
But an analysis of the symbol relation reveals aspects of truth
which go far beyond the notion of structural similarity which
the symbolic logicians speak of. Two other traits of the thing
are discovered and affirmed: one that it *is;* two that it is *something.*

Walker Percy, "Metaphor as Mistake"

3a. Whenever an ancient cult image, the pattern on a brooch, a
broken column or a painted potsherd asks to be interpreted, any
historian worth his salt will try to make sense of it in such terms
as his creative imagination suggests. But a critical mind will
not rest with this vision. He will watch for further evidence to
fit it into the image of the lost culture. Usually, of course, such
further evidence is available in one form or another, and the
historian's task is precisely to fit it all together into a context

that "makes sense." And so intensely does his imagination become engaged that he begins to people the past with men who might have created those very brooches and done those very deeds of which the sources tell us. There is much to be admired in this effort of the imaginative historian to "wake the dead" and to unriddle the mute language of the monuments. But he should never conceal from himself that his method is circular. The physiognomic unity of past ages which he reads from their various manifestations is precisely the unity to which the rules of his game have committed him. It was he who unified the clues in order to make sense of them.

E. H. Gombrich, "Physiognomic Perception"

3b. There is no isolated event. Any event is connected with other events, those which brought it about and those which it brings about. Nor does connection of events in itself make a story, let alone history. To form a story, the *connection* of happenings must have some substratum, or focus, something to which it is related, something to whom it happens. This something, or somebody, to which, or whom, a connection of events relates, is what gives the plain connection of events an actual, specific *coherence*, what turns it into a story. But such specific coherence is not given of itself, it is given by a perceiving and comprehending mind. It is created as a *concept*, i.e., as a meaning. Thus, to make even a simple story, three factors are indispensable: connection of events, relatedness of this connection to something, or somebody, which gives the events their specific coherence and creates the concept which means a meaning. What I propose to demonstrate in the following is that the questioning of and the questing after a meaning of history both beg the question. There is no story, there is no history without meaning.

Erich Kahler, *The Meaning of History*

3c. To control the interpretation of an individual work of art by a "history of style," which in turn can only be built up by interpreting individual works may look like a vicious circle. It is, indeed, a circle though not a vicious but a methodical one. Whether we deal with historical or natural phenomena, the individual observation assumes the character of a "fact" only when it can be related to other analogous observations in such a way that the whole series "makes sense." This "sense" is, therefore, fully capable of being applied, as a control, to the interpretation of a new individual observation within the same range of phenomena. If, however, this new individual observation definitely refuses to be interpreted according to the "sense" of the series, and if an error proves to be impossible, the "sense" of the series will have to be re-formulated to include the new observation.

Erwin Panofsky, *Studies in Iconology*

3d. [Biologists] usually proceed in such a way that from certain facts gained by analysis we sketch a picture of the whole organism, which in turn, so long as we encounter discrepancies between this picture and factual experience, stimulates further questions and investigations. Upon the basis of new inquiries the picture of the whole is again modified, and the process of discovering new discrepancies and making new inquiries follows, and so on. By such empirical procedure in a dialectic manner, a progressively more adequate knowledge of the nature of the organism, of its "essence," is acquired, and an increasingly correct evaluation of the observed facts, and of whether or not they are essential to the organism is obtained. . . . As skepticism toward a naive copy-theory of knowledge grew, and as it was realized that "empirical" facts are not a simple expression of reality but are also produced through the method of investigation, it became more and more clear that it was the task of natural science to transcend the "empirical" facts and create images, "symbols," which are suited for gaining a coherent understanding of the "facts."

Kurt Goldstein, *Human Behavior*

4a. A perpetual doubting and a perpetual questioning of the truth of what we have learned is not the temper of science. If Einstein was led to ask not "What is a clock?" but "How, over great distances and with great precision, do we synchronize clocks?" that is not an illustration of the scepticism of science; it exemplifies rather the critical reason creating a new synthesis from paradoxes, anomalies, and bewilderments, which experiments carried on with new precision and in a new context brought into being.

J. Robert Oppenheimer, *Science and the Common Understanding*

4b. . . . What I know, what is certain, what I cannot deny, what I cannot reject—this is what counts. I can negate everything of that part of me that lives on vague nostalgias, except this desire for unity, this longing to solve, this need for clarity and cohesion. I can refute everything in this world surrounding me that offends or enraptures me, except this chaos, this sovereign chance and this divine equivalence which springs from anarchy. I don't know whether this world has a meaning that transcends it. But I know that I do not know that meaning and that it is impossible for me just now to know it. What can a meaning outside my condition mean to me? I can understand only in human terms. What I touch, what resists me—that is what I understand. And these two certainties—my appetite for the absolute and for unity and the impossibility of reducing this world to a rational and reasonable principle—I also know that I cannot reconcile them. What other truth can I admit without lying, without bringing in a hope I lack and which means nothing within the limits of my condition.

Albert Camus, *The Myth of Sisyphus*

4c. . . . It is essential that we distinguish the viewpoint of the scientist from that of the acting person. The superior wisdom of the scientist may unfortunately blind him to the process of growth that is actually taking place. The scientist's frame of reference is like the frame of an omniscient being: to him all things have time, place and determined orbits. But this frame is definitely not the frame of the acting person. The situation is much like that of the watcher from the hilltop who sees a single oarsman on the river below. From his vantage point the watcher notes that around the bend of the river, unknown as yet to the oarsman, there are dangerous rapids. What is present to the watcher's eye still lies in the future for the oarsman. The superior being predicts that soon the boatman will be portaging his skiff —a fact now wholly unknown to the boatman who is unfamiliar with the river's course. He will confront the obstacle when it comes, decide on his course of action, and surmount the difficulty. In short, the actor is unable to view his deeds in a large space-time matrix as does an all-wise God, or the less wise demigods of science. From his point of view he is working within a frame of choice, not of destiny. As psychologists, we ought to know, and do know, that the way a man defines his situation constitutes for him its reality. Choice for him is a paramount fact; how matters appear to the watcher on the hill is irrelevant. It is because existentialism takes always the acting person's point of view that it insists so strongly upon the attribute of freedom in man's nature.

Gordon Allport, *Becoming*

4d. However, in choosing a subject and an object radically different from one another, anthropology runs a risk: that the knowledge obtained from the object does not attain its intrinsic properties but is limited to expressing the relative and always shifting position of the subject in relation to that object. It may very well be, indeed, that so-called ethnological knowledge is condemned to remain as bizarre and inadequate as that which an exotic visitor would have of our own society. The Kwakiutl Indian whom Boas sometimes invited to New York to serve him as an informant was quite indifferent to the panorama of skyscrapers and of streets ploughed and furrowed by cars. He reserved all his intellectual curiosity for the dwarfs, giants and bearded ladies who were exhibited in Times Square at the time, for automats, and for the brass balls decorating staircase banisters. . . . All these things challenged his own culture, and it was that culture alone which he was seeking to recognize in certain aspects of ours.

Claude Lévi-Strauss, The Scope of Anthropology